Baselines under the International Law of the Sea

The Law of the Sea

Volumes published in this Brill Research Perspectives title are listed at *brill.com/rpls*

Baselines under the International Law of the Sea

Reports of the International Law Association Committee on Baselines under the International Law of the Sea

Edited by

Coalter G. Lathrop
J. Ashley Roach
Donald R. Rothwell

TUTA SUB AEGIDE PALLAS 1683

BRILL

LEIDEN | BOSTON

This paperback book edition is simultaneously published as issue 2.1–2 (2018) of *Law of the Sea*, DOI:10.1163/24519359-12340005.

The Library of Congress Cataloging-in-Publication data is available online at http://catalog.loc.gov
LC record available at http://lccn.loc.gov/2019931038

Typeface for the Latin, Greek, and Cyrillic scripts: "Brill". See and download: brill.com/brill-typeface

ISBN 978-90-04-39813-9 (paperback)
ISBN 978-90-04-39814-6 (e-book)

This book is printed on acid-free paper and produced in a sustainable manner.

Contents

Baselines under the International Law of the Sea: Reports of the International Law Association Committee on Baselines under the International Law of the Sea 1

Coalter G. Lathrop, J. Ashley Roach, and Donald R. Rothwell

Abstract 1
Keywords 2
Introduction 2
I Baselines under the International Law of the Sea (Sofia Report, 2012) 3
A *Report* 4
I Introduction 4
II The Normal Baseline: Origin, Significance, and Interests 6
A *Origin* 6
B *Significance* 8
C *Interests* 13
III The Normal Baseline: Existing Law 15
A *Interpreting Article 5* 15
1 General Rule 15
2 Supplementary Means 18
B *International Judicial Decisions* 24
C *The Normal Baseline in Municipal Law* 30
1 National Legislation 30
2 National Judicial Decisions 35
D *Expert Views on the Normal Baseline* 41
E *Reefs and Low-Tide Elevations* 45
F *General Conclusion* 47
IV The Existing Law Applied in a Changing World 47
A *Territorial Gain: Harbour Works, Coastal Protection, Land Reclamation* 48
1 Harbour Works 48
2 Coast Protective Works: Artificial Conservation of the Baseline 50
3 Land Reclamation: Artificial Extension of the Baseline 51
B *Sea Level Rise and Coastal Erosion* 53
V Conclusions 57
VI Annex: Actual Low-Water Line vs. Charted Low-Water Line 58

B *Resolution No. 1/2012: Baselines under the International Law of the Sea* 61

II Baselines under the International Law of the Sea (Sydney Report, 2018) 62

A *Report* 63

I Background 63

II Straight Baselines 66

A *Relevant Historical Background to Article 7, LOSC* 66

B *LOSC Text* 67

C *Analysis of Article 7, LOSC* 68

1 Text 68

2 State Practice 71

3 Case Law 77

4 Commentary by Publicists 80

III Straight Baselines and Bays 82

A *Relevant Historical Background* 82

B *Article 10: LOSC Text* 83

C *Analysis of Article 10* 84

1 Text 84

2 State Practice 84

3 Case Law 86

4 Commentary by Publicists 88

IV Straight Baselines and Low-Tide Elevations 90

A *Relevant Historical Background* 90

B *Article 13: LOSC Text* 90

C *Analysis of Article 13* 90

1 Text 90

2 State Practice 92

3 Case Law 93

4 Commentary by Publicists 95

V Combination of Methods in Drawing Baselines 96

A *Relevant Historical Background* 96

B *Article 14: LOSC Text* 96

C *Analysis of Article 14* 96

1 Text 96

2 State Practice 97

3 Case Law 98

4 Commentary by Publicists 98

VI Archipelagic Baselines 98

A *Relevant Historical Background* 98

B *United Nations Conferences on the Law of the Sea: I, II, III* 99
C *LOSC Text: Article 47* 99
D *Analysis of Article 47* 101
1 Text 101
2 State Practice 102
3 Case Law 105
4 Commentary by Publicists 106
VII Distinctions among Islands, Rocks, and Low-Tide Elevations 107
VIII Distinct Island Issues 109
A *Oceanic Islands* 109
B *Offshore Archipelagos* 110
IX Settlement of Disputes with Respect to Straight and Archipelagic Baselines 112
X Final Observations and Conclusions 113
A *Straight Baselines and Diplomatic Protests* 114
B *Straight Baselines* 115
C *Internal Waters and Straight Baselines* 120
D *Bays and Straight Baselines* 120
E *Low-Tide Elevations and Straight Baselines* 121
F *Combination of Methods in Drawing Baselines* 121
G *Archipelagic Baselines* 122
H *Final Observations* 124
B *Dissenting Report by Sienho Yee* 125
C *Appendix 1 – Straight Baseline Segments* 126
D *Appendix 2 – Straight Baselines State Practice* 153
E *Appendix 3 – Archipelagic States* 156
F *Resolution 1/2018: Committee on Baselines under the International Law of the Sea* 161
G *Annex: Sydney Conclusions on Baselines under the International Law of the Sea* 162
References (Sofia Report 2012 Normal Baseline) 165
References (Sydney Conference 2018 Final Report [Straight Baselines]) 170
Editor Biographies 177

Baselines under the International Law of the Sea

Reports of the International Law Association Committee on Baselines under the International Law of the Sea

*Coalter G. Lathrop**
Sovereign Geographic
coalter@sovereigngeographic.com

*J. Ashley Roach***
Chair, ILA Committee on Baselines under the International Law of the Sea
jashleyr@yahoo.com

*Donald R. Rothwell****
ANU College of Law
Donald.Rothwell@anu.edu.au

Abstract

Between 2008–2018 the International Law Association (ILA) Committee on Baselines under the International Law of the Sea produced two reports on the normal baseline (2012) and straight and archipelagic baselines (2018). The Sofia Report (2012) is organised around the interpretation of Article 5 of the 1982 United Nations Convention on the Law of the Sea (LOSC) concerning the normal baseline. Under the leadership of Committee Chair Judge Dolliver Nelson, the Committee was asked to identify the existing law on the normal baseline and to assess the need for further clarification or development of that law in light of substantial coastal change. The Report applies the rules of treaty interpretation, including an assessment of the ordinary meaning of the terms of the treaty and, because those leave the meaning ambiguous, the preparatory works of the normal baseline provision. The Report then turns to address the application of the existing law to changing coasts and concludes that the law on the normal baseline is inadequate to address problems of substantial territorial loss. The Sydney Report (2018) is organised around a common methodology in assessing Articles 7, 8, 10, 13, 14 and 47 of the LOSC concerning straight baselines, closing lines, and straight

* Rapporteur (2008–2012).
** Committee Chair (2012–2018).
*** Rapporteur (2012–2018).

 | DOI:10.1163/9789004398146_002

archipelagic baselines. Each analysis seeks to provide some background to the drafting of the Article, analysis of the text, assessment of state practice, relevant case law, and a summary of the commentary by publicists. The Report then moves to address certain cross-cutting or global issues that are relevant to a contemporary analysis of straight and archipelagic baselines, before reaching conclusions.

Keywords

UNCLOS – baselines – normal baseline – low-water mark – straight baseline – closing lines – archipelagic baselines – archipelagic states – state practice

Introduction

The International Law Association (ILA), founded in 1873, has a long-standing tradition of its Committees undertaking independent research and analysis on contemporary international law issues. The ILA has in recent decades always had at least one Committee whose work focussed on the law of the sea and in 2008 the Committee on Baselines under the International Law of the Sea was formed. The Committee's work has been in two phases. The Committee's first report under its original mandate addressed the normal baseline in the law of the sea and was considered at the ILA's 75th Sofia Conference (2012) and was endorsed as *Baselines under the International Law of the Sea* (Sofia Conference 2012).

Two matters were identified during the conclusion of that phase. The first was a recognition that substantial territorial loss resulting from sea-level rise is an issue that extends beyond baselines and the law of the sea and encompasses consideration at a junction of several parts of international law. In response a new ILA Committee on International Law and Sea Level Rise was established. The second was the desirability of further exploration of the international law of the sea addressing "straight baselines" under an extended mandate of the Committee on Baselines under the International Law of the Sea. The ILA Committee on Baselines under the International Law of the Sea therefore had its mandate expanded to consider these issues, and it deliberated on these matters during 2012–2018.

The baseline is the starting point from which all maritime claims are asserted. As the law of the sea has developed customary international law, decisions of international courts, and eventually treaties have recognised that while the normal baseline is the low-water mark, coastal States are also entitled to draw straight baselines along certain parts of their coast and closing lines across bays. With the recognition granted to archipelagic States by the 1982 United Nations Convention on the Law of the Sea, those States are also entitled to draw archipelagic baselines that connect the islands that make up the State. The mix of custom and treaty law governing baselines has resulted in a variety of state practice concerning issues such as the determination of the low-water mark, the length of straight baselines, excessive straight baseline claims, and the impact of fringing islands. Baselines have also been the subject of diplomatic protest, and consideration by international courts and tribunals.

The two Final Reports of the ILA Committee on Baselines under the International Law of the Sea, and associated Conference Resolutions, are now reproduced from Sofia (2012) and Sydney (2018) so as to allow for greater dissemination of the Committee's work and scholarly analysis. We acknowledge the contributions made by Committee members in the preparation of these reports, and especially detailed comments and feedback provided in writing and at inter-sessional meetings of the committee. Where possible, alternate and dissenting views have been taken into account.

1 Baselines under the International Law of the Sea (Sofia Report, 2012)

Members of the Committee:
Judge Dolliver Nelson (UK): *Chair*
Coalter Lathrop (USA): *Rapporteur*

Judge D.H. Anderson (UK)
Alternate: Mr Tim Daniel
Gilberto Marcos Antonio Rodrigues (Brazil)
Dr Nuno Antunes (Portugal)
Professor Frida Armas Pfirter (Argentina)
Dr Kaare Bangert (Denmark)
Emmanuelle Cabrol (France)
Mr C.M. Carleton (UK)
Alternate: Dr Edwin Egede
Ms Simona Drenik (Slovenia)
Professor Erik Franckx (HQ)
Professor Teresa Infante-Caffi (HQ)
Dr Marie Jacobsson (Sweden)
Professor Atsuko Kanehara (Japan)
Professor Natalie Klein (Australia)

Professor Doris Koenig (Germany)
Alternate: Professor Nele Matz-Lueck
Professor B. Kwiatkowska (Netherlands)
M. Richard Meese (France)
Professor John Noyes (USA)
Mr Simon Olleson (UK)
Alternate: Mr Joshua Brien
Dr A.G. Oude Elferink (Netherlands)
Professor Alexander Proelss (Germany)
Michael Reed (USA)
Captain J. Ashley Roach (Nominee of Chair)
Professor Donald Rothwell (Australia)
Alternate: Professor Gillian Triggs
Professor Alfred H.A. Soons (Netherlands)
Professor Norio Tanaka (Japan)
Professor Davor Vidas (Norway)
Alternate: Mr Oystein Jensen (Norway)
Professor George Walker (USA)
Professor Sienho Yee (HQ)

A *Report*

1 Introduction

The International Law Association Committee on Baselines under the International Law of the Sea was formed with the approval of the ILA Executive Council in November 2008, with Judge Dolliver Nelson appointed as Chair and Dr Alex Oude Elferink as Rapporteur.[1] In the autumn of 2009, Dr Oude Elferink relinquished his position, and Mr Coalter Lathrop was approved as Rapporteur of the Committee.[2] The four-year mandate of the Committee ends in 2012.

The Committee was established with a two-part mandate: first, to "identify the existing law on the normal baseline" and, second, to "assess if there is a need for further clarification or development of that law".[3] The need to identify, and possibly clarify or develop, the existing law concerning the normal baseline arises in response to possible sea level rise that has been predicted to accompany

1 *Minutes of Meeting of Executive Council*, Nov. 15, 2008, Charles Clore House, London.

2 Many Committee members made significant contributions to this Report. Special acknowledgment is due to Committee member Michael Reed, whose research and drafting formed the basis for text related to the *travaux préparatiores* of Article 5, United States practice, and state practice more generally, and who contributed significant research and drafting to other parts of this Report.

3 *Proposal for the establishment of a new committee on baselines*, para. 7 [hereinafter *Proposal*].

the phenomenon of climate change, and the effects this may have in particular upon low-lying, small island developing states.[4] The need also arises with respect to the artificial extension of existing coasts[5] (for example, through land reclamation projects). In addition to concerns raised by these phenomena, the importance of identifying the existing law on the normal baseline was highlighted in two recent maritime delimitation cases – *Nicaragua* v. *Honduras* (ICJ Judgment 2007)[6] and *Guyana* v. *Suriname* (Annex VII Arbitral Tribunal award 2007)[7] – in which the location of the normal baseline was in question.[8] Finally, the normal baseline is of fundamental importance for the construction of other types of baselines that do not follow the sinuosities of the coast, including straight baselines, archipelagic baselines, and bay and river closing lines.[9] These 'straight line' baselines are not considered in any detail in this report. The normal baseline along ice-covered coast is also not dealt with in this Report.[10] The Committee notes that straight baselines and baselines along ice-covered coasts could be the subjects of additional reports produced under a new or extended mandate.

In order to satisfy its mandate, the Committee drafted an internal discussion document for consideration at the August 2010 ILA biennial meeting in The Hague. The Committee considered the internal discussion document in a closed meeting and in an open working session held from 18–19 August 2010. A draft final report was produced on the basis of those discussions, and taking

4 *Id.* para. 4.

5 *Id.* para. 5.

6 Territorial and Maritime Dispute between Nicaragua and Honduras in the Caribbean Sea (Nicaragua v. Honduras), 2007 ICJ 659 (Oct. 8).

7 Award of the Arbitral Tribunal in the Matter of an Arbitration between Guyana and Suriname (Guyana v. Suriname), 47 ILM 166 (2008) (Sept. 17, 2007), *available at* http://www.pca-cpa.org/upload/files/Guyana-Suriname%20Award.pdf.

8 *See Proposal, supra* note 3, para. 2.

9 *See id.* para. 3. These 'straight line' baselines include Article 7 straight baselines, Article 9 baselines across the mouths of rivers, Article 10 bay closing lines, and Article 47 archipelagic baselines. It should be noted that the low-water line serves as the anchor for these 'straight line' baselines. To be valid in international law each of these baselines – which deviate from the location of the normal baseline – still must attach to or link up with the low-water line at their endpoints, and intermediate turning points. So, while the focus of this report is on the normal baseline, the issues raised here between the charted and actual low-water line are no less important for locating the other baselines contemplated in the Convention.

10 The issue of the normal baselines along ice-covered coasts was introduced during the open working session of 19 August 2010. *Baselines under the International Law of the Sea*, REPORT OF THE 74TH CONFERENCE 827, 833 (2010) (Noyes). The question of whether ice may be treated as 'land' under certain circumstances is not resolved.

into account comments from Committee Members and non-members, and also responses of Committee Members to an *ad hoc* series of questions formulated by the Rapporteur focusing on issues of state practice concerning baselines. The draft final report was circulated to Committee Members on 18 January 2012 and was discussed during an inter-sessional Committee meeting convened in Hamburg, Germany on 16–17 March 2012. A revised draft final report was subsequently submitted to the Committee on 18 May 2012, and this final report was submitted to ILA headquarters in advance of the 8 June 2012 deadline. This final Report takes account of comments submitted by Committee Members both during and subsequent to the Hamburg inter-sessional meeting.

This Report introduces the issues, identifies the existing law concerning the normal baseline, and suggests possible clarification or development of that law. The Committee has set out the relevant background information on the origin and significance of the normal baseline and has sought to highlight the interests of various actors in the location of the baseline (Section II). The Committee has investigated the meaning of the conventional law of normal baselines, including an analysis of the *travaux préparatiores*, and an assessment of other sources of law. On the basis of this analysis, the Committee has stated its conclusions concerning the existing law on the normal baseline (Section III). The Committee considers the impact on the normal baseline of territorial gain and territorial loss from, for example, the construction of coastal defenses or the effects of sea level rise (Section IV). Finally, the Committee's assessment of the need for further clarification or development of the law of normal baselines is set forth (Section V). The Annex to this Report provides a brief description of the technical reasons for the difference – in some circumstances – between the charted low-water line and the actual low-water line.

II The Normal Baseline: Origin, Significance, and Interests

A *Origin*

Article 5 of the United Nations Convention on the Law of the Sea (UNCLOS or the 1982 Convention) defines the normal baseline. The normal baseline article is concise, providing that:

> Except where otherwise provided in this Convention, the normal baseline for measuring the breadth of the territorial sea is the low-water line along the coast as marked on large-scale charts officially recognized by the coastal State.[11]

11 United Nations Convention on the Law of the Sea, Dec. 10, 1982, 1833 UNTS 397. The first clause in this article refers to other baseline provisions within the Convention, including Article 7 (straight baselines), Article 9 (mouths of rivers), and Article 10 (bays).

Although seemingly straightforward, the Committee notes that the concise language of Article 5 has been interpreted and applied in two ways:

(1) the normal baseline is the low-water line depicted on the charts officially recognized by the coastal State; or

(2) the normal baseline is the low-water line along the coast at the vertical, or tidal, datum indicated on the charts officially recognized by the coastal State.[12]

The application of the first interpretation would lead to the conclusion that the charted low-water line is the legal normal baseline and the chart itself is the legal document that determines the position of that baseline irrespective of the physical realities of the coast. The second interpretation would support a conclusion that the actual low-water line is the legal normal baseline and that charts, although not insignificant, are not determinative of the location of the normal baseline under Article 5 of the 1982 Convention. Under the latter interpretation adjudicators may consider evidence of the physical coastal realities or the actual coastal configuration notwithstanding the depiction of the normal baseline on officially recognized charts.

Prescott and Schofield have framed this issue, referring to several prominent members of this Committee, including Christopher Carleton, Alex Oude Elferink, and Michael Reed. They write:

> Under normal circumstances it might be considered that the low-water line shown on a chart officially recognized by a country is the baseline from which its territorial sea is measured and that this will prevail in any dispute. That is certainly the attitude of the British and Dutch governments (Carleton, pers. comm., 2001; [Oude] Elferink, pers. comm., [May] 2001). According to this view it is the chart that is the legal document determining the position of the normal baseline and this remains the case even where the coastline's configuration has changed. Thus, if the coastline has altered, but it has not been published, the legal baseline is that on the published chart. Where this is the case, the normal baseline will only come to reflect the physical change in the coastline if a fresh

12 The concept of vertical or tidal datums is instrumental to understanding the baselines issue. "In UNCLOS analysis, 'datum (vertical)' or 'vertical datum' means any level surface, e.g., mean sea level, taken as a surface of reference from which elevations may be reckoned". DEFINITIONS FOR THE LAW OF THE SEA: TERMS NOT DEFINED BY THE 1982 CONVENTION 163 (George K. Walker ed., 2012). See the Annex to this Report for a complete explanation of datums and how they impact the location of the normal baseline and the depiction of that line on nautical charts.

> survey is undertaken and the chart correspondingly updated (Carleton and Schofield, 2001: 24–25).
>
> However, Reed (2000: 180) records that members of the International Law Commission, during the preparation of draft articles for the 1958 Convention, expressed views that if the charted baseline departed appreciably from the actual low-water line the chart could be challenged in any legal tribunal. There does not appear to be any precise definition of the term 'appreciably' found in the *travaux préparatoires*. Reed records that in domestic cases even minor deviations have been raised and taken into account[13] (Reed, 2000: 182).

The Committee notes that the issue of the interpretation of Article 5 is largely academic. It is often the case that the application of either interpretation will result in the same line or in lines that differ in very minor ways. In these circumstances the issue addressed herein does not arise or is not one with which the law concerns itself – *de minimis non curat lex*. However, in some circumstances the application of the competing interpretations could result in normal baselines that are appreciably different – in absolute spatial terms – or that are different in small but important ways.[14]

The question before the Committee is, in essence, whether the Article 5 normal baseline is a line on a chart (the charted low-water line) or a line on the 'ground' (the actual low-water line). And, depending on the answer to that question, what are the implications when this rule is applied in practice in a variety of current and readily foreseeable situations involving territorial loss or gain? Recognizing that the location of these two lines can be substantially different, the Committee notes that the interpretation of Article 5 may have significant real-world consequences.

B *Significance*

The baseline is the legal expression of a state's coast, which, in turn, functions as an intermediary for the land territory of a coastal State in the determination of maritime zones and the generation of maritime rights and jurisdiction. As the International Court of Justice noted, "[t]he land is the legal source of

---

13 Victor Prescott & Clive Schofield, The Maritime Political Boundaries of the World 101 (2d ed. 2005).

14 For example, the transformation of a low-tide elevation into a fully submerged feature could result from only a small physical change but could significantly reduce the size of a state's territorial sea.

the power which a State may exercise over territorial extensions to seaward".[15] Weil expands on this fundamental notion, writing that maritime rights "have been based on two principles which have acquired an almost idiomatic force ...: the land dominates the sea and it dominates it by the intermediary the coastal front."[16] The ICJ emphasized the importance of the coast in this context:

> What distinguishes a coastal State with [maritime] rights from a land-locked State which has none, is certainly not the landmass, which both possess, but the existence of a maritime front in one State and its absence in the other. The juridical link between the State's territorial sovereignty and its rights to certain adjacent maritime expanses is established by means of its coast.[17]

The Committee notes that the coast, and the baseline to the extent that it represents the coast,[18] is foundational to the very concept of maritime jurisdiction.

The baseline issue may be conceptualized in a number of ways. For example, the baseline plays three distinct roles. First, the baseline divides land territory, including internal waters, from the territorial sea.[19] The navigational rights of flag states and the rules relating to jurisdiction over foreign vessels differ substantially between internal waters and the territorial sea. Specifically, the right of innocent passage does not exist in internal waters, with one exception.[20] Coastal State regulations may also differ between these two zones. It is

---

15 North Sea Continental Shelf (Federal Republic of Germany/Denmark; Federal Republic of Germany/Netherlands), 1969 ICJ 3, 51 (Feb. 20).

16 PROSPER WEIL, THE LAW OF MARITIME DELIMITATION – REFLECTIONS 50 (1989). Weil borrows the phrase "the land dominates the sea" from the *North Sea* judgment. *North Sea, supra* note 15, at 51.

17 Continental Shelf (Libyan Arab Jamahiriya/Malta), 1985 ICJ 13, 41 (June 3).

18 The term 'coast' is broader than the term 'baseline', but undoubtedly the low-water line is part of the coast. 'Coast' is defined as "the edge or margin of land next to the sea". DEFINITIONS, *supra* note 12, at 130. An earlier version of the International Hydrographic Organization glossary defines "coast" as "The sea-shore. The narrow strip of land in immediate contact with any body of water, including the area between high- and low-water lines". *Quoted in id.* at 131.

19 *See* United Nations Convention on the Law of the Sea, *supra* note 11, art. 8(1) ("[W]aters on the landward side of the baseline of the territorial sea form part of the internal waters of the State".).

20 *See id.* art. 8(2) ("Where the establishment of a straight baseline in accordance with the method set forth in article 7 has the effect of enclosing as internal waters areas which had not previously been considered as such, a right of innocent passage as provided in this Convention shall exist in those waters".).

therefore important for citizens and foreigners alike to know where the line of division – the baseline – is located.

Second, the outer limits of the territorial sea,[21] contiguous zone,[22] exclusive economic zone,[23] and, under certain circumstances, the continental shelf[24] are measured from the baseline and are delineated on the basis of that measurement. Here too, the rights and duties of the coastal state and of other ocean users will differ substantially depending upon the jurisdictional zone.[25] A coastal state's exploitation of offshore natural resources and a flag state's navigation through maritime areas provide two examples of activities for which the associated rights and duties differ substantially depending upon the jurisdictional zone in which those activities occur.

Third, baselines are often the starting point for determining title to maritime areas subject to overlapping coastal state claims.[26] It is this third role – the role of baselines in the bilateral delimitation of maritime boundaries – that, at least in part, prompted the formation of this Committee.[27] Parties in two recent maritime delimitation cases argued, among other things, "that the baselines depicted on the chart did not reflect the situation on the ground".[28] Other

21 *Id.* art. 3.

22 *Id.* art. 33(2).

23 *Id.* art. 57.

24 *Id.* art. 76(1), (5) & (6).

25 In some federal states the federated states or entities within the country may have jurisdiction over certain maritime areas off their coasts. While the rules governing the relationship between the federal and regional powers within a federation are not part of international law, the relationship can give rise to judicial consideration of international law rules (such as those governing baselines) within municipal legal systems.

26 In *Romania* v. *Ukraine* the Court distinguishes the role of baselines in the delineation of the outer limits of maritime zones from their role in the delimitation of a boundary between two states. Maritime Delimitation in the Black Sea (Romania v. Ukraine), 2009 ICJ 61, 108 (Feb. 3) ("The Court observes that the issue of determining the baseline for the purpose of measuring the breadth of the continental shelf and the exclusive economic zone and the issue of identifying base points for drawing an equidistance/median line for the purpose of delimiting continental shelf and exclusive economic zone between adjacent/opposite States are two different issues".).

27 Historically, the word 'delimitation' has been used to refer to the bilateral process of boundary making between two neighboring coastal states and to the unilateral process of establishing the outer limits of various maritime zones. Here we use the word 'delimitation' to refer only to the former and the word 'delineation' to refer to the latter. Where, in quotations, 'delimitation' has been used to refer to the establishment of outer limits, we note this use for the sake of clarity.

28 *Proposal, supra* note 3 (referring to *Nicaragua* v. *Honduras* and *Guyana* v. *Suriname*).

cases have raised related issues.[29] As noted above, it is land territory, with the coast as intermediary, which generates entitlements to maritime area. As such, coastal geography is of paramount importance in delimiting boundaries between coastal states with overlapping claims to maritime areas.

The territorial sea delimitation provisions of the 1958 Convention and 1982 Convention refer to baselines.[30] With an exception for historic title and other special circumstances, Article 15 of the 1982 Convention provides that:

> [w]here the coasts of two States are opposite or adjacent to each other, neither of the two States is entitled, failing agreement between them to the contrary, to extend its territorial sea beyond the median line every point of which is equidistant from the nearest points *on the baselines* from which the breadth of the territorial seas of each of the two States is measured.[31]

As a consequence, the location of the baseline is a primary consideration in the delimitation of lateral or opposite territorial sea boundaries. In contrast, the 1982 Convention delimitation provisions for the exclusive economic zone and continental shelf do not refer to baselines as a starting point. However, the maritime delimitation jurisprudence appears to give a procedural presumption to the construction of a provisional delimitation line measured from baselines.[32]

These three roles – (1) division of territory/internal waters from territorial sea, (2) delineation of outer limits of maritime jurisdictional zones, and (3) delimitation of boundaries dividing one state's maritime area from another state's maritime area – may also be separated or grouped on the basis of their

---

29 *See, e.g.*, Continental Shelf (United Kingdom/France), XVIII RIAA 271 (Mar. 14, 1978); Award of the Arbitral Tribunal in the second stage of the proceedings between Eritrea and Yemen (Maritime Delimitation) (Eritrea/Yemen), XXII RIAA 335 (Dec. 17, 1999); Maritime Delimitation and Territorial Questions between Qatar and Bahrain (Qatar v. Bahrain), 2001 ICJ 40 (Mar. 16); Land and Maritime Boundary between Cameroon and Nigeria (Cameroon v. Nigeria: Equatorial Guinea intervening), 2002 ICJ 303 (Oct. 10); *Romania* v. *Ukraine*, *supra* note 26; Dispute concerning delimitation of the maritime boundary between Bangladesh and Myanmar in the Bay of Bengal (Bangladesh/Myanmar), ITLOS Case No. 16 (Mar. 14, 2012).

30 Convention on the Territorial Sea and the Contiguous Zone, art. 12, Apr. 29, 1958, 516 UNTS 206.

31 United Nations Convention on the Law of the Sea, *supra* note 11, art. 15 (emphasis added).

32 *See Romania* v. *Ukraine*, *supra* note 26; *Bangladesh/Myanmar*, *supra* note 29. In practice, courts and tribunals have disregarded specific base points in delimitations that would be legitimate base points for measuring the outer limits of maritime zones. *See, e.g.*, Ukraine's Serpents' Island, Romania's Sulina Dyke, and Bangladesh's Saint Martin's Island.

unilateral or bilateral aspects. The first and second roles of baselines share a common characteristic: they both establish the outer limits of coastal state jurisdiction beyond which flag states or the international community enjoy different rights from those enjoyed in various coastal zones. In these two roles, the establishment, maintenance, notification, and use of the baseline are prerogatives of the coastal state.[33] The baseline, although it impacts interests beyond the coastal state, is largely a unilateral concern weighted heavily toward the interests of the coastal state. It is not, however, purely unilateral. The inherent tension between unilateral prerogative and multilateral interest is captured in the *Fisheries* case. The ICJ wrote:

> The delimitation of sea areas has always an international aspect; it cannot be dependent merely upon the will of the coastal State as expressed in its municipal law. Although it is true that the act of delimitation [of baselines and outer limits] is necessarily a unilateral act, because only the coastal State is competent to undertake it, the validity of the delimitation with regard to other States depends upon international law.[34]

In contrast, in the delimitation role a coastal state's baseline is a bilateral concern, and it is, in the case of adjudication, the court or tribunal's prerogative to determine the location of baselines and, in some instances, to disregard a claimed baseline in part or in its entirety.[35]

Lastly, baseline rules may be considered in light of two different contexts in which they are applied. The first is when a coastal State defines and regulates the status of its territorial sea and other maritime zones, usually by means of domestic legislation. Here, the baseline rules are intended to be applied in a domestic setting and on an enduring basis. The second is when a base point or subsection of a baseline is subject to examination at a particular time, for example, following an arrest or incident at sea or in the context of maritime boundary negotiations or litigation. In these latter circumstances, baseline

33 *See, e.g.*, United Nations Convention on the Law of the Sea, *supra* note 11, arts. 3 ("Every State has the right to establish the breadth of its territorial sea … measured from baselines determined in accordance with this Convention".), 5 ("charts officially recognized by the coastal State"), and 14 ("The coastal State may determine baselines in turn by any of the methods provided for…".).

34 Fisheries (United Kingdom v. Norway), 1951 ICJ 116, 132 (Dec. 18) (addressing the unilateral act of declaring straight baselines; however, the same issues apply with respect to normal baselines).

35 *See Romania* v. *Ukraine*, *supra* note 26 (disregarding points on Romania's straight baseline, including the seaward end of Sulina dyke); *Nicaragua* v. *Honduras*, *supra* note 6 (disregarding Honduran straight baselines).

rules are applied in a much more restricted context where questions of evidence assume greater importance.

These different roles of baselines and conceptualizations of the issue do not affect the Committee's assessment of the existing law on the normal baseline. However, they may affect the manner in which a baseline question is posed or – in the event of litigation – the way in which a challenge to a baseline is framed, including the possible litigants and venue. For example, bilateral delimitation cases are heard in public international law forums, while claims challenging the right of coastal States to enforce its laws in areas defined on the basis of distance from baselines are more likely to be heard in the national courts of the enforcing coastal State. It is not surprising therefore that the issue of baselines has come to the attention of the ILA following various international maritime delimitation cases.[36]

C *Interests*

Many different interests are at play with respect to the location of baselines. Churchill and Lowe, referring to the desirability of precise baseline rules, highlight the role of state self-interest: the interest of the coastal State in moving baselines seaward against the interest of all other States. They write:

> If the rules are not sufficiently precise, it may be possible for a State to draw its baselines in a generous manner, thus pushing the outer limit of its territorial sea and other zones seawards and bringing greater areas of sea within internal waters, thus reducing the areas of sea available for use by other States.[37]

Of course, it is not just internal waters, but the extent of all maritime zones measured from baselines that would be affected by the coastal State's 'generous' drawing of its baselines. In a subsequent delimitation of overlapping zones, these baselines might be challenged by a neighboring state.

Sub-state political units may have an interest in the location of the baseline if it separates or is linked to the line separating their areas from the area of the state. This is the situation as between the United States of America and

36 Klein notes that "[i]t is most typical that a challenge to baselines will ensue in the context of a delimitation between States with opposite or adjacent coasts". NATALIE KLEIN, DISPUTE SETTLEMENT IN THE UN CONVENTION ON THE LAW OF THE SEA 268 (2005).

37 R.R. CHURCHILL & A.V. LOWE, THE LAW OF THE SEA 32 (3d ed. 1999).

its coastal federated states, and has given rise to several cases before the U.S. Supreme Court in which the location of the baseline was at issue.[38]

Private actors may have an interest in the location of baselines and the outer limits of zones measured therefrom. Consider, for example, a vessel fishing in the vicinity of the outer limit of the exclusive economic zone, or a lessee with a license to explore or exploit natural resources within, but not beyond, the outer limit of a state's maritime area. Any private actor involved with maritime transportation will have an interest in the location of baselines and outer limits, as would defendants raising certain jurisdictional defenses in the courts of a coastal State. In all of these examples, private actors may find themselves contesting the coastal State's official baseline, perhaps on the grounds that it does not reflect the physical realities of the actual low-water line.

Prescott and Schofield note that

> [i]n practice it seems likely that the dispute over whether the charted or actual low-water line should prevail will only arise in two situations. The first is when a country realises that the actual line lies significantly seawards of the charted line. The second is when a foreigner, accused of improperly entering a maritime zone, realises that the actual line lies significantly landwards of the low-water line shown on the chart.[39]

As demonstrated in maritime delimitation cases there is a third situation in which a coastal state may contest its neighbor's asserted baseline when it realizes that the actual line lies significantly *landwards* of the charted line.

Finally, there is a special category of coastal State with an existential interest in this issue. The Committee refers here to the low-lying, small island developing states that may be particularly vulnerable to the effects of sea level rise. It is possible that some of these States could lose the entirety of their territory to the sea, and thereby the basic qualifications of statehood itself.[40] The plight of these States contributed to the formation of this Committee, and, certainly, they have a unique interest in the subject of this Report. The existing law of the

---

38 *See infra* section III.C.2.

39 PRESCOTT & SCHOFIELD, *supra* note 13, at 101.

40 Susin Park, *Climate Change and the Risk of Statelessness: The Situation of Low-lying Island States* (UNHCR, May 2011) ("The Intergovernmental Panel on Climate Change (IPCC) thus concluded that '[s]ea-level rise impacts on the low-lying Pacific Island atoll States of Kiribati, Tuvalu, Tokelau and the Marshall Islands may, at some threshold, pose risks to their sovereignty or existence''. [quoting IPCC, Climate Change 2007, Fourth assessment report, Report of the international working group II, *Impacts, adaptation and vulnerability* 736]).

normal baseline as it affects the interests of small island developing states is addressed in Section IV.B.

III The Normal Baseline: Existing Law

In an effort to identify the existing law concerning the normal baseline, the Committee has applied the rules of treaty interpretation to Article 5 of the 1982 Convention, including a review of its predecessor provision – Article 3 of the 1958 Convention – and the relevant *travaux préparatoires*. The Committee begins this section with the results of that exercise (III.A). The treatment of the normal baseline in international judicial decisions (III.B) and in municipal legislation and litigation (III.C) provides important perspectives on the existing law, as do the writings of legal and technical experts (III.D). We complete our study of the existing law with an assessment of two other normal baseline articles, Article 6 (reefs) and Article 13 (low-tide elevations) (III.E), before providing our general conclusions on the existing law (III.F).

A *Interpreting Article 5*

1 General Rule

The Committee begins with the text of Article 5 and the interpretive rules of Articles 31 (general rule of interpretation) and 33 (interpretation of treaties authenticated in two or more languages) of the Vienna Convention on the Law of Treaties.[41] In English, Article 5 reads:

> Except where otherwise provided in this Convention, the normal baseline for measuring the breadth of the territorial sea is the low-water line along the coast as marked on large-scale charts officially recognized by the coastal State.[42]

---

41 Vienna Convention on the Law of Treaties, May 23, 1969, 1155 UNTS 331.

42 United Nations Convention on the Law of the Sea, *supra* note 11.
In French:
"Sauf disposition contraire de la Convention, la ligne de base normale à partir de laquelle est mesurée la largeur de la mer territoriale est la laisse de basse mer le long de la côte, telle qu'elle est indiquée sur les cartes marines à grande échelle reconnues officiellement par l'Etat côtier."
In Spanish:
"Salvo disposición en contrario de esta Convención, la línea de base normal para medir la anchura del mar territorial es la línea de bajamar a lo largo de la costa, tal como aparece marcada mediante el signo apropiado en cartas a gran escala reconocidas oficialmente por el Estado ribereño."
In Chinese:

The text of this provision, which is equally authoritative in Arabic, Chinese, English, French, Russian, and Spanish,[43] must be interpreted "in good faith in accordance with the ordinary meaning to be given to the terms of the treaty in their context and in the light of its object and purpose",[44] with the presumption that the provision has "the same meaning in each authentic text".[45]

As noted above, the English version of Article 5 could lead to two different meanings of "the normal baseline for measuring the breadth of the territorial sea": (1) the low-water line along the coast (the actual low-water line), or (2) the low-water line as marked on charts officially recognized by the coastal State (the charted low-water line). Put more simply, the charted line could *be* the legal normal baseline or the charted line could *illustrate* the legal normal baseline.

The Committee has reached the view that an analysis of the equally authentic texts in other languages provides no indication regarding which meaning should prevail. The Spanish equivalent of the phrase "as marked on" is, "*tal como aparece marcada mediante el signo apropiado en*" (as marked/shown by the appropriate symbol on). The French equivalent of the phrase "as marked on" is "*telle qu'elle est indiquée sur*" (as it is indicated on).[46] The Spanish and French may indicate that the charted line is meant to be a representation, depiction, or illustration of the normal baseline, not the normal baseline itself. In contrast, the Chinese and Russian texts are in line with the English version, which seems to emphasize the charted line. For lack of linguistic expertise, the Committee has not analyzed the Arabic text.

"除本公约另有规定外，测算领海宽度的正常基线是沿海国官方承认的大比例尺海图所标明的沿岸低潮线。"

In Russian:

"Если иное не предусмотрено в настоящей Конвенции, нормальной исходной линией для измерения ширины территориального моря является линия наибольшего отлива вдоль.

берега, указанная на официально признанных прибрежным государством морских картах крупного масштаба."

43 *Id.* art. 320. *See also* Responsibilities and Obligations of States Sponsoring Persons and Entities with Respect to Activities in the Area (Request for Advisory Opinion submitted to the Seabed Disputes Chamber) paras. 208–17, ITLOS Case No. 17 (Feb. 1, 2011).

44 Vienna Convention on the Law of Treaties, *supra* note 41, art. 31(1).

45 *Id.* art. 33(3).

46 In both the French and Spanish texts, the same phrasing is used in Article 6 (reefs) as in Article 5, while in the English version Article 5 and Article 6 differ. In English, Article 6 reads "as shown by the appropriate symbol on". This might lead to the conclusion that the English phrases, "as marked on" and "as shown by the appropriate symbol on", were intended to have the same meaning in both Articles.

The interpretation of Article 5 may be assisted by a review of Article 7 (straight baselines), and the apparent exception made in Article 7(2), which provides:

> Where because of the presence of a delta and other natural conditions the coastline is highly unstable, the appropriate points may be selected along the furthest seaward extent of the low-water line and, *notwithstanding subsequent regression of the low-water line*, the straight baseline shall remain effective until changed by the coastal State in accordance with this Convention.[47]

The Committee notes that this provision distinguishes between the actual low-water line and the representational version of that low-water line (here, the straight baseline constructed by connecting appropriate turning points on a low-water line that no longer exists in its original location). Article 7(2) allows – in very particular circumstances – for the representational version to remain effective despite the fact that it does not reflect the actual low-water line. This appears to support the interpretation that, with this one exception, in conditions of physical change the baseline must reflect the actual low-water line. However, Article 7(2) also lends weight to the role of the coastal State in recognizing and depicting its own baselines. In the Article 5 context, this might include depiction of the normal baseline in the form of revised or updated "large-scale charts officially recognized by the coastal State," irrespective of physical changes to the coast.

The other related provisions of the 1982 Convention that the Committee considers may assist in the interpretation of Article 5 are the 'notice' or 'publicity' provisions of Article 16(1) and Article 47(8). Both articles address the role of charts in depicting artificial, straight-line baselines determined in accordance with Article 7 (straight baselines), Article 9 (mouths of rivers), Article 10 (bays), and Article 47 (archipelagic baselines), respectively. Both articles provide that baselines drawn in accordance with these articles "shall be shown on charts of a scale or scales adequate for ascertaining their position".[48] Here, the role of charts is to allow others to ascertain the position of the artificial baseline. Publicity of these baselines through charts provides notice of their location for mariners and other interested parties. What is particularly noteworthy is that these publicity provisions do not apply, and there is no equivalent provision that does apply, to the publicity of charts depicting the Article 5 normal baseline.

47 United Nations Convention on the Law of the Sea, *supra* note 11, art. 7(2) (emphasis added).
48 *Id.* arts. 16(1) and 47(8).

2 Supplementary Means

The treatment of charts and the low-water line in these articles seems to indicate that the Article 5 normal baseline is the actual low-water line, not the representational, charted low-water line. However, the supplementary means of interpretation contained in Article 32 of the Vienna Convention are also available, and the Committee has applied these means to this interpretation exercise. In this regard, the Committee recalls that supplementary means of interpretation – namely a review of the *travaux préparatoires* – may be applied to confirm a meaning determined pursuant to Article 31, or to determine a meaning where the Article 31 interpretation "leaves the meaning ambiguous or obscure; or leads to a result which is manifestly absurd or unreasonable".[49] The Committee has applied the supplementary means of interpretation for all three of the reasons outlined above: that is, to confirm that the actual low-water line is the normal baseline; to clarify the roles of charts and the charted line in Article 5, which remain ambiguous; and to avoid the manifestly absurd or unreasonable results that might arise from certain interpretations and applications of Article 5.[50]

The *travaux préparatoires* reveal that the original role of the charted line was neither to *illustrate* nor to *be* the normal baseline. Instead, charts and the charted line played an indirect role in defining the word 'low-water' in what has now become the Article 5 phrase 'low-water line'.

The language adopted in Article 5 of the 1982 Convention is substantially the same as in Article 3 of the 1958 Convention on the Territorial Sea and Contiguous Zone (the 1958 Convention),[51] which reads:

> Except where otherwise provided in these articles, the normal baseline for measuring the breadth of the territorial sea is the low-water line along

49 Vienna Convention on the Law of Treaties, *supra* note 41, art. 32.

50 Absurd or unreasonable results might arise in two situations. First, if the charted line were the legal normal baseline and the Article 5 chart no longer reflected the physical reality of the coast, the maritime zones generated from that baseline would no longer correspond to the territory from which they were derived. In circumstances of significant territorial loss this would defy the fundamental principle of international law that maritime rights are subsidiary rights derived from title to territory leading to an absurd result: maritime zones without territory. Second, if the legal normal baseline (the actual low-water line) and outer limits measured therefrom were subject to revision with each minute physical change to the coast, this would impose an insurmountable burden on coastal states and mariners alike. In tandem with the principle *de minimis non curat lex*, nautical charts perform an important stabilizing role in this regard. They provide the most authoritative depiction of the normal baseline and enjoy a presumption of accuracy.

51 Convention on the Territorial Sea and the Contiguous Zone, *supra* note 30.

the coast as marked on large-scale charts officially recognized by the coastal State.

The only change from the 1958 Convention was the replacement of the words 'these articles' with 'this Convention' in the first line. No substantive alteration was intended. This understanding is confirmed in the *Virginia Commentary*, which notes that "[i]n the Main Trends Working Paper (Source 9), Provision 4, Formula A, repeated article 3 of the 1958 Convention, and became the basis for the final text of the 1982 Convention".[52]

Article 5 was not new in 1982, nor was Article 3 new in 1958. Baselines were considered during preparations for the 1930 Hague Codification Conference (1930 Conference), and though that Conference adopted no convention on the law of the sea, draft articles were produced, including draft articles on baselines.[53] Those draft articles formed the basis of the work by the International Law Commission on the law of the sea in the 1950s,[54] which culminated in the 1958 Conventions, including the Convention on the Territorial Sea and Contiguous Zone. The 1930 draft article dealing with the normal baseline formed the basis of Article 3 of the 1958 Convention. In turn, Article 3 was adopted nearly *verbatim* as Article 5 of the 1982 Convention. The Committee finds no evidence of an intention to change the meaning of the normal baseline provision in all of that time.

In its infancy, the baseline discussion focused on the distinction between what we now refer to as normal and straight baselines. In 1929, in advance of the 1930 Conference, the conference preparatory committee distributed a questionnaire to governments that included the following inquiry: "Along the coasts. Is the line that of low tide following the sinuosities of the coast; or a line drawn between the outermost points of the coast, islands, islets or rocks; or

52 2 UNITED NATIONS CONVENTION ON THE LAW OF THE SEA, 1982: A COMMENTARY 88 (Satya N. Nandan & Shabtai Rosenne eds., 1993). *See also* CHURCHILL & LOWE, *supra* note 37, at 32 (stating that the baselines provisions of the 1958 Convention "were not only binding on parties to the Convention, but in most respects were also regarded … as representing the rules of customary international law. Thus it is not surprising to find that the Law of the Sea Convention … simply repeats most of the 1958 Convention's [baseline] provisions *verbatim*…".); DEFINITIONS, *supra* note 12, at 114 (referring to 1982 Convention, Article 5 and noting of 1958 Convention, Article 3 that "Article 3 applies the same rule").

53 CHURCHILL & LOWE, *supra* note 37, at 32–33.

54 *See Summary Records of the Fourth Session*, [1952] 1 Y.B. Int'l L. Comm'n 143, UN Doc. A/CN.4/SER.A/1952 (Special Rapporteur François, Regime of the Territorial Sea, noting that he had "tak[en] as a basis the work of the The Hague Conference").

some other line?"[55] A substantial majority of responding states opined that the 'line of low tide following the sinuosities of the coast' is the proper baseline.[56] However, it was immediately clear that a treaty provision that merely referred to the 'line of low tide' would be inadequate.[57] The line of low tide is defined by a vertical datum, or chart datum, and, as Germany pointed out in its questionnaire response, there were at least six datums in use at the time which might be used to identify the 'line of low tide'.[58] These six datums would lead to six different 'lines of low tide' along the same coast. To add to the problem there was no international agreement as to which of these datums should be used for charting purposes. At that time, nautical charts provided the only visual representation of the 'line of low tide'.

The problem facing the preparatory committee and the Hague conferees in 1929 and 1930 was, in short, the issue of vertical datums, specifically the fact that several different vertical datums were in use by the charting agencies of participating States. In order to describe the 'line of low tide' with any precision, the vertical datum would also have to be specified. But, if a single vertical datum were specified, a significant number of coastal States' charts would cease to reflect the legal baseline or 'line of low tide' at that specified vertical datum, requiring expensive, time-consuming updates. The solution was to decline to identify a single datum and, instead, to ratify any reasonable datum already in use. Germany was the first to suggest this solution in its response to the pre-conference questionnaire: "The German Government considers

---

55 Excerpt of *Bases of Discussion Drawn up for the Conference by the Preparatory Committee, II. Territorial Waters*, League of Nations Doc. C.74.M.39.1929.V. (1929), *reprinted in Official Documents: Conference for the Codification of International Law*, 24 AM. J. INT'L L. SUPP. 29 (1930).

56 *Id.* at 30. The ICJ, in a recent case, notes the exceptional nature of straight baselines: "the method of straight baselines, which is an exception to the normal rules for the determination of baselines, may only be applied if a number of conditions are met. This method must be applied restrictively". *Qatar* v. *Bahrain*, *supra* note 29, at 103. In 1929, Norway was a notable exception, taking an early position in support of what we now refer to as straight baselines.

57 *See Bases of Discussion*, *supra* note 55, at 30 ("Various replies call attention to the different meanings which can be given to the expression 'low water'. This is a question of a technical character which must be brought to the notice of the Governments…".).

58 *Bases of Discussion Drawn up for the Conference by the Preparatory Committee, II. Territorial Waters*, League of Nations Doc. C.74.M.39.1929.V. (1929) at 35. Germany pointed out that "different methods are employed in the existing marine charts of the various States to fix the 'spring-tide low-water level', which corresponds to the 'low-water mark'". It continued, noting that "[a] number of other criteria are also adopted by the various countries to determine the base line, *e.g.*, 'mean water', the 'line of mean low-water spring-tides', the 'spring-tide low-water line during the equinoxes', the 'low-water level' and the 'mean sea-level'".

in 1953. Commission member Amado (Brazil) captured the discussion in 1952 noting, "the proviso should be deleted, since, if the low-water mark in official charts departed appreciably from the line of mean low-water spring tides, those charts would not be accurate and their validity would be questioned by any legal tribunal".[65] Commission member Yepes (Colombia) did not agree with the deletion, but noted that "if a dispute arose as to whether a chart did or did not 'appreciably' depart from that criterion, it could be referred to an international tribunal".[66] Commission member Scelle (France) pointed out that, even with the proviso, the article "would not exclude charts which were unacceptable on other grounds, as being out of date, for instance".[67]

In 1953, a Committee of Experts was convened at the invitation of François. He drafted a questionnaire in light of the outstanding technical issues faced by the Commission in 1952. Importantly, the Report of the Committee of Experts warns that "these replies are given from the technical point of view, bearing in mind in particular *the practical difficulties of the navigator*".[68] The first question posed to the Committee was "[a]ssuming the territorial sea to be measured from the low-water line, what line might then preferably be taken as such?"[69] Considering the context arising from the 1930 draft text and from the previous year's debate, it is clear that the experts were being asked to identify the preferred vertical datum for defining low-water. Still without international agreement on a single datum for charting purposes, the experts declined to answer the question with a specific vertical datum and answered instead that "the base-line for measuring the territorial sea should be the low-water line along the coast as marked on the largest-scale chart available, officially recognized by the coastal State".[70] The "largest-scale chart available" is the chart that any prudent navigator would have referred to while navigating near the coast. The experts also agreed that the proviso regarding the mean low-water spring tides was unnecessary and that there was no danger that omitting the provision "might tempt governments unreasonably to extend their low-water lines on their charts".[71]

65 *Id.* at 172.

66 *Id.* at 178.

67 *Id.* (emphasis added).

68 *Rapport du Comité d'experts sur certaines questions d'ordre technique concernant la mer territoriale*, [1953] 2 Y.B. Int'l L. Comm'n 77, UN Doc. A/CN.4/SER.A/1953/Add.1, English translation *reprinted in* 2 UNITED NATIONS CONVENTION ON THE LAW OF THE SEA, 1982: A COMMENTARY 59 (Myron H. Nordquist ed., 2003).

69 *Id.*

70 *Id.*

71 *Id.*

The Commission incorporated the Experts' answers. Article 4 of the 1956 ILC draft articles (soon to become Article 3 of the 1958 Convention) read:

> Subject to the provisions of article 5 [straight baselines] and to the provisions regarding bays and islands, the breadth of the territorial sea is measured from the low-water line along the coast, as marked on large-scale charts officially recognized by the coastal State.[72]

The commentary accompanying this article indicates that the unresolved problem of different vertical datums continued to influence the thinking of the Commission through 1956. In that commentary the Commission noted the following:

> The traditional expression "low-water mark" may have different meanings; *there is no uniform standard by which States in practice determine this line.* The Commission considers that it is permissible to adopt as the base line the low-water mark as indicated on large-scale charts officially recognized by the coastal State. The Commission is of the opinion that the omission of detailed provisions such as were prepared by the 1930 Codification Conference is hardly likely to induce Governments to shift the low-water lines on their charts unreasonably.[73]

As noted above, Article 3 was adopted *verbatim* in the text of Article 5 of the 1982 Convention. To the extent that the wording of Article 5 is vague, the Committee considers that this was deliberate, and was intended to 'paper over' the practical difficulties resulting from the absence of a universally agreed vertical datum for defining low water. The insertion of the reference to charts was intended to address these difficulties, and was not intended to give primacy to the charted line.

B *International Judicial Decisions*

The manner in which international courts and tribunals have dealt with the normal baseline is also informative. The Committee recalls that two international judicial decisions were specifically referred to in the proposal for the establishment of this Committee: the ICJ judgment in *Nicaragua* v. *Honduras*

72 *Report of the International Law Commission to the General Assembly*, [1956] 2 Y.B. Int'l L. Comm'n 253, 266, UN Doc. A/CN.4/SER.A/1956/Add.1.

73 *Id.* at 267 (emphasis added).

and the arbitral award in *Guyana* v. *Suriname*.[74] In both cases, the parties argued "that the baseline depicted on the chart did not reflect the situation on the ground".[75] The Committee accordingly addresses the baseline issues raised in *Guyana* v. *Suriname* and *Nicaragua* v. *Honduras* before turning to other international judicial decisions.

The arbitration between Guyana and Suriname involved the delimitation of a lateral maritime boundary from the land boundary terminus of the adjacent coastal states out to the 200 nautical mile outer limit. In this region of north-eastern South America massive shoals of soft 'sling mud' originating in the mouth of the Amazon River are carried slowly along the coast from east to west by the Guyana Current toward the mouth of the Orinoco River. These shoals of mud are substantial and "the presence of these mud banks complicates survey work along the coast".[76] One large shoal of mud, attached to Suriname's coast near Vissers Bank, contributed to the charted low-water line depicted on the most recent large-scale chart of the area officially recognized by Suriname: Netherlands Hydrographic Office Chart 2218 (2005 ed.). The newly charted low-water line was located several kilometers seaward of the charted line shown on previous charts of the area. In the arbitration, Suriname selected a base point on Vissers Bank – point S14 – as depicted on Chart 2218, and Guyana challenged point S14 on the grounds that the charted low-water line on Chart 2218 did not represent the actual coastal configuration of Vissers Bank.[77]

Guyana contended that the new chart inaccurately depicted Suriname's low-water line, supported that contention with additional map and satellite evidence,[78] urging the Tribunal to disregard the chart.[79] Suriname countered with an explanation of how the new chart had been constructed noting that data were used from older charts, aerial photography, and ship-based echo sounders, and that Chart 2218 was "produced in accordance with the

74 Several Committee members were involved in these cases as counsel, advocates, and advisers. The Committee Chair, Judge Dolliver Nelson, was President of the Annex VII tribunal in *Guyana* v. *Suriname*, *supra* note 7.

75 *Proposal*, *supra* note 3, para. 2.

76 *The production of the June 2005 edition of chart NL 2218*, Annex SR43, Rejoinder of Suriname, *Guyana* v. *Suriname*, *supra* note 7, *available at* http://server.nijmedia.nl/pca-cpa.org/upload/files/SR%20Annexes%2041-44.pdf.

77 Reply of Guyana, *Guyana* v. *Suriname*, *supra* note 7, at 40, *available at* http://www.pca-cpa.org/upload/files/GUYANA%20Reply%20brief%20volume%20I.pdf.

78 *Analysis of Recent Shoreline Revisions to the 2005 Edition of Dutch Nautical Chart NL 2218*, Annex R2, Reply of Guyana, *Guyana* v. *Suriname*, *supra* note 7, *available at* http://www.pca-cpa.org/upload/files/GR%20Annex%20R02-a.pdf.

79 Reply of Guyana, *supra* note 77, at 40 n.31 ("It is plain that the hastily-prepared June 2005 version of chart NL 2218 should be given no weight".).

requirements for the safety of navigation, the primary purpose of nautical charts".[80]

The Tribunal, faced with the argument that the low-water line marked on the large-scale chart officially recognized by the coastal State was not an accurate reflection of the actual low-water line, did not simply accept the charted line as the legal normal baseline of Suriname, but instead admitted evidence from both parties regarding the accuracy of that line. After consideration of the evidence, the Tribunal rejected Guyana's challenge to the charted line, explaining that "[t]he Tribunal is not convinced that the depiction of the low-water line on chart NL 2218, a chart recognised as official by Suriname, is inaccurate. As a result, the Tribunal accepts the basepoint on Vissers Bank, Suriname's basepoint S14".[81]

For the purposes of this Report, the relevance of this case centers on the approaches of the parties and the Tribunal to the question of charts. In this regard, the Committee notes that neither party contended that the chart was dispositive, even though it was a large-scale chart officially recognized by the coastal State. Instead, both sides introduced evidence in support of, or against, the accuracy of the chart and, specifically, the charted low-water line. The Tribunal accepted the evidence, weighed it, and reached conclusions based upon it – most notably that the party challenging the officially recognized large-scale chart had not convinced the Tribunal of the inaccuracy of the contested chart. All participants proceeded on the assumption that officially recognized charts may be challenged before an international tribunal and that the actual location of a baseline may be determined by that body.[82]

Two conclusions arise from *Guyana* v. *Suriname* regarding charts and the normal baseline. First, the charted low-water line may be challenged before an

80 *The production of the June 2005 edition of chart NL 2218, supra* note 76.

81 *Guyana* v. *Suriname, supra* note 7, para. 396.

82 The Commission on the Limits of the Continental Shelf, a scientific and technical body formed pursuant to Annex II of the Law of the Sea Convention, is not a judicial body and lacks the authority to determine the location of baselines. This is set out in the Commission's guidelines:

"3.3.1. The Commission is not entitled by the Convention to issue any recommendations with respect to the delineation of baselines from which the breadth of the territorial sea is measured. Its role is limited to a potential request for information about the geodetic position and definition of the baselines used in a submission made by a coastal State.

3.3.2. There are only two instances in which the Commission might request geodetic information about baselines. First, it must be satisfied that the test of appurtenance has been positively met. Secondly, if the 350 M limit is employed as a constraint in a submission, the Commission might also find it useful to make recommendations in relation to the methodology employed in the delineation of this limit."

Scientific and Technical Guidelines of the Commission on the Limits of the Continental Shelf, CLCS/11 (May 1999).

international tribunal on the basis that it does not reflect accurately the actual low-water line. Second, the officially recognized chart is presumed accurate and the burden of proof is on the party challenging that chart.

The other international judicial decision mentioned in the Committee proposal – the judgment in *Nicaragua* v. *Honduras* – dealt with different baseline questions. Here too adjacent coastal states sought to resolve their lateral maritime boundary off unstable coasts. The instability in this case was created by sediment transported down the border river to its deltaic mouth at Cape Gracias a Dios. The parties agreed that sediment transport caused the delta "as well as the coastline to the north and south of the Cape, to exhibit a very active morpho-dynamism".[83] The Court also recognized that, generally, there was a process of accretion in the delta area by which the actual low-water line continued to move seaward.[84]

Here, the charted low-water line was not at issue – the Court does not once mention nautical charts or the charted low-water line in the judgment. In fact, it does not appear that the parties in *Nicaragua* v. *Honduras* introduced nautical charts into evidence, nor does it appear that they argued their positions on the basis of charts or the charted low-water lines. Instead, both parties introduced satellite imagery of the mouth of the Rio Coco to demonstrate the location of the actual low-water line. Nonetheless, two conclusions regarding baselines may be gleaned from the Court's judgment. First, despite the fact that Honduras had deposited a list of coordinates of its straight baseline turning points mere months after Nicaragua filed its Application in this case, the Court did not regard them as viable base points because they no longer reflected the actual coastal configuration.[85] Second, invoking Article 5 of the 1982 Convention, the Court concluded that a base point that is not on the actual low-water line "cannot be properly used as a base point".[86] Both of these conclusions support the interpretation that the actual low-water line is the Article 5 normal baseline.

Baseline issues have arisen in other international judicial decisions. With respect to the "international aspect" of baselines, the 1951 judgment in *Fisheries* is directly on point. That judgment was quoted above for the proposition that "[t]he delimitation of sea areas has always an international aspect; it cannot be dependent merely upon the will of the coastal State as expressed in its municipal law". This is undoubtedly the passage Hudson was referring to in 1952 when

83 *Nicaragua* v. *Honduras*, *supra* note 6, at 742.

84 *Id.*

85 *See id.* at 743.

86 *Id.* ("This point, even if it can be said to appertain to Honduras, is no longer in the mouth of the River Coco and cannot be properly used as a base point [see UNCLOS, Art. 5.]".).

he pointed out that "to accept a line indicated on official charts ... would be inconsistent with the judgment of the Court."[87] Although the case addressed a challenge to straight baselines, *Fisheries* is consistent with the perspective that the charted line cannot stand as an unchallengeable fact simply because a coastal state recognizes, officially, the chart on which that line appears. This would allow the normal baseline to be established "merely upon the will of the coastal State".

In *Qatar* v. *Bahrain* the International Court of Justice was faced with several features whose status as either an island or a low-tide elevation was ambiguous.[88] In the confined geographic context of the case, islands would be taken into account in the delimitation while many low-tide elevations would not.[89] The Court began its analysis by recalling "that under the applicable rules of international law the normal baseline for measuring [the breadth of the Territorial Sea] is *the low-water line along the coast* (Art. 5, 1982 Convention on the Law of the Sea)".[90] The manner in which the Court dealt with the feature named Qit'at Jaradah is particularly instructive:

> 191. Another issue on which the Parties have totally opposing views is whether Qit'at Jaradah is an island or a low-tide elevation.
>
> ....
>
> 193. Qatar maintains that Qit'at Jaradah is not, and has never been, reflected on nautical charts as an island but always as a low-tide elevation....
>
> 194. Bahrain commissioned an expert to examine the geographical situation; this expert concluded that Qit'at Jaradah – though small in size – is permanently above water, and is thus an island....
>
> 195. ... *The Court has carefully analysed the evidence submitted by the Parties* and weighed the conclusions of the experts referred to above.... On these bases, the Court concludes that the maritime feature of Qit'at Jaradah satisfies the above-mentioned criteria and that it is an island which should as such be taken into consideration for the drawing of the equidistance line.[91]

---

87 *Summary Records of the Fourth Session*, *supra* note 54, at 173.

88 *Qatar* v. *Bahrain*, *supra* note 29.

89 *See id.* at 102 ("The Court, consequently, is of the view that in the present case there is no ground for recognizing the right of Bahrain to use as a baseline the low-water line of those low-tide elevations which are situated in the zone of overlapping claims, or for recognizing Qatar as having such a right".).

90 *Id.* at 97 (emphasis added).

91 *Id.* at 98–99 (emphasis added).

Despite the chart evidence indicating that Qit'at Jaradah was a low-tide elevation, the Court concluded – on the basis of evidence other than charts – that Qit'at Jaradah was an island.[92]

In *Cameroon* v. *Nigeria* the Court drew a short maritime boundary segment constructed from two base points, one each on the low-water lines of Nigeria and of Cameroon.[93] The Court relied on a chart in order to identify the coordinates of those points. The Court wrote:

> In the present case the Court has determined that the land-based anchorage points to be used in construction of the equidistance line are West Point and East Point, as determined on the 1994 edition of British Admiralty Chart 3433. These two points, situated respectively at 8° 16′ 38″ longitude east and 4° 31′ 59″ latitude north and 8° 30′ 14″ longitude east and 4° 30′ 06″ latitude north, correspond to the most southerly points on the low-water line for Nigeria and Cameroon....[94]

This was the only current large-scale chart available to the Court, both parties had depicted their maritime boundary positions on an earlier version, and neither party challenged the accuracy of the low-water line as depicted.[95]

Similar circumstances arose in the most recent delimitation case. In *Bangladesh* v. *Myanmar*, baselines played a minor role in the pleadings and no role in the Tribunal's decision. Despite being situated in a region with notoriously unstable coasts, both parties relied on British Admiralty Chart 817 to determine their baselines and base points, and neither party challenged the accuracy of the chart. The Tribunal adopted baselines and base points from Chart 817 in its decision.[96]

Other cases currently pending before international courts and tribunals are likely to contain baseline issues, in particular the need to prove the location of the normal baseline and the existence or status of particular features.

---

92 The Court followed the same approach to charts as evidence of baselines elsewhere in the judgment. *See id.* at 98 ("After careful analysis of the various reports, documents and charts submitted by the Parties...").

93 *Cameroon* v. *Nigeria*, *supra* note 29.

94 *Id.* at 443.

95 When it was later discovered that the chart did not reflect the actual low-water line at the time of the judgment as a result of coastal change, the parties entered into negotiations to adjust the boundary to reflect the actual low-water line.

96 *Bangladesh/Myanmar*, *supra* note 29, para. 156 ("The Tribunal sees no reason to depart from the common approach of the Parties on the issue of base points. Accordingly, it will draw an equidistance line from the low-water line indicated on the Admiralty Chart 817 used by the Parties".).

The parties in *Nicaragua* v. *Colombia* have presented the Court with different positions on the status of Quitasueño related to the measurement of the high-water line on that feature.[97] The outstanding maritime delimitation between Bangladesh and India is before an Annex VII tribunal that will undoubtedly be faced with baseline questions.[98]

C *The Normal Baseline in Municipal Law*

The treatment of the normal baseline in municipal legislation and judicial decisions provides an additional perspective on the existing law on the normal baseline, in particular on the role of charts. In this regard, the Committee has carried out a comprehensive survey of municipal baseline legislation.[99] A summary of that survey is provided (III.C.1). The Committee has also investigated national judicial decisions in several states in which municipal courts were confronted with baselines questions. The treatment by national courts of those questions is briefly reviewed (III.C.2).

1 National Legislation

The Committee has undertaken to identify, categorize, and provide representative examples of a robust sample of relevant state practice through a survey of the practice of Committee members' home States, among other States. This research indicates that a number of approaches are taken to the question of baselines, in particular to the statutory definition of the baseline and to the role of charts in defining, publicizing, and proving the baseline.

---

97 *See* Rejoinder of Colombia, Territorial and Maritime Dispute (Nicaragua v. Colombia), at 84, para. 3.2 ("according to Colombia it has the status of a group of islands and other features as defined in the law of the sea; for Nicaragua, on the other hand, it is a submerged bank"). For additional information see the Court's website at http://www.icj-cij.org.

98 For additional information about the case between Bangladesh and India, see the website of the Permanent Court of Arbitration at http://www.pca-cpa.org.

99 During the 2010 Committee working session, it was suggested that "data on state practice should be included" in this report. REPORT, *supra* note 10, at 832 (Yee). Several Committee members have provided such data from their home states. Publications of the UN Division for Ocean Affairs and the Law of the Sea have also been excellent sources of information. *See, e.g.*, BASELINES: NATIONAL LEGISLATION, *supra* note 62; UN DIVISION FOR OCEAN AFFAIRS AND THE LAW OF THE SEA, NATIONAL LEGISLATION ON THE TERRITORIAL SEA, THE RIGHT OF INNOCENT PASSAGE AND THE CONTIGUOUS ZONE, UN Sales No. E.95.V.7 (1995); UN OFFICE FOR OCEAN AFFAIRS AND THE LAW OF THE SEA, NATIONAL CLAIMS TO MARITIME JURISDICTION: EXCERPTS OF LEGISLATION AND TABLE OF CLAIMS, UN Sales No. E.91.V.15 (1992); UN Division for Ocean Affairs and the Law of the Sea, *Maritime Space: Legislation and Treaties* (online database), *available at* http://www.un.org/Depts/los/LEGISLATIONANDTREATIES/index.htm.

We have identified four approaches taken by States for defining their normal baselines: (1) the normal baseline is described with no reference to a charted line;[100] (2) the normal baseline is described with an explicit reference to a charted line;[101] (3) the normal baseline is described with an implied reference to a charted line;[102] and (4) the State does not have a normal baseline.[103]

Some States define their normal baseline without reference to the charted line. These States may refer to a chart publication requirement or the use of charts as evidence of the line, but they do not define the baseline itself on the basis of charts of a charted line. Statutory definitions of the baseline from the laws of Australia,[104] France,[105] and Grenada[106] demonstrate this approach.

100 States in this category include: Australia, Bahamas, Barbados, Belize, Benin, Bulgaria, Cameroon, Chile, Columbia, Congo, Costa Rica, Cyprus, Dominican Republic, Djibouti, El Salvador, Equatorial Guinea, Eritrea, France, Gambia, Germany, Greece, Grenada, Guatemala, Haiti, Honduras, Iceland, Iran, Iraq, Ireland, Italy, Ivory Coast, Jordan, Kiribati, Kuwait, Latvia, Lebanon, Madagascar, Maldives, Mauritania, Mauritius, Monaco, Morocco, Namibia, Nauru, New Zealand, Oman, Papua New Guinea, Poland, Romania, Saint Kitts & Nevis, Saint Lucia, Saudi Arabia, Senegal, Sierra Leone, Slovenia, Somalia, Sri Lanka, Suriname, South Africa, Spain, Sweden, Tonga, Tunisia, Turkey, United Arab Emirates, United Kingdom, Russian Federation, Venezuela, and Yugoslavia.

101 States in this category include: Argentina, Brazil, Cook Islands, Denmark, Guyana, Ghana, Japan, Liberia, Malaysia, Micronesia, Mozambique, Myanmar, Netherlands, Niue, Portugal, Republic of Korea, Russia, Samoa, Sudan, Syria, Trinidad & Tobago, Turkey, Tuvalu, Tanzania, Vanuatu, and Yemen.

102 States in this category include: Bahrain, Brunei, Qatar, and United States of America.

103 States in this category include: Antigua & Barbuda, Cambodia, Cape Verde, China, Comoros, Cuba, Ecuador, Egypt, Estonia, Faroe Islands, Fiji, Finland, Guinea-Bissau, Indonesia, Jamaica, Kenya, Lithuania, Malta, Norway, Philippines, Saint Vincent & Grenadines, Sao Tome & Principe, Seychelles, Solomon Islands, and Viet Nam.

104 "[T]he baseline from which the breadth of the part of the territorial sea adjacent to the mainland of Australia is to be measured is the line constituted by the following: (a) the low-water line along the coast, except where that low-water line is landward of a line mentioned in paragraph (b) [river closing line], (c) [bay closing line], (d) [straight baseline] or (e) [historic bay closing line]…". Seas and Submerged Lands (Territorial Sea Baseline) Proclamation (2006) (Australia) § 6, *available at* http://www.comlaw.gov.au/Details/F2006L00525.

105 "The baselines are the low-water mark as well as straight baselines and closing lines of bays as determined by decree". Delimitation of French Territorial Waters, Law No. 71-1060 (1971) (France) art. 1, *available at* http://www.un.org/Depts/los/LEGISLATIONANDTREATIES/PDFFILES/FRA_1971_Law.pdf (*"Les lignes de base sont la laisse de basse mer ainsi que les lignes de base droites et les lignes de fermeture des baies qui sont determines par décret"*.).

106 "The baselines, for the purpose of measuring the breadth of the territorial sea, shall be (a) the low-water line; or (b) [straight archipelagic baselines]". Territorial Sea and Maritime Boundaries Act, No. 25 (1989) (Grenada) § 4(1), *available at* http://www.un.org/Depts/los/LEGISLATIONANDTREATIES/PDFFILES/grd_act_25_1989.pdf.

Other States define their normal baseline with an express reference to charts or the charted line. In doing so, these States tend to adopt a version of the language of Article 5 of the 1982 Convention. Where the language of Article 5 is adopted, the role of charts and the charted line is made no less ambiguous. Statutory definitions of the baseline from the laws of Brazil,[107] Japan,[108] and the Netherlands[109] demonstrate this approach.

Still other States define their baselines with an implied reference to a charted line. For example, when the phrase "determined in accordance with international law" is utilized to describe the normal baseline, it indicates the adoption of the relevant rules and provisions to which the coastal State is bound pursuant to its international law obligations. For the preponderance of coastal States this obligation is codified in the 1982 Convention, Article 5; for others the same rule is codified in the 1958 Convention, Article 3. Statutory definitions of the baseline from the laws Bahrain,[110] Brunei,[111] and the United States[112] demonstrate this approach.

---

107 "The Brazilian territorial sea is ... measured from the low-water line along the Brazilian coast, as marked on large-scale charts officially recognized by Brazil". The Territorial Sea, the Contiguous Zone, the Exclusive Economic Zone and the Continental Shelf, Law No. 8.617 (1993) (Brazil) art. 1, *available at* http://www.un.org/Depts/los/LEGISLATIONANDTREATIES/PDFFILES/BRA_1993_8617.pdf.

108 "2.... the baseline ... shall be the low-water line along the coast.... 6. The low-water line along the coast referred to in paragraph 2 ... shall be the line[] marked on large-scale charts published by the Maritime Safety Agency". Enforcement Order of the Law on the Territorial Sea and the Contiguous Zone (Cabinet Order No. 210 of 1977, as amended by Cabinet Order No. 383 of 1993, Cabinet Order No. 206 of 1996 and Cabinet Order No. 434 of 2001) (Japan) art. 2, 66 LOS BULL. 71 (2008).

109 "The territorial sea of the Netherlands shall extend to a line, each point on which lies twelve international nautical miles ... seawards of the nearest point on the low-water line along the coast.... The low-water line shall be defined as the line indicating the depth of 0 metres on the large-scale Dutch sea charts issued upon the instructions of the Minister of Defense". Territorial Sea (Demarcation) Act (1985) (Netherlands) § 1, Staatsblad, 1985, 129. An electronic version is available on the following site of the Dutch government: http://wetten.overheid.nl/BWBR0003748/.

110 "The breadth of the territorial sea of the State of Bahrain shall be twelve nautical miles, measured from baselines drawn in accordance with the United Nations Convention on the Law of the Sea, 1982". Decree-Law No. 8 (1993) (Bahrain) art. 1, *available at* http://www.un.org/Depts/los/LEGISLATIONANDTREATIES/PDFFILES/BHR_1993_Decree.pdf.

111 "[The breadth of the territorial waters] shall be measured in accordance with international law". Territorial Waters Act (1982) (Brunei) § 2(2), *available at* http://www.un.org/Depts/los/LEGISLATIONANDTREATIES/PDFFILES/BRN_1982_Act.pdf.

112 "The territorial sea of the United States henceforth extends to 12 nautical miles from the baselines of the United States determined in accordance with international law". Territorial Sea of the United States, Proclamation (1988) (United States), *available at*

Finally, for some states their entire baseline consists of Article 7 straight baselines or Article 47 archipelagic baselines. These States need not, and often do not, mention charts in their statutory description because both straight baselines and archipelagic baselines may be, and typically are, described using lists of geographical coordinates.[113]

The Committee's survey of national legislation indicates that many coastal States do not include charts or the charted line in the legal description of the normal baseline. The non-use of charts to describe the normal baseline does not detract from or conflict with the two other roles nautical charts play in national baseline legislation: (1) to publicize or give notice of baselines and associated outer limits to interested parties in the domestic and international spheres; and (2) to prove the location of the baseline when challenged.

Unlike the notice provisions of Articles 16 and 47 of the 1982 Convention, which require coastal states to depict their straight and archipelagic baselines "on charts of a scale or scales adequate for ascertaining their position", notice requirements in national legislation often do not distinguish between normal baselines and artificial, straight baselines.[114]

The 1982 Convention does not specify that the depiction of baselines on nautical charts is conclusive in proving the location of a coastal State's baseline. Some states, however, expressly refer in their national legislation to the role of charts, and the weight to be given to charts, as evidence of the baseline.[115] Among these states, the weight of charts as evidence varies significantly

---

http://www.un.org/Depts/los/LEGISLATIONANDTREATIES/PDFFILES/USA_1988_Proclamation.pdf.

113 United Nations Convention on the Law of the Sea, *supra* note 11, arts. 16(1) and 47(8).

114 *See, e.g.*, Delimitation of Marine Waters Act, No. 32 (1978) (Solomon Islands) art. 8(1), *available at* http://www.un.org/Depts/los/LEGISLATIONANDTREATIES/PDFFILES/SLB_1978_Act.pdf ("The Minister shall cause all closing lines, baselines and other lines drawn under the provisions of this Act for the purpose of determining the limits of the internal waters, territorial seas and exclusive economic zone of Solomon Islands to be clearly indicated on charts of a scale or scales adequate for them to be readily determined and shall give due publicity to such charts...".).

115 These provisions appear in the legislation of the following states: Barbados, Brunei, Grenada, Namibia, New Zealand, Saint Kitts & Nevis, Saint Lucia, Samoa, Seychelles, Solomon Islands, Sri Lanka, Tuvalu, and United Kingdom.

from mere 'evidence'[116] to '*prima facie* evidence'[117] to 'sufficient evidence'[118] to 'conclusive evidence'.[119] In one example, certified charts "shall be judicially noticed for all purposes of the law as indicating the baselines from which the territorial waters shall be measured".[120]

---

116 *See, e.g.*, Maritime Areas Act, No. 3 (1984) (St. Kitts & Nevis) §§ 19 & 20, *available at* http://www.un.org/Depts/los/LEGISLATIONANDTREATIES/PDFFILES/KNA_1984_Act.pdf ("§19. The Minister shall cause to be prepared such charts … as he thinks fit showing … (b) the baseline of the territorial sea.… § 20. A document, purporting to be certified by the Minister to be a true copy of a chart … prepared pursuant to section 19, shall be received in any Proceedings as evidence of any matter shown in the document, but without prejudice to the right to adduce evidence in rebuttal".). *See also* Territorial Sea and Maritime Boundaries Act, No. 25 (1989) (Grenada), *supra* note 106, §§ 28 & 29; Maritime Zones Act (1999) (Samoa) § 10(2), *available at* http://www.un.org/Depts/los/LEGISLATIONANDTREATIES/PDFFILES/WSM_1999_MaritimeZ.pdf; Delimitation of Marine Waters Act, No. 32 (1978) (Solomon Islands), *supra* note 114, § 8(2); Marine Zones (Declaration) Act (1983) (Tuvalu) §§ 13 & 14, *available at* http://www.un.org/Depts/los/LEGISLATIONANDTREATIES/PDFFILES/TUV_1983_Act.pdf.

117 *See, e.g.*, Territorial Sea and Exclusive Economic Zone Act, No. 3 (1990) (Namibia) § 2(2), *available at* http://www.un.org/Depts/los/LEGISLATIONANDTREATIES/PDFFILES/NAM_1990_Act.pdf ("(b) Any baseline referred to in this section may be marked or indicated by appropriate symbols on scale charts officially recognized by Namibia; (c) In any proceedings before a court of law any chart referred to in paragraph (b) shall be *prima facie* evidence of the matters referred to therein".). *See also* Territorial Waters Act, (1982) (Brunei), *supra* note 111, § 4(1); Maritime Zones Law, No. 22 (1976) (Sri Lanka) § 14, *available at* http://www.un.org/Depts/los/LEGISLATIONANDTREATIES/PDFFILES/LKA_1976_Law.pdf.

118 *See, e.g.*, Territorial Sea and Exclusive Economic Zone Act, No. 28 (1977, as amended by Act No. 146 of 1980) (New Zealand) § 31, *available at* http://www.un.org/Depts/los/LEGISLATIONANDTREATIES/PDFFILES/NZL_1980_Act.pdf ("(1) For the purposes of this Act, in any proceedings in any Court the line of low water for any area depicted on the charts … shall be sufficient evidence of the line of the low-water mark for that area. (2) For the purpose of this Act … a certificate … that any specified chart is a chart referred to in subsection (1) of this section shall be admissible as evidence of the matters stated in the certificate".).

119 *See, e.g.*, Maritime Zones Act, No. 2 (1999) (Seychelles) §§ 27 & 28, *available at* http://www.un.org/Depts/los/LEGISLATIONANDTREATIES/PDFFILES/SYC_1999_Act2.pdf ("§ 27. The President shall cause to be prepared charts … as the President thinks fit, showing … (a) the baselines, low-water lines and any closing lines.… § 28. A document purporting to be certified by the President to be a true copy of a chart … prepared pursuant to section 27 shall be received in any proceedings as conclusive evidence of any matter referred to in that section and shown in the document".). *See also* Territorial Sea Act (1987) (United Kingdom) § 1(3), *available at* http://www.un.org/Depts/los/LEGISLATIONANDTREATIES/PDFFILES/GBR_1987_Act.pdf.

120 Territorial Waters Act, No. 1977-26 (1977) (Barbados) § 4(3), *available at* http://www.un.org/Depts/los/LEGISLATIONANDTREATIES/PDFFILES/BRB_1977_26.pdf ("(3) Where baselines are prescribed under subsection (2) [straight baselines] the Minister shall cause

Many of the states that give nautical charts significant weight as evidence of baselines do not include charts or the charted line in their statutory definitions of the normal baseline. Moreover, several states that expressly recognize charts as evidence only refer to the charts as evidence of their artificial, 'straight line' baselines, and not of the normal baseline.[121] To the extent that a conclusion may be drawn from the relatively scarce and disparate provisions related to charts as evidence in national legislation, it appears that in most municipal legal systems nautical charts are accorded no special legal role in proving the location of the normal baseline and merely provide a source of evidence to prove a disputed fact. However, in practical terms, in particular where charts have been specially produced to publicize a baseline as required by national law, nautical charts may be the best evidence of the baseline location. It must be acknowledged that in some national systems charts do hold a special position as evidence. The wide range of approaches to charts as evidence is demonstrated by a brief review of national judicial decisions related to baselines.

2 National Judicial Decisions

Analyzing statutory language may be informative, but its utility is augmented when this language is applied in municipal judicial decisions.[122] Unfortunately, these decisions have been more difficult to access than legislation. The Committee has been able to find a total of eight relevant decisions from Australia (1), the Netherlands (2), Nigeria (1), the United Kingdom (1), and the United States (3).

These decisions fall into two categories: law enforcement cases in which the decisions are related to an act by a mariner, such as a fisherman, accused of violating a coastal state law applicable within a certain distance of a baseline; and title cases in which the decisions are related to ownership of resource rights, usually to mineral resources, as between a federal government and one of its federated states the spatial extent of which is defined by, or in relation

---

the baselines ... to be marked on a scaled map or chart and such map or chart *shall be judicially noticed for all purposes of the law* as indicating the baselines from which the territorial waters shall be measured…".) (emphasis added). However, only those charts showing the Barbados straight baselines are subject to judicial notice.

121 *See, e.g.*, Barbados, Seychelles, and Solomon Islands.

122 Committee member Yee expresses concern about the probative value of municipal judicial decisions: "I do not believe that the practice of the judicial organs of some States examining the appropriateness of the charts recognized by their own governments should be given much weight. To the extent that one branch of the government can examine the work of another branch, one has to wonder which act is the final one as far as the determination of the baseline is concerned. It seems that only the examination or not, or how such an examination is done, by a foreign organ is of value in our inquiry".

to, baselines. In the law enforcement category, the interests are short term, the activity is ephemeral and difficult to detect (often involving repetitive behavior by multiple individuals), and certainty, publicity, and prior notice of lines and limits are desirable for the orderly conduct of activities in and beyond the relevant maritime zone. In the title category, the interests are longer term, the actors fewer, and the location of the activity or interest is fixed. Most importantly, the title category of cases tends to involve a dispute between equals while the law enforcement category of cases is characterized by a power imbalance between the state and an individual.

In some municipal jurisdictions the burden of proof falls on the state as a result of this power imbalance. In our scenario this means that the state must prove every element of a crime in order to prevail, including the location of the conduct relative to the baseline, and the defendant may challenge that evidence with evidence to the contrary. As indicated by the statutory language related to charts as evidence surveyed above and the Dutch jurisprudence reviewed here, this is not true of all municipal law jurisdictions. It does, however, appear to be universally acknowledged that, once publicized through officially recognized charts, the baseline location shown on those charts may not be challenged by the coastal state itself in law enforcement cases. The state is estopped from contesting its own officially recognized depiction of baselines. Here, it seems, the charted line reigns supreme.

The national judicial decisions reviewed below draw from both law enforcement and title cases. The preponderance of the decisions seem to indicate that the normal baseline exists even in the absence of officially recognized charts depicting it, that where the charted line does appear on officially recognized charts its accuracy may be challenged, and that, in some cases, the charted line may be found to be inaccurate on the basis of evidence to the contrary.

In the Australian case of *Chia Hsing* v. *Rankin* the defendant was accused of having in his charge a foreign fishing vessel within a declared fishing zone (measured from Australia's normal baseline). The defendant argued that there could be no fishing zone because Australia had not marked the baseline on large scale charts pursuant to Article 3 of the 1958 Convention. In that decision, Chief Justice Barwick of the High Court of Australia wrote of the low-water line:

> That line does not depend for its existence and significance upon any chart. The precise position of that line is a fact to be determined if occasion demands by a court of law. No doubt a hydrographer's chart will provide cogent evidence of that fact, and a chart conforming to the specification in Art. 3 of the Treaty may be decisive internationally, particularly

> if a conventional baseline were adopted. But the fact of the low water mark cannot depend upon the existence of any such chart.[123]

In the same case Justice Gibbs observed:

> In any case it is impossible to suppose that it was intended by the Geneva Convention that the existence of a territorial sea should be dependent upon the existence of officially recognized large-scale charts showing the low-water line.... Article 3 of the Geneva Convention must be regarded as doing no more than provide a means by which the low-water line may be evidenced. If there are charts of the kind mentioned they provide evidence (perhaps conclusive) of the position of the low water line.[124]

The Australian High Court appears to take the view that the low-water line exists independent of charts, but that officially recognized, large-scale charts (if available) would provide strong evidence of the location of that line. Nigerian courts appear to take a similar view. In the case *A-G of the Federation* v. *A-G of Abia State and 35 Others*, in which the federal government failed to tender charts in support of its baseline position, Judge Ogundare (JSC) opined "In my humble view ... the seaward boundary of a littoral State as we are called to determine in this case, is a matter of law. What becomes factual, and on which evidence will be required to prove, is the actual location of that boundary".[125]

In the United States, officially recognized nautical charts are susceptible to challenge. The United States Supreme Court has, on several occasions, addressed disputes between the United States Government and coastal federated states of the United States that raise the baselines issue. The issue arises in the United States because each of its coastal states was granted mineral rights seaward to three nautical miles from the coast.[126] When the Court was asked to define the 'coast' for purposes of that grant it concluded that "[t]he [1958] Convention on the Territorial Sea and the Contiguous Zone ... provides such definitions. We adopt them for purposes of the Submerged Lands Act. This

123 Chia Hsing v. Rankin, (1978) 141 CLR 182, 192, *available at* http://www.austlii.edu.au/au/cases/cth/HCA/1978/56.html.

124 *Id.* at 195.

125 Edwin Egede, *The Nigerian Territorial Waters Legislation and the 1982 Law of the Sea Convention*, 19(2) INT'L J. MARINE & COASTAL L. 151, 160 (2004), *quoting* [2002] 6 NWLR (Part 764), at 542, 643–44.

126 Submerged Lands Act, 43 USC §§ 1301, 1311. There are some exceptions to the three-mile rule for certain states.

establishes a single coastline for both the administration of the Submerged Lands Act and the conduct of our future international relations…".[127]

Three United States Supreme Court decisions demonstrate the view within the United States municipal legal system that officially recognized charts may be used as evidence of the baseline, but that they are not dispositive of that fact: *United States* v. *Louisiana*, *United States* v. *California*, and *United States* v. *Alaska*.[128] In a case involving sedimentary deposits from the Mississippi River that altered the shape of the mainland coastline, and alternately created and destroyed offshore islands and low-tide elevations, Louisiana argued that the drafters of the 1958 Convention, Article 3, purposely adopted the charted line, believing that it would err on the side of navigational safety and that the United States Government should not be allowed to disprove its own official charts. The Supreme Court disagreed, and both sides were allowed to introduce the best available evidence to prove the present location of the actual low-water line.[129]

California, having found errors in United States Government charts that worked to California's advantage,[130] contended that "pursuant to Article 3 [of the 1958 Convention], the United States is bound by these charts…".[131] The Supreme Court's Special Master recommended that the nautical charts not be treated as conclusive evidence,[132] and the Court agreed.[133]

Finally, Alaska and the United States disagreed as to the status of an offshore feature in the Arctic Ocean near the Prudhoe Bay oil field known as Dinkum Sands. Alaska contended that Dinkum Sands was an island generating Alaskan rights to mineral resources within three nautical miles. The United States contended that it was not an island and generated no rights for the state. In 1950 Dinkum Sands had been observed by hydrographic surveyors, and charted as an island, but in 1955 a naval vessel reported that Dinkum Sands no longer stood above mean high water. The following year the official United States nautical

---

127 United States v. California, 381 US 139, 165 (1965).

128 Committee member Yee expresses particular concern about the value of United States practice in this analysis: "The complicated dynamics of the relationship between the United States and its component states cast doubt on the value of the U.S. practice in dealing with federal-state relations as practice within the meaning of Article 38(1)(b) of the ICJ Statute".

129 United States v. Louisiana, 394 US 11, 40–41 n.48 (1969), and 420 US 529 (1975).

130 Most of those errors resulted from the unintended use of coastal piers as base points for generating three-mile arcs to describe the territorial sea and California's Submerged Lands Act outer limits.

131 United States v. California, Report of the Special Master 25 (Aug. 20, 1979).

132 *Id.*

133 United States v. California, 447 US 1, 6–7 (1980).

chart of the area was updated to depict Dinkum Sands as a low-tide elevation, not an island. The feature has been charted as a low-tide elevation ever since.[134] In *United States* v. *Alaska*, the parties introduced extensive evidence regarding the feature's elevation, composition and transiency, including chart evidence. Relying on this updated evidence the Special Master concluded that Dinkum Sands was not an island.[135] The Supreme Court agreed.[136] In this case nautical charts were offered as evidence, but the parties and the Court did not rely on them to determine the status of Dinkum Sands. Instead an extensive updated survey was conducted, at a cost of approximately $2.5 million, on the understanding that nautical charts are not conclusive.

The courts in the Netherlands have a different opinion of charts as evidence. In a pair of cases the District Court of Amsterdam took a highly deferential view of the role of officially recognized charts in proving the location of baselines. The two decisions of 29 June 2007 dealt with the relationship between the charted low-water line and the actual low-water line.[137] In both cases the defendants argued that they were not fishing inside the 12-nautical-mile zone because a low-tide elevation, which was included in the current official large-scale chart, actually no longer existed. As a consequence, they argued, the location where they were accused of committing a violation was no longer within 12 nautical miles of the actual low-water line. The District Court rejected this plea in identical terms in the two cases, observing that:

134 For a period of nearly 30 years the charted status of Dinkum Sands as a low-tide elevation did not correspond with the depiction of Alaska's three-mile zone or the United States three-mile territorial sea. Rather than treating it as a low-tide elevation situated beyond three nautical miles from Alaskan territory, the US Baselines Committee charged with charting the limits of the territorial sea continued to treat it as an island generating a territorial sea. Apparently, one member of the Baseline Committee persuaded the whole Committee to treat Dinkum Sands as an island based solely on his personal observation of Dinkum Sands as a member of the 1949–1950 survey party. United States v. Alaska, 511 US 1, 28 (1997). That depiction of the Dinkum Sands territorial sea outer limits was corrected by the Baseline Committee in 1984. Minutes of Baseline Committee Meeting of July 17, 1984. From the international perspective the issue became moot in 1988 when the United States extended the breadth of its territorial sea from three nautical miles to 12 nautical miles. Dinkum Sands is well within 12 nautical miles of two islands and the United States mainland and generates territorial sea regardless of its status as an island or a low-tide elevation.

135 United States v. Alaska, No. 84 Original, October Term, 1995, Report of Special Master J. Keith Mann of March 1996, at 227–310.

136 United States v. Alaska, 511 US 1, 22–31 (1997).

137 This concerned cases 13/501817–05 and 13/500730–05 (A) & 13/994290–06 (B). The Dutch text of the two decisions can be accessed through http://rechtspraak.nl.

> *In law the chart officially published by the authorities is determinative.* On the date of the charges the chart dated 3 January 2002 applied, with the 12-mile zone that had been determined also taking into account the low-tide elevation off Schouwen. That the defendant had received information that the boundary would shift and that this apparently was already indicated on the plotter he was using (alongside the "old" boundary), does not change the fact that until 22 December 2004, the date of publication of the new nautical chart 110, *de jure* a different situation applied. The defendant, being an experienced fisherman, had at least to have been aware of this.[138]

This outcome reflects the language of the Territorial Sea Demarcation Act, which is quite clear with respect to the charted line.[139] It is also in conformity with the view of the Netherlands executive branch. In a press release on a separate matter the Ministry of Defense observed "A change in the actual coastline thus has no effect, until it is included in the nautical chart".[140]

It appears that the courts in the United Kingdom may sit somewhere between the Australia/Nigeria/United States and Netherlands positions, allowing that charts may be challenged, but giving them primacy as evidence. There, the best known baselines case is *Post Office* v. *Estuary Radio Ltd.*[141] The question before the Court was whether Red Stone Radio Tower, located in the Thames estuary, was within either the internal waters (here, a juridical bay) or the territorial sea of the United Kingdom, a determination that hinged on the location of the low-water line.[142] The trial Court ultimately ruled for the Crown, but not before noting:

> I would have thought that the best evidence of what is the low-water line along the coast would be found on the large-scale charts officially recognized by the coastal state … and that *prima facie* there would be

138 Translation by Committee members Oude Elferink, Soons, and Kwiatkowska (emphasis added).

139 *See* Territorial Sea (Demarcation) Act (1985) § 1(2), *available at* http://www.un.org/Depts/los/LEGISLATIONANDTREATIES/PDFFILES/NLD_1985_DemarcationAct.pdf ("The low-water line shall be defined as the line indicating the depth of 0 meters on the large-scale Dutch sea charts issued upon the instructions of the Minister of Defence".).

140 Maritieme zones gewijzigd door aanleg Maasvlakte 2 (press release of 22 Dec. 2009), *available at* http://www.defensie.nl/actueel/nieuws/2009/12/22/46142802/Maritieme_zones_Noordzee_gewijzigd_door_aanleg_Maasvlakte_2 (translation by Committee members Oude Elferink, Soons, and Kwiatkowska) (emphasis added).

141 [1967] 3 All English Reports 663.

142 *Id.* at 665.

> good ground for accepting those as accurate until they were shown to be inaccurate; but I agree with counsel for the defendants that *it is open to a party to bring forward evidence and say; the chart is inaccurate, that which it shows is not there.*[143]

The appellate Court upheld the trial Court's decision. With respect to finding the natural entrance points of the juridical bay on that low-water line, the appellate Court concluded that "[t]he only simple and convenient way in which they can do this is by visual inspection and measurement of the officially recognised charts of the claimant state".[144]

The Committee notes that a single conclusion is difficult to glean from the small sample of cases with widely variable parties and fact patterns. At one end of the spectrum are the Australian, Nigerian, and United States cases reviewed, in which charts have been viewed as a source of evidence for proving the fact of the normal baseline location. At the other end is the Dutch approach, in which the officially recognized chart has been declared 'determinative' of the baseline. The British approach appears to lie somewhere in the middle of the spectrum. As a practical matter the Dutch and British reliance on charts may be understood against the back drop of widely-publicized, frequently-updated nautical charts issued by unusually diligent hydrographic services.[145]

D *Expert Views on the Normal Baseline*

The preponderance of the scholarship in this area appears to support the view that charts are not determinative of the naturally ambulatory normal baseline, although this view is not universally held. Alexander writes: "Normal baselines may change over time as the low-water line changes because of erosion, deposition or the emplacement of human-made structures on the shore. Official baselines have been, and will continue to be challenged by affected parties".[146]

143 *Id.* at 675 (emphasis added).

144 *Id.* at 683.

145 The example of the Netherlands raises the question does the regularity of chart updating change the application of the normal baseline rule? The Dutch rule that "[i]n law the chart officially published by the authorities is determinative" would lead to bizarre and indefensible results in coastal states where charts have not been updated for, literally, centuries. This question circles back to the 1952 argument of French ILC member Scelle, who noted that outdated charts might be unacceptable. On this basis, Committee member Oude Elferink suggests that "Article 5 indicates that a coastal State in principle is entitled to rely on the low-water line as depicted on its nautical charts but this may not be the case if an area is not regularly surveyed and the relevant nautical chart is outdated".

146 Lewis M. Alexander, *Baseline Delimitations and Maritime Boundaries*, 23 VA. J. INT'L L. 503, 535 (1983).

Beazley, writing about the technical considerations in maritime boundary delimitation notes that:

> both the 1958 and 1982 Conventions specify that the large-scale charts officially recognized by the coastal state are the appropriate documents from which to determine the position of the 'normal baseline'.... In some cases, however, existing charts have been thought to be inadequate. It may be that the existing charts were held to be on too small a scale or based on surveys too old to truly represent the current situation.[147]

In these situations, states turn to other evidence of the location of the baseline, including aerial photography, large-scale land maps, or new coastal surveys.[148]

Caron, referring to the outer limits of maritime zones as 'boundaries', writes:

> maritime boundaries under the 1982 Convention generally are contingent upon the continued existence of the baseline. If the baseline moves, the boundary moves. If a baseline point such as an exposed rock disappears, the boundary generated by that point also disappears. Although this is obviously an important principle, it often goes unstated.[149]

Caron arrives at this conclusion through an analysis of other provisions in the Convention, in particular Article 7(2). He concludes that "in other than article 7(2) situations, the outer boundary of the exclusive economic zone, the contiguous zone, and the territorial sea are ambulatory in that they will move with the baselines from which they are measured".[150] Caron maintains this perspective on the existing law of the normal baseline in subsequent writing, but argues that the rules should be changed in the interest of efficiency and stability.[151]

---

147 Peter Beazley, *Technical Considerations in Maritime Boundary Delimitations*, *in* 1 INTERNATIONAL MARITIME BOUNDARIES 243, 245 (Jonathan I. Charney & Lewis M. Alexander eds., 1993).

148 *Id.* These types of evidence are not inherently better than nautical charts, but where no recent large-scale nautical chart is available they may be of some utility.

149 David D. Caron, *When Law Makes Climate Change Worse: Rethinking the Law of Baselines in Light of a Rising Sea Level*, 17 ECOLOGY L.Q. 621, 634 (1990).

150 *Id.* at 635.

151 David D. Caron, *Climate Change, Sea Level Rise and the Coming Uncertainty in Oceanic Boundaries: A Proposal to Avoid Conflict*, *in* MARITIME BOUNDARY DISPUTES, SETTLEMENT PROCESSES, AND THE LAW OF THE SEA 1 (Seoung-Yong Hong & Jon M. Van Dyke eds., 2009).

O'Connell asserts that "[t]here is no doubt that changes in the shoreline, however and how quickly effected, result in changes in the baseline from which the territorial sea is measured".[152] Reed sums up the situation succinctly: "It is the actual low-water line and not the charted line that is to be used as the baseline under the Convention". Reed continues:

> In practice, the charted line is clearly the starting point in each effort to locate the low-water line.
>
> ....
>
> A final element of the normal low-water line must be mentioned, that being its ambulatory nature.... As the baseline ambulates, so does each of the maritime zones measured from it.
>
> ... Although the chart may provide a presumption of that line's location, extrinsic evidence will be permitted to prove its actual location and no particularly oppressive burden of proof seems to be required.[153]

Sohn and Noyes, writing about the ambulatory nature of outer limits measured from baselines, write: "Perfect stability, however, is impossible when the coastline is used as the baseline. The territorial sea 'will remain ambulatory because it is measured from an impermanent feature – the natural coastline'".[154] Soons also indicates that the outer limits of most maritime zones will move with movement of the baseline.[155] He suggests that loss of maritime area resulting from landward movements of the baseline can be prevented through the "artificial conservation of the baseline",[156] but that "[a]s far as the low-water line is concerned, this means the construction or reinforcement of sea defences (shoreline protection)".[157] Soons does not suggest that artificial conservation of the baseline can be achieved by publishing, recognizing, or maintaining charts that depict a low-water line that does not reflect the physical realities of the coast.

---

152 D.P. O'Connell, 2 The International Law of the Sea 682 (I.A. Shearer ed., 1984).

153 Michael W. Reed, 3 Shore and Sea Boundaries 182–85 (2000).

154 Louis B. Sohn & John E. Noyes, Cases and Materials on the Law of the Sea 235 (2004) (quoting Robert D. Hodgson & Robert W. Smith, *The Informal Single Negotiating Text (Committee II): A Geographical Perspective*, 3 Ocean Dev. & Int'l L. 225, 234 [1976]).

155 A.H.A. Soons, *The Effects of a Rising Sea Level on Maritime Limits and Boundaries*, 37(2) Neth. Int'l L. Rev. 207, 216–18 (1990).

156 *Id.* at 222.

157 *Id.*

Finally, a group of technical experts assembled by the United Nations examined the baselines provisions of the 1982 Convention and concluded, among other things, that "[t]he low-water line along the coast is a fact irrespective of its representation on charts. The territorial sea exists even if no particular low-water line has been selected or if no charts have been officially recognized".[158] It defines the 'low-water line' as "the intersection of the plane of low-water with the shore," and distinguishes the 'low-water mark on a chart' as "the line depicting the level of chart datum".[159]

On the other side of the ledger are several technical experts who assert that the charted line is the normal baseline irrespective of changes to the actual low-water line. Kapoor and Kerr state that "once the normal baseline has been established and cartographically depicted on large scale charts, it remains in place until such time as it is redrafted, irrespective of whether or not the actual low-water line has physically moved".[160] Carleton and Schofield appear to agree with Kapoor and Kerr's interpretation of Article 5. They write:

> It is, however, worth recognising that Article 5 refers to the low-water line along the coast "*as marked on large-scale charts officially recognised by the coastal state*". It is therefore the chart that is the legal document determining the position of the normal baseline and this remains the case even where the coastline has, in reality, changed. Thus, if the coastline has altered, but it has not been published, the legal baseline is still that on the published chart. Where this is the case, the normal baseline will only come to reflect the physical change in the coastline if a fresh survey is undertaken and the chart correspondingly updated.[161]

---

158 UN OFFICE OF OCEAN AFFAIRS AND LAW OF THE SEA, BASELINES: AN EXAMINATION OF THE RELEVANT PROVISIONS OF THE UNITED NATIONS CONVENTION ON THE LAW OF THE SEA 3, UN Sales No. E.88.V.5 (reissued 1989) [hereinafter BASELINES: AN EXAMINATION]. For a list of the experts, see Appendix II at 66–68. *See also* TORSTEN GIHL, THE BASELINE OF THE TERRITORIAL SEA 129 (1967) ("The coast is, of course, the place where the land and the sea meet, and where the area of the sea that will be subjected to the state's sovereignty consequently begins.... The situation of the coast is a geographical fact. The coast lies where it lies...".).

159 BASELINES: AN EXAMINATION, *supra* note 158, at 2.

160 D.C. KAPOOR & ADAM J. KERR, A GUIDE TO MARITIME BOUNDARY DELIMITATION 31 (1986).

161 Christopher Carleton & Clive Schofield, *Developments in the Technical Determination of Maritime Space: Charts, Datums, Baselines, Maritime Zones and Limits*, 3(3) IBRU MARITIME BRIEFING 24–25 (2001) (emphasis in original). *See also* DAVID ANDERSON, MODERN LAW OF THE SEA – SELECTED ESSAYS 454 (Leiden: Martinus Nijhoff, 2008) ("The low-water line remains fixed to the extent that the chart remains current; however, the low-water line may change as a result of new surveys or the adoption of a different

These authors appear to be of the minority view that the charted line is the Article 5 normal baseline.

E *Reefs and Low-Tide Elevations*

Two other provisions in the 1982 Convention address particular situations in which the normal baseline may be used, Article 6 (reefs) and Article 13 (low-tide elevations).[162] Once Article 5 is interpreted and the meaning of "the normal baseline" is agreed, these two provisions hold no mystery. However, reefs and low-tide elevations are highly susceptible to coastal change, and these provisions merit brief comment. Article 13 provides:

> 1. A low-tide elevation is a naturally formed area of land which is surrounded by and above water at low tide but submerged at high tide. Where a low-tide elevation is situated wholly or partly at a distance not exceeding the breadth of the territorial sea from the mainland or an island, the low-water line on that elevation may be used as the baseline for measuring the breadth of the territorial sea
> 2. Where a low-tide elevation is wholly situated at a distance exceeding the breadth of the territorial sea from the mainland or an island, it has no territorial sea of its own.

Under this provision, whether a naturally-formed feature may be included in the baseline depends on its height relative to the vertical datum *and* its horizontal location relative to the nearest mainland or island. In order to be included, some part of the feature must be above water at low tide as defined by the low-water datum. Absent this characteristic, the feature would not have a low-water line. Some drying part of the feature as defined by its low-water line

---

chart datum or the extension of the breadth of the territorial sea from say three to twelve miles – followed, in each case, by the production of new charts. This link between the low-water mark and the chart was made in 1930 by the Hague Conference and maintained by the ILC, the Geneva Convention and the LOS Convention".).

162 Some regard Article 9 (mouths of rivers) and Article 10 (bays) as normal baseline provisions. *See, e.g.*, Christopher Carleton, *Problems Relating to Man-made Basepoints under UNCLOS*, *presented at* CURRENT PROBLEMATIC ISSUES IN THE LAW OF THE SEA (Dublin, 3–4 June 2010). Other sources include only Articles 5, 6, and 13 under a consideration of normal baselines. *See, e.g.*, BASELINES: AN EXAMINATION, *supra* note 158, at v. River and bay closing lines are not straight baselines. They are not governed by Article 7 and are not subject to the Article 8(2) exception to which certain Article 7 straight baselines are subject. The river mouth and bay closing lines are not, however, baselines that follow the sinuosities of the low-water line. Instead, they are artificial 'straight line' baselines that must 'attach' to, or start and end at points on the low-water line.

must also be within the territorial sea generated from the nearest mainland or island. Without both of these qualities a low-tide elevation does not contribute to the normal baseline. Therefore, an otherwise unqualified low-tide elevation situated within the territorial sea of a qualified low-tide elevation does not contribute to the baseline.

Changes in sea level, or other natural processes, that lead to the total submersion of an otherwise qualified low-tide elevation could have an impact on the location of the normal baseline and of outer limits measured from that feature.[163] Similarly, changes in the coastal configuration of the nearest mainland or island could have the effect of placing a previously qualified low-tide elevation outside the territorial sea and therefore unable to contribute to the generation of the territorial sea outer limit. Of course, accretion along a mainland or island coast could bring a low-tide elevation within the territorial sea. Alternatively, if a feature were to rise above water even at high tide, a low-tide elevation could transform into an island with its own baseline, irrespective of its distance from other territory.[164]

Article 6 contains an exception to the distance from mainland or island requirement for reefs and provides:

> In the case of islands situated on atolls or of islands having fringing reefs, the baseline for measuring the breadth of the territorial sea is the seaward low-water line of the reef, as shown by the appropriate symbol on charts officially recognized by the coastal State.

As with Article 5, the low-water line is the normal baseline and charts may be used to depict or show that line. The reef need only rise above low-water,[165] but unlike low-tide elevations that do not meet the requirements of Article 6, the Article 6 reef need not be within the territorial sea or any specified distance from the reference island.

The analysis of the normal baseline generated by these features does not differ from the analysis of Article 5. The normal baseline is the actual low-water line, not the charted line. The baselines on these features may not be preserved solely through the publication of a chart depicting them.

---

163 See the controversy surrounding the status of Dinkum Sands as an island or low-tide elevation, *supra* note 135 and associated text.

164 *See Qatar* v. *Bahrain*, *supra* note 29.

165 *See Eritrea/Yemen*, *supra* note 29, at 368 (citing to the language of Article 6, the Tribunal concludes that "[a] reef that is not also a low-tide elevation appears to be out of the question as a base point…".).

F *General Conclusion*

The Committee concludes that the legal normal baseline is the actual low-water line along the coast at the vertical datum, also known as the chart datum, indicated on charts officially recognized by the coastal State. The phrase "as marked on large-scale charts officially recognized by the coastal State" provides for coastal State discretion to choose the vertical datum at which that State measures and depicts its low-water line. The charted low-water line illustrates the legal normal baseline, and in most instances and for most purposes the charted low-water line provides a sufficiently accurate representation of the normal baseline. As a matter of evidence for proving the location of the normal baseline the charted line appears to enjoy a strong presumption of accuracy. However, where significant physical changes have occurred so that the chart does not provide an accurate representation of the actual low-water line at the chosen vertical datum, extrinsic evidence has been considered by international courts and tribunals in order to determine the location of the legal normal baseline.

IV The Existing Law Applied in a Changing World

The baseline issues that arose in the two international cases cited in the Committee Proposal and reviewed in Section III.B resulted from natural changes to the shape of the coast: migrating banks of sling mud and accretion at the mouth of a river. Human-induced change can also impact the shape of coasts and the location of the intersection between land and sea at low-water. The Committee Proposal acknowledges such possibilities observing:

> Climate change and the resulting sea level rise are impacting on the normal baselines. Low lying small island developing states may in particular be negatively affected by this phenomenon.... Human activities in the sea are increasing. This among others concerns the artificial extension of existing coasts, which may have a huge impact on the location of the normal baseline.[166]

In this section the Committee considers the existing law of the normal baseline in relation to territorial gain resulting from human-made structures and the artificial conservation or extension of existing coasts (IV.A) and territorial loss in relation to sea level rise (IV.B).

---

166 *Proposal, supra* note 3, paras. 4 and 5.

A *Territorial Gain: Harbour Works, Coastal Protection, Land Reclamation*

1 Harbour Works

The case that harbour works constitute part of the normal baseline is fairly clear cut.[167] Article 11 (ports) speaks directly to this subset of artificial structures. It reads:

> For the purpose of delimiting the territorial sea, the outermost permanent harbour works which form an integral part of the harbor system are regarded as forming part of the coast. Off-shore installations and artificial islands shall not be considered as permanent harbour works.

That is to say, the structures referred to in the first sentence are to be considered part of the coast along which the low-water line is the baseline from which the territorial sea and other maritime zones are measured. This treatment of harbour works is not new to the 1982 Convention. Identical or similar provisions were offered at the 1930 Conference and again in ILC drafts preceding the 1958 Convention. In fact, commentary to the ILC's 1954 draft article on ports indicated that the "article is consistent with the positive law now in force".[168] Nonetheless, there has been some debate as to which structures qualify under this provision.

Authorities have tended to define 'harbour works' with examples. Jessup recommended that stone jetties and breakwaters connected with the shore should extend the outer limit of the territorial sea.[169] Pearcy cited 'piers and breakwaters' as the most common examples of harbour works, but cautioned that they must be connected to the shore or an installation on the shore.[170] However, several decades later the group of technical experts assembled by the United Nations to examine the baseline provisions of UNCLOS included "jetties,

167 Shalowitz opined that "this provision is open to interpretation as to what constitutes a 'harbour system' and 'harbour works'", but there has been surprisingly little controversy associated with either term. SHALOWITZ, *supra* note 61, at 229–30. Shalowitz was referring to Article 8 of the 1958 Convention on the Territorial Sea and the Contiguous Zone, *supra* note 30, but that article is identical to UNCLOS Article 11. Nor has a structure's 'permanence' been controversial. The Committee has found no international situation in which a structure has been denied 'harbour work' status on the basis of impermanence.

168 *Report of the International Law Commission to the General Assembly*, [1954] 2 Y.B. Int'l L. Comm'n 140, 155, UN Doc. A/CN.4/SER.A/1954/Add.1.

169 PHILIP C. JESSUP, THE LAW OF TERRITORIAL WATERS AND MARITIME JURISDICTION 69–70 (1927).

170 G. Etzel Pearcy, *Measurement of the Territorial Sea*, 40 DEP'T ST. BULL. No. 1044, at 963 (June 29, 1959).

moles, quays or other port facilities, coastal terminals, wharves, breakwaters, sea walls, etc.",[171] emphasizing that "[t]his would include features like *detached* breakwaters".[172] A later UN publication emphasized that same point.[173]

Walker includes 'piers' in a list otherwise identical to the UN technical experts' list.[174] Sohn and Noyes cite an ILC member's comment that the Commission's recognition of "jetties and piers" as part of the baseline assumed that those features "would be of such a type as to constitute a physical part of the coastline", and those authors go on to point out that the United States Supreme Court declined to include open-pile piers on the California coast as part of the baseline, in part on the reasoning that they provided no coast protective function.[175]

Other authorities have identified coastal projects that, they contend, should not be assimilated to harbour works or form part of the coast. These include: piers that do not provide a coast protective function, such as open pile piers,[176] bridges,[177] causeways,[178] and dredged channels.[179] The ILC questioned the sta-

171 BASELINES: AN EXAMINATION, *supra* note 158, at 54.

172 *Id.* at 33 (emphasis added).

173 "Under Article 11, '*the outermost permanent harbour works which form an integral part of the harbor systems*' are regarded as forming part of the coast. This would include features such as detached breakwaters...". UN DIVISION FOR OCEAN AFFAIRS AND THE LAW OF THE SEA, HANDBOOK ON THE DELIMITATION OF MARITIME BOUNDARIES 7, UN Sales No. E.01.V.2 (2000). *See also* Carleton, *supra* note 162, at 5 ("Providing the structures are considered to be an integral part of the harbour system, even constructions such as detached moles or breakwaters would form an integral part of the harbour and be a legitimate part of the normal baseline".). This understanding is important because without it detached breakwaters would arguably be treated as artificial islands and ineligible as base points.

174 DEFINITIONS, *supra* note 12, at 216.

175 SOHN & NOYES, *supra* note 154, at 278 n.3 (referring to United States v. California, 447 US 1, 8 [1980]). *But see* Carleton, *supra* note 162, at 10 ("State practice would indicate that [single jetties of pile construction] are usually considered to be harbour installations under Article 11 and as such form a legitimate part of the normal baseline".).

176 United States v. California, 447 US 1, 8 (1980). *But see* Carleton, *supra* note 162, at 19 ("This is a unique judgment and particular to the United States, reflecting the administration's reluctance to extend State maritime jurisdiction".).

177 Pearcy, *supra* note 170, at 966–67.

178 *See id.*

179 Louisiana argued that dredged offshore channels leading to ports constitute harbour works and should be treated as baselines for the territorial sea. The Supreme Court, reasoning that dredged channels are below water at all times and do not possess a low-water line, concluded that they are not part of the 'coast'. United States v. Louisiana, 394 US 11, 38 (1969).

tus of "a jetty extending several kilometers into the sea", but declined to state an opinion, purportedly because of the rareness of the situation.[180]

This last category was considered in *Romania* v. *Ukraine* where the seaward end of Romania's Sulina dyke (extending 7.5 kilometers into the sea) was proposed as a base point to be used in the delimitation with Ukraine.[181] The International Court of Justice considered the work of the ILC in 1956, writing:

> In the light of the above, the ILC did not, at the time, intend to define precisely the limit beyond which a dyke, jetty or works would no longer form "an integral part of the harbour system". The Court concludes from this that there are grounds for proceeding on a case-by-case basis, and that the text of Article 11 of UNCLOS and the *travaux préparatoires* do not preclude the possibility of interpreting restrictively the concept of harbour works so as to avoid or mitigate the problem of excessive length identified by the ILC. This may be particularly true where, as here, the question is one of delimitation of areas seaward of the territorial sea.[182]

While the Court did not reject the use of the seaward end of the dyke in Romania's baseline system for the purpose of measuring the breadth of the territorial sea, it did reject the dyke as a base point from which to measure an equidistance boundary with Ukraine.[183]

2 Coast Protective Works: Artificial Conservation of the Baseline

The Committee recalls that in 1956, the ILC commented that "[p]ermanent structures erected on the coast and jutting out to sea (such as jetties and coast protective works) are assimilated to harbour works".[184] McDougal and Burke take a similar position for certain coast protective works writing, "[t]here would seem to be no substantial objection to assimilating 'coast protective works' to harbor installations even when they are isolated structures if, as is usually the

180 *Report of the ILC (1956)*, *supra* note 72, at 270.

181 Sulina dyke may be better described as a pair of parallel training walls designed to maintain water depth and access to the river port of Sulina. Contrary to the Court's conclusion that Sulina dyke serves no "direct purpose in port activities" (*Romania* v. *Ukraine*, *supra* note 26, para. 138), Carleton argues that the only reason to build a training wall such as Sulina dyke "is to facilitate the safe navigation of vessels to and from a river port". Carleton, *supra* note 162, at 28.

182 *Romania* v. *Ukraine*, *supra* note 26, para. 134.

183 *Id.* paras. 137–38.

184 *Report of the ILC (1956)*, *supra* note 72, at 270.

case, they are not extensive".[185] Shalowitz includes "structures along the seacoast at inlets or rivers for protective purposes", but does not specify whether they must have a functional relationship with a harbour system.[186]

It is not clear whether coast protective works that do not form an integral part of a harbour system would be assimilated to harbour works under Article 11 or would be considered part of the Article 5 'coast' independent of Article 11. Notwithstanding, in practice these structures have been taken to form part of the coast. Prescott and Schofield observe that "[s]ometimes protecting walls will lie *along* the coast and cover the normal low-water line rather than jutting out significantly into the sea. Nevertheless they are clearly to be regarded as part of the baseline from which territorial waters are measured".[187] Carleton writes of dykes, levees, berms, and seawalls "[w]here these constructions abut directly onto the sea they effectively form part of the State's coast. In these circumstances it is also considered that they form a legitimate part of the State's coastline and can be used as territorial sea basepoints".[188]

Although there is a clear requirement under Article 11 that harbour works be an "integral part of a harbour system", the Committee finds no authority to suggest that coast protective works must be associated with harbors in order to qualify as part of the coast and, therefore the normal baseline. To the contrary, Soons – referring to "artificial conservation of the baseline" – writes that "[a]rtificial conservation of the coastline, including that of islands, is fully permitted under public international law: this is proved by abundant State practice".[189]

3 Land Reclamation: Artificial Extension of the Baseline

Artificial extension of the baseline appears to receive a similar treatment.[190] Here too, what little state practice there is indicates that artificial extensions of the coast serve to extend the normal baseline.

---

185 Myres McDougal & William Burke, The Public Order of the Oceans 422–23 (1962). *But see* Carleton, *supra* note 162, at 13 (referring to the coast protective works of the Netherlands which cover 17 percent of the coastline and yet are "considered to be part of the normal baseline".).

186 Shalowitz, *supra* note 61, at 292.

187 Prescott & Schofield, *supra* note 13, at 135.

188 Carleton, *supra* note 162, at 13.

189 Soons, *supra* note 155, at 222.

190 Artificial extension of the coast should be distinguished from territorial gain resulting from natural means such as accretion and land rise, or post-glacial rebound. These natural modes of territorial gain would extend the low-water line when they occur in coastal areas.

Carleton cites examples from the Netherlands, United Arab Emirates, Singapore, and Japan,[191] and concludes that "[p]rovided the reclaimed land is an integral part of the mainland or an island, State practice would indicate that it is acceptable to consider it as part of the State's coast for the generation of maritime limits".[192] Malaysia, upon instituting proceedings against Singapore in *Land Reclamation*, appeared to believe that Singapore's land reclamation projects would impact the location of Singapore's baseline for the purpose of a delimitation between their opposite coasts. Malaysia's concern indicates that Malaysia considered that such a reconfiguration of Singapore's coasts would functionally and legally extend Singapore's baseline seaward to Malaysia's disadvantage in a delimitation of maritime spaces between the opposite states.

The United States Supreme Court considered the issue with respect to a spoil bank made of dredged material that attached to and extended offshore from the natural coastline. Louisiana contended that the artificial extension should be considered part of the state's coast while the United States argued that it should not on the theory that spoil banks are not useful and are likely to be short-lived. The Court rejected this argument, noting simply, "it suffices to say that the [1958] Convention contains no such criteria",[193] and the spoil bank was included as part of the baseline.

In the Netherlands, the impact of artificial extensions of the baseline on the normal baseline has been considered in connection with the adoption of the Territorial Sea Demarcation Act. A Dutch Parliamentary Commission asked whether an artificial extension of the coast would lead to a shift of the normal baseline. The Minister of Foreign Affairs answered that it would.[194] This approach has been consistently followed by the Netherlands. A recent example is provided by the latest extension of the Port of Rotterdam. There, land reclamation extended the coast a couple of kilometers seaward and this also has led to a shift in the low-water line.[195]

From the foregoing the Committee concludes that existing international law recognizes harbour works as described above, any coast protective work

191 Carleton, *supra* note 162, at 19–22.

192 *Id.* at 22.

193 United States v. Louisiana, 394 US 11, 41 (1969).

194 Determination of the boundaries of the territorial sea of the Netherlands (Act boundaries Netherlands territorial sea); Note in response to the report (Tweede Kamer [1982–1983] 17 654, No. 7, at 8).

195 *See further* Maritieme zones gewijzigd door aanleg Maasvlakte, *supra* note 140, at 2. A figure illustrating the shift in the low-water line and the corresponding shift in maritime limits is included in a figure forming part of the press release, *available at* http://www.defensie.nl/_system/handlers/generaldownloadHandler.ashx?filename=/media/detail_ENC_NL50132A_2009_tcm46-142800.pdf.

which extends above the chart datum, and any human-induced extension of the natural coast, as part of the coast for the purposes of Article 5. As such, the normal baseline moves, sometimes seaward, with the resulting changes in coastal configuration.

B *Sea Level Rise and Coastal Erosion*

In the Committee's view, it follows that if the legal baseline changes with human-induced expansions of the actual low-water line to seaward, then it must also change with contractions of the actual low-water line to landward. These contractions could occur, for example, from the actual loss of land through erosion or from rising sea levels that, over time, would submerge coastlines and associated territory. In theory, these contractions could occur to such an extent that the entire territory, and actual low-water line, of low-lying small island nations would be below the vertical datum, thereby eliminating entirely the normal baseline and any entitlement to maritime zones generated from the baseline. Even if such an extreme scenario were not to arise, the Committee considers that the likelihood that some offshore low-lying small islands will be completely submerged will still remain, which will give rise to debate as to whether a coastal state loses the totality of its entitlement to claim a normal baseline from territory that has become submerged. Islands presently above the water surface at high tide may, as a result of sea level rise, disappear at high tide and become low tide elevations, resulting in the feature being reclassified from an island to an insular feature.[196]

This may be the unavoidable consequence of using the actual low-water line as the baseline from which maritime zones are measured, but it is a consequence that authors seem to agree reflects the existing law of the normal baseline. Caron and Soons reach this conclusion.[197] Rayfuse has also written recently on the topic of the disappearing state, baselines, and the impact on maritime entitlements.[198] Schofield and Arsana have also addressed this issue,

---

196 Clive Schofield & I. Made Andi Arsana, *Imaginary Islands? Options to Preserve Maritime Jurisdictional Entitlements and Provide Stable Maritime Limits in the Face of Coastal Instability*, 6th IHO-IAG ABLOS Conference, 25–27 October 2010, at 6, *available at* http://www.iho.int/mtg_docs/com_wg/ABLOS/ABLOS_Conf6/ABLOS_Conf6.htm.

197 *See* Caron (1990), *supra* note 149; Caron (2009), *supra* note 151; Soons, *supra* note 155.

198 *See* Rosemary Rayfuse, *W(h)ither Tuvalu? International Law and Disappearing States*, University of New South Wales Faculty of Law Research Series, 2009, Paper 9, *available at* http://law.bepress.com/unswwps/flrps09/art9/; Rosemary Rayfuse, *Sea Level Rise and Maritime Zones: Preserving the Maritime Entitlements of 'Disappearing' States*, *in* THREATENED ISLAND NATIONS: LEGAL IMPLICATIONS OF RISING SEAS AND A CHANGING CLIMATE (M.B. Gerrard & G.E. Wannier eds., forthcoming 2012) (citing manuscript of this chapter).

with particular reference to the impact of sea level rise on islands.[199] These authors agree that under the existing law the normal baseline would disappear along with any territory that it once circumscribed and the maritime entitlements it once generated if that territory submerges below the relevant vertical datum. Short of actual physical protection of the coast the authors do not find that the existing law provides for any other way to protect the maritime interests of states threatened with a total loss of territory.

Unlike most of the scenarios considered above in which possible differences between the charted and actual low-water lines are small and the effects local – sling mud banks, deltaic accretion, other forms of accretion and erosion, land reclamation projects, or the construction of harbour works – the prospect of significant sea level rise carries with it problems of global scale and effect and serious existential implications for some states. Among these problems are negative impacts on maritime boundaries negotiated in reliance on normal baselines in existence at the time of a delimitation,[200] and the outer limits of a State's maritime zones proclaimed in reliance upon a normal baseline. Under these circumstances, a question arises as to whether the existing law of normal baselines would or should apply.

Considering the possibility of total loss of territory and all maritime rights, Caron, Soons, Rayfuse, Jesus, Schofield and Arsana, and Hayashi have proposed changes to existing international law. The Committee notes that the implementation of these proposals would undoubtedly create serious challenges to fundamental principles of the law of the sea (such as, for example, the principle that "the land dominates the sea"[201]),[202] notwithstanding that the proposals seek to promote stability, particularly regarding the preservation of the outer limits of maritime zones. In this respect, Jesus argues that "a substantial rise in sea level, whatever the cause, should not entail the loss of States'

199 Schofield & Arsana, *supra* note 196. *See also* Clive Schofield, *Shifting Limits? Sea Level Rise and Options to Secure Maritime Jurisdictional Claims*, 3 Carbon & Climate L. Rev. 405, 408 (2009); Moritaka Hayashi, *Sea-Level Rise and the Law of the Sea: Future Options, in* The World Ocean in Globalisation 187 (Davor Vidas & Peter Johan Schei eds., 2011).

200 José Luís Jesus, *Rocks, New-born Islands, Sea Level Rise and Maritime Space, in* Negotiating for Peace – Liber Amicorum Tono Eitel 599, 602 (Jochen Frowein *et al.* eds., 2003); Schofield, *supra* note 199, at 406; Katherine Houghton *et al.*, *Maritime Boundaries in a Rising Sea*, 3 Nature Geoscience 813 (2010) (discussing case studies).

201 *See supra* note 15 and associated text.

202 Jenny Grote Stoutenburg, *Implementing a New Regime of Stable Maritime Zones to Ensure the (Economic) Survival of Small Island States Threatened by Sea-Level Rise*, 26 Int'l J. Marine & Coastal L. 263, 271–75 (2011).

ocean space and their rights over maritime resources, already recognized by the 1982 Convention and by the community of nations".[203]

After acknowledging that States may protect their coasts through the creation or reinforcement of sea defenses, Soons suggests that "[a] less expensive, but probably also less dependable means for these States to prevent negative consequences as a result of sea level rise ... is to contribute towards the creation of a new rule of customary international law which allows coastal States in case of sea level rise to maintain the original outer limits of their maritime zones".[204] In order to succeed, these States would need to "gain approval for this practice in the relevant international fora".[205]

Caron notes that "[i]n the case of a rising sea level, the law of baselines gives rise to a legal feedback that increases the potential for the waste of resources as well as private and interstate conflict".[206] Like Soons, he acknowledges that states may "preserve their rights and entitlements by committing resources to stabilize that aspect of the physical world which is threatened by climatic change [that is, the baseline]".[207] He continues noting the inefficiencies of preserving baselines, "not because the aspect itself is valuable, but rather because the entitlements are valuable, and those entitlements, for purely conventional reasons, require its preservation".[208] In order to address the problems of inefficiency and conflict, Caron suggests modifying the rule and concludes "that states should move toward permanently fixing ocean boundaries".[209]

Rayfuse also acknowledges that "[c]urrent international law does not adequately address the continued maintenance of [maritime] entitlements in the context of sea level rise,"[210] and suggests that "a more lasting solution to the challenges to coastal states posed by sea level rise will require the international community to adopt new positive rules of international law to freeze existing baseline claims".[211] She continues: "For states whose very existence is threatened, recognition of a new category of state, able to capitalize on existing maritime entitlements, will also be needed".[212] According to this author, a freezing of maritime zone outer limits "would be consistent with, and would

203 Jesus, *supra* note 200, at 601.
204 Soons, *supra* note 155, at 231.
205 *Id.*
206 Caron (2009), *supra* note 151, at 2.
207 *Id.* at 13.
208 *Id.*
209 *Id.* at 14 (using the term 'boundaries' to refer to the outer limits of maritime zones).
210 Rayfuse (2012) (manuscript), *supra* note 198, at 12.
211 *Id.* at 12–13.
212 *Id.* at 13. *But see* Julia Lisztwan, *Stability of Maritime Boundary Agreements*, 37 YALE J. INT'L L. 153 (2012) (offering a competing view on the equities of freezing existing baselines

significantly assist in, the promotion and achievement of the LOSC objectives of peace, stability, certainty, fairness, and efficiency in ocean governance".[213] Rayfuse concludes that, considering the possibility of total loss of territory and all associated maritime rights, recognition of the concept of the 'deterritorialised state' might provide an equitable solution to the legal problems involved in sea level rise.[214]

Schofield and Arsana consider that one option to resolve this issue would be to "legally fix or declare the location of normal baselines and/or the maritime limits derived from them".[215] While considering the potential for unilateral state practice in this area to develop new customary law, they assert that a "preferable approach would be to seek multilateral agreement on, effectively, a revised legal regime applicable to normal baselines".[216]

The Committee concludes that the existing law of the normal baseline applies in situations of significant coastal change caused by both territorial gain and territorial loss. Coastal states may protect and preserve territory through physical reinforcement, but not through the legal fiction of a charted line that is unrepresentative of the actual low-water line.

All coastal States face the threat of territorial loss as a result of predicted sea level rise. When coastal territory submerges below the selected low-water datum, the normal baseline would retreat, and in extreme cases would be lost. As indicated in the proposal establishing this Committee, low-lying, small-island developing states are likely to be the most severely affected by this phenomenon. If current predictions of sea level rise are realized, some States will become completely submerged. The resulting deterritorialization will likely mean, among other things, a total loss of baselines and of the maritime zones generated by coastal territory and measured from those baselines. Should the issue of deterritorialization fall to be considered by the international community at least in part as a baseline issue, the existing law of the normal baseline does not offer an adequate solution.

Here the Committee raises the possibility of deterritorialization in the context of Article 5 baselines, but the loss of a State's territory to rising sea levels is not primarily a baseline or law of the sea issue. Substantial territorial loss is a much broader issue encompassing concerns of statehood, national identity, refugee status, state responsibility, access to resources,

considering that zones preserved under such rules would otherwise have reverted to the commons).

213 Rayfuse (2012) (manuscript), *supra* note 198, at 6.

214 *Id.* at 9–13.

215 Schofield & Arsana, *supra* note 196, at 11.

216 *Id.*

and international peace and security. This issue requires consideration by a committee established for the specific purpose of addressing this range of concerns. The work of that committee should take into account the spirit of the modern law of the sea in which the interests of differently situated states are balanced. That committee should also recall the aims of the Convention: to strengthen peace, security, cooperation, and friendly relations among nations in conformity with the principles of justice and equal rights; to take account of the interests and needs of humankind as a whole; and to promote the economic and social advancement of all peoples of the world considering the special interests and needs of developing countries.

V Conclusions

The Committee concludes that the legal normal baseline is the actual low-water line along the coast at the vertical datum, also known as the chart datum, indicated on charts officially recognized by the coastal State. The phrase "as marked on large-scale charts officially recognized by the coastal State" provides for coastal State discretion to choose the vertical datum at which that State measures and depicts its low-water line. The charted low-water line illustrates the legal normal baseline, and in most instances and for most purposes the charted low-water line provides a sufficiently accurate representation of the normal baseline. As a matter of evidence for proving the location of the normal baseline the charted line appears to enjoy a strong presumption of accuracy. However, where significant physical changes have occurred so that the chart does not provide an accurate representation of the actual low-water line at the chosen vertical datum, extrinsic evidence has been considered by international courts and tribunals in order to determine the location of the legal normal baseline.[217, 218]

---

217 Committee member Oude Elferink does not subscribe to the Committee's conclusion on the interpretation of Article 5 of the United Nations Convention on the Law of the Sea and aspects of the analysis leading up to that conclusion.

218 Committee member Yee would like to emphasize the following: "Article 5 says that the normal baseline is 'the low-water line along the coast as marked on large-scale charts officially recognized by the coastal State'. It is neither 'the low-water line along the coast', pure and simple, nor the line 'as marked on large-scale charts officially recognized by the coastal State', pure and simple. The conclusions of the Committee have the effect of interpreting 'as marked on large-scale charts officially recognized by the coastal State' out of Article 5, despite the lip service paid to it under the guise of giving the charts 'a strong presumption of accuracy'. To the extent that the phrase 'as marked on large-scale charts officially recognized by the coastal State' was put in the provision (or its predecessor) to address the difficulty resulting from the lack of a universal standard for determining the low-water line, and to the extent that this difficulty has not yet disappeared (that is to say,

The Committee concludes that the normal baseline is ambulatory, moving seaward to reflect changes to the coast caused by accretion, land rise, and the construction of human-made structures associated with harbour systems, coastal protection and land reclamation projects, and also landward to reflect changes caused by erosion and sea level rise. Under extreme circumstances the latter category of change could result in total territorial loss and the consequent total loss of baselines and of the maritime zones measured from those baselines. The existing law of the normal baseline does not offer an adequate solution to this potentially serious problem.

The Committee recommends that the issue of the impacts of substantial territorial loss resulting from sea level rise be considered further by a Committee established for the specific purpose of addressing the wide range of concerns it raises.

VI Annex: Actual Low-Water Line vs. Charted Low-Water Line

This Annex explains the technical reasons there may be differences between the actual and charted low-water lines. Walker provides the following definition of 'low-water line':

(a) In UNCLOS, the phrases "low-water line" and "low-water mark" are synonymous. They mean the intersection of the plane of low water with the shore, or the line along a coast or beach to which the sea recedes at low tide.

(b) It is the normal practice for the low-water line to be shown as an identifiable feature on nautical charts unless the scale is too small

---

there is still no universal standard for determining the low-water line on the coast), there is no justification for downplaying this phrase. A proper interpretation of Article 5 must give effect to both components: (1) 'the low-water line along the coast' and (2) 'as marked on large-scale charts officially recognized by the coastal State'. This requires at least that the coastal State's choice of any reasonable method, which need not be the best method in the view of a *post-facto* decision-maker, to determine the low-water line on the coast as well as its reasonable operations to achieve such a determination under that method, be respected, if the coastal State's determination is open to examination. For example, if a coastal State has determined its low-water line by using Method A, it should not be assessed subsequently by using Method B. In short, if there is any reasonable ground for, or any reasonable method that can result in, the coastal State's decision, that decision should be respected or be given deference. International judicial decisions that have not addressed these points have not tackled the issues head-on and as a result their value is questionable. The so-called 'strong presumption of accuracy' does not give any special weight to the recognition of the chart by the coastal State, as it seems that, according to the Committee, the presumption is rebutted whenever the chart is shown not to reflect physical reality accurately".

to distinguish it from the high-water line or where there is no tide so that the high and low water lines are the same.

(c) The actual water level taken as low water for charting purposes is known as the level of chart datum.[219]

When the "identifiable feature on nautical charts" (the charted line) does not accurately reflect the "intersection of the plane of low water with the shore" (the actual line), the difference between the two may be attributed to any combination of the following: (1) the actual low-water line is elusive; (2) coastal zones are highly dynamic zones experiencing constant morphologic change; (3) the main purpose of nautical charts is safety of navigation; and (4) there is a significant lag time in the charting process.

Elusive line. The low-water line is the line of intersection of the sea with the coast at low tide. This is problematic for two reasons: (1) the line of intersection between land and sea is constantly in flux, and (2) there is no international agreement on a mandatory universal low tide datum.[220] The line of intersection between land and sea is constantly in flux at several different spatial and temporal scales. At the micro-spatial/micro-temporal scale wave action changes this line of intersection by the second or minute. At the macro-spatial/macro-temporal scale this line of intersection changes by virtue of erosion, accretion, dredging, land reclamation, and sea level changes. At an intermediate scale this line of intersection changes over the course of a single tidal cycle. The tidal cycle, which is easily observed over the course of hours, also exhibits longer-term, seasonal, annual, and decadal fluctuations.

The changes caused by the tidal cycle can be fixed by identifying the single vertical, or tidal, datum to represent 'low water'. This vertical datum is the 'zero level' to which elevation and depth measurements are reduced. The intersection of the land with the sea – at that chosen level – is the low-water line. The low-water line thus defined is an elusive feature if not a purely conceptual construct. For example, the vertical datum recommended by the International

---

219 DEFINITIONS, *supra* note 12, at 239.

220 *But see Datums and Bench Marks*, RESOLUTIONS OF THE INTERNATIONAL HYDROGRAPHIC ORGANIZATION 35 (2d ed. 2010 [updated to Mar. 2012]), IHO Res. 3/1919 (last amended by circular letter 19/2008), para. 2(a), *available at* http://www.iho.int/iho_pubs/misc/M3-E-MARCH12.pdf ("It is further resolved that the Lowest Astronomical Tide (LAT), or as closely equivalent to this level as is practically acceptable to Hydrographic Offices, be adopted as chart datum where tides have an appreciable effect on the water level".). For an analysis of vertical datums, see Nuno Sergio Marques Antunes, *The Importance of the Tidal Datum in the Definition of Maritime Links and Boundaries*, 2(7) (IBRU) MARITIME BRIEFINGS (2000).

Hydrographic Organization for use on nautical charts – the lowest astronomical tide (LAT) – is defined as "[t]he lowest tide level which can be predicted to occur under average meteorological conditions and under any combination of astronomical conditions".[221] The actual low-water line defined using the LAT datum will only be visible once every full metonic cycle of 18.6 years provided the meteorological conditions are normal. This means the low-water line will actually be underwater during all but the very lowest tides. Proving the existence of something that does not make an appearance but once every two decades presents obvious difficulties.

Morphologic change. In addition to tidal fluctuation, the coastal zone is an area of constant physical change brought about by the forces of wind and water. These forces contribute to the actual change in the morphology, or shape, of the coast. Some coastal areas are highly dynamic; others are less so. This will affect the rate of morphologic change. Coastal material – sand, mud, pebbles, rock, coral reef, mangrove, etc. – will also influence the rate at which the change occurs. Morphologic change, which creates territorial loss and gain through erosion and accretion, can be slowed (and sometimes inadvertently accelerated elsewhere) by the construction of coastal defenses. Morphologic change and its relationship to the chart-making process contributes to the problem addressed by this Committee.

Safety of navigation. The primary purpose of nautical charts is safety of navigation. As a result, the focus of new surveys, updates and corrections to charts is on navigational hazards and navigational aids, not necessarily on changes to coastal configuration. Nautical charts err on the side of caution. The vertical datums to which depths are referenced on a chart are chosen because they represent the worst case tidal scenario, not because they reflect the reality of the low-tide line under normal or average conditions. Finally, hydrographic agencies focus their resources on updating and producing large-scale charts of high traffic areas. This leaves less-traveled stretches of coast under-researched and uncorrected even if these areas are important for the purposes of defining outer limits of maritime zones or delimitating boundaries with neighbors.

Production time lag. Conceptually the low-water line is fixed by the selection of a vertical datum from which to measure depths and elevations. This hydrographic fiction neutralizes the impact of tidal fluctuation but does not neutralize the impact of morphologic change to the coast. To the extent that coastal change occurs and charts are not updated to reflect that change, differences between the actual and charted low-water line will arise. In order to minimize these differences, detection and depiction of coastal change must

221 *Datums and Bench Marks*, *supra* note 218.

occur rapidly. However, even with modern detection technology (for example, satellite sensors, global positioning systems, and aerial photography) and analysis and depiction technology (for example, geographic information systems (GIS) and electronic chart display and information systems [ECDIS]) charting agencies are not able to achieve real-time chart making and distribution. To the contrary, there are coasts in the world for which the best available charted low-water line is based on surveys made in the 19th century. In these circumstances coastal changes that have occurred in the interim will not be reflected in the charted low-water line.

B *Resolution No. 1/2012: Baselines under the International Law of the Sea*

The 75th Conference of the International Law Association held in Sofia, Bulgaria, 26 to 30 August 2012:

HAVING CONSIDERED the Report of the Committee on Baselines under the International Law of the Sea;

APPRECIATING the work done by the Committee in identifying the existing law concerning the normal baseline and assessing the need for further clarification or development of that law;

NOTING the conclusions of the Committee, in particular addressing:

1. The text and legislative history of Article 5 of the 1982 United Nations Convention on the Law of the Sea and its predecessor Article 3 of the 1958 UN Geneva Convention on the Territorial Sea and Contiguous Zone;
2. The origin of the phrase "as marked on large-scale charts officially recognised by the coastal State" in Article 5;
3. The treatment of the normal baseline in international judicial decisions;
4. The approaches adopted in national legislation and judicial decisions concerning the description of, publication of and sources of evidence to prove the location of the normal baseline;
5. The implications of the existing law of the normal baseline in situations of territorial gain resulting from human-made structures and the artificial conservation or extension of existing coasts;
6. The implications of the existing law of the normal baseline in situations of territorial loss resulting from sea-level rise;
7. The recognition that substantial territorial loss resulting from sea-level rise is an issue that extends beyond baselines and the law of the sea, and encompasses consideration at a junction of several parts of international

law, including such fundamental aspects as elements of statehood under international law, human rights, refugee law, and access to resources, as well as broader issues of international peace and security; and

8. The acknowledgement that the above issue requires consideration by a committee established for the specific purpose of addressing this broad range of concerns;

REQUESTS the Secretary-General of the International Law Association to forward the Committee's Report together with this Resolution to the Secretary-General of the United Nations with the request that they be brought to the attention of States Parties to the United Nations Convention on the Law of the Sea, other interested States, the International Court of Justice, the International Tribunal for the Law of the Sea, the Permanent Court of Arbitration and other interested parties.

II Baselines under the International Law of the Sea (Sydney Report, 2018)

Members of the Committee:
Captain J. Ashley Roach (American): *Chair*
Professor Donald R. Rothwell (Australia): *Rapporteur*

Judge D.H. Anderson (British)
Alternate: Mr Tim Daniel
Dr Gilberto Marcos Antonio Rodrigues (Brazil)
Dr Nuno Antunes (Portugal)
Professor Frida Armas Pfirter (Argentina)
Dr Kaare Bangert (Denmark)
Mr John Brown (British: *Nominee of the Chair*)
Ms Emmanuelle Cabrol (France)
Alternate: Dr Paul von Mühlendahl
Mr C.M. Carleton (British)
Alternate: Dr Edwin Egede
Dr Robin Cleverly (British)
Dr Simona Drenik (Slovenia)
Professor Erik Franckx (HQ)
Dr Antoine Grima (HQ)
Professor Maria Teresa Infante-Caffi (Chile)
Ambassador Marie Jacobsson (Sweden)

Professor Atsuko Kanehara (Japan)
Alternate: Dr Kentaro Nishimoto
Professor Natalie Klein (Australia)
Professor Barbara Kwiatkowska (Netherlands)+
Professor Doris Koenig (Germany)
Professor Suzanne Lalonde (Canada)
Mr Coalter Lathrop (American)
Dr Atip Latipulhayat (Indonesia)
Mr Richard Meese (France)
Professor Alina Miron (France)
Judge Dolliver Nelson (British: *Nominee of the Chair*)*
Professor John Noyes (American)
Mr Simon Olleson (British)
Professor Alex G. Oude Elferink (Netherlands)
Professor Alexander Proelss (Germany)
Professor Norio Tanaka (Japan)#
Professor Davor Vidas (Norway)
Alternate: Dr Oystein Jensen
Professor George Walker (American)
Professor Sienho Yee (HQ)

A *Report*

I Background

1. The International Law Association (ILA) Committee on Baselines under the International Law of the Sea was formed with the approval of the ILA Executive Council in November 2008. The Committee's final report was considered at the Sofia Conference (2012) and in Resolution No. 1/2012 the 75th Conference of the ILA noted the conclusions of the Committee and requested the Secretary-General of the ILA to forward the Report to relevant Parties. The Committee's original four-year mandate ended in 2012.

2. Two matters were identified during the conclusion of the final report in 2012. The first was a recognition that substantial territorial loss resulting from sea-level rise is an issue that extends beyond baselines and the law of the sea and encompasses consideration at a junction of several parts of international law. In response, a proposal for the establishment of a new ILA Committee on International Law and Sea Level Rise was submitted to ILA and endorsed

+ Professor Kwiatkowska passed away on 3 February 2015.
* Judge Nelson passed away on 18 July 2016.
# Professor Tanaka passed away on 12 November 2014.

by the Executive Council. The second was the desirability of further exploration of the international law of the sea addressing "straight baselines" under an extended mandate of the Committee on Baselines under the International Law of the Sea. It was therefore proposed that the ILA Committee on Baselines under the International Law of the Sea have its mandate expanded for a further 4 years during which time it would consider the following matters:

1. The interpretation and relevant state practice of Article 7 of the 1982 United Nations Convention on the Law of the Sea regarding the method adopted by States of drawing straight baselines.
2. The interpretation and relevant state practice of Article 8(2) of the 1982 United Nations Convention on the Law of the Sea regarding the effect arising from the establishment of straight baselines within waters previously not considered internal waters and the consequences thereof for innocent passage.
3. The interpretation and relevant state practice of Article 10 of the 1982 United Nations Convention on the Law of the Sea relating to the method adopted by States of drawing straight baselines within a bay.
4. The interpretation and relevant state practice of Article 13 of the 1982 United Nations Convention on the Law of the Sea as it relates to the method adopted by States in relying upon low-tide elevations in the drawing of straight baselines, and the consistency of that practice with Article 7(4) of the Convention.
5. The interpretation and relevant state practice of Article 14 of the 1982 United Nations Convention on the Law of the Sea as it relates to the matters noted above with respect to how States rely upon a combination of methods in determining baselines, including the normal baseline as provided for in Article 5 of the Convention and as considered in the Committee's 2012 Sofia Conference Report.
6. The interpretation and relevant state practice of Article 47 of the 1982 United Nations Convention on the Law of the Sea regarding the method adopted by States in the drawing of archipelagic baselines.

3. The then Director of Studies asked the Executive Council to agree to an extended mandate until 2016 and that extension was duly granted.[1] At the March 2016 Inter-sessional meeting of the Committee it was decided to seek an extension of the Committee's mandate for a further two years. The

1 International Law Association, Executive Council Meeting Minutes, 10 November 2012.

Director of Studies approved the work plan for 2016–2018, during which time the Committee also considered the following issues:

1. The interpretation of Article 7(2) with respect to deltas and unstable coastlines;
2. The meaning of "main islands" in Article 47(1);
3. The legal consequences arising when the status of an archipelagic State and that State's capacity to proclaim archipelagic baselines is disputed; and
4. The significance and relevant state practice with respect to Article 50 and the drawing of closing lines for the delimitation of internal waters within an archipelagic State.

In March 2018 an Inter-sessional meeting of the Committee was held in Singapore hosted by the National University of Singapore where a draft of this report was subject to review.

4. This Final Report is organised around a common methodology in assessing the key articles under consideration by the Committee: Articles 7, 8, 10, 13, 14 and 47 of the 1982 United Nations Convention on the Law of the Sea (LOSC).[2] Each analysis seeks to provide some background to the drafting of the Article, analysis of the text, assessment of state practice, relevant case law, and a summary of the commentary by publicists. The Report then moves to address certain cross-cutting or global issues that are relevant to a contemporary analysis of straight and archipelagic baselines, before reaching conclusions. This Final Report consolidates much of the historical background to and commentary by publicists found in the First Report (2014) and Second Report (2016). Those Reports can be found on the ILA website which archives the work of this Committee.[3] The Committee has been able in this Final Report to take into account recent developments arising from the decisions of international courts and tribunals. The 2016 *South China Sea* case[4] before an Annex VII LOSC Arbitral Tribunal was an important decision with respect to a number of the questions the Committee had under review. This Final Report makes reference to relevant aspects of the unanimous decision of the Annex VII LOSC Arbitral

2 United Nations Convention on the Law of the Sea (LOSC), 1833 UNTS 397.

3 See also International Law Association, *Report of the Seventy-Sixth Conference, Washington 2014* (International Law Association, London: 2014) 202–240.

4 *In the Matter of an Arbitration before An Arbitral Tribunal Constituted Under Annex VII to the 1982 United Nations Convention on the Law of the Sea between The Republic of the Philippines and the People's Republic of China*, PCA Case no. 2013-19, Award of 12 July 2016 (2016 South China Sea Arbitration).

Tribunal in the *South China Sea* case. The Committee notes that China did not participate in the proceedings before the Tribunal and makes no observations regarding the jurisdiction of the Tribunal to determine the matters before it.[5]

5. While the Committee has sought to be comprehensive in its analysis, by reason of the limitations imposed by its mandate and the length of this Final Report, it has not been possible to consider all possible issues. A detailed analysis of Article 8(2) can be found in the Second Report (2016). Likewise, a more detailed analysis of commentary by publicists can be found in the First Report (2014) and Second Report (2016). Aspects of the report need to be read along with Appendix 1, 2, and 3 which are attached. The leading publication on the history of the negotiation of individual articles in the LOSC remains the *Virginia Commentaries*,[6] and the recent *United Nations Convention on the Law of the Sea: A Commentary*[7] provides a more contemporary analysis of individual articles. Finally, in this Report the terms "miles" and "nautical miles" have been used interchangeably.[8]

II Straight Baselines

A *Relevant Historical Background to Article 7, LOSC*

6. The origin of Article 7 can be found first in the decision of the International Court of Justice (ICJ) in the *Fisheries* case,[9] second in the work of the International Law Commission (ILC) including the Draft Articles on the Law of the Sea, and third in the deliberations of the First United Nations Conference on the Law of the Sea (UNCLOS I) that resulted in adoption of the 1958 Convention on the Territorial Sea and the Contiguous Zone.[10] This detailed historical background can be found in the First Report (2014).

5 Committee member Yee objects to the Final Report's references to the award without noting the critical study of the award published as Chinese Society of International Law "The South China Sea Arbitration Awards: A Critical Study" (2018) 17 *Chinese Journal of International Law* 210–748; a copy of this study was received after the Draft Final Report was circulated to the Committee members.

6 Satya N. Nandan and Shabtai Rosenne (eds.), *United Nations Convention on the Law of the Sea 1982: A Commentary* Vol. II (Martinus Nijhoff, Dordrecht/Boston/London: 1993).

7 Alexander Proelss (ed.), *United Nations Convention on the Law of the Sea: A Commentary* (C.H. Beck/Hart/Nomos, München/Oxford/Baden-Baden: 2017).

8 George Walker (ed.), *Definitions for the Law of the Sea: Terms Not Defined by the 1982 Convention* (Martinus Nijhoff, Leiden/Boston: 2012) 247 comments: "Mile" or "nautical mile", wherever appearing in UNCLOS, means the international nautical mile, i.e. 1852 meters or 6076.115 feet, corresponding to 60 nautical miles per degree of latitude.

9 *Fisheries* (United Kingdom v. Norway) [1951] ICJ Rep. 116.

10 *Convention on the Territorial Sea and the Contiguous Zone*, 516 UNTS 206.

B *LOSC Text*

7. During negotiations at the Third United Nations Conference on the Law of the Sea (UNCLOS III) on the matter of straight baselines, emphasis was given to seeking to repeat the essential elements of Article 4 of the Convention on the Territorial Sea and the Contiguous Zone, albeit with appropriate modifications to reflect changes in the structure of the draft Convention negotiating text. The most significant adjustment to the text of the original article was a proposal to take into account the circumstances of highly unstable coastlines. Bangladesh was a strong supporter of such a change, and made a number of proposals at various stages of the conference negotiations.[11] The Bangladesh proposal was ultimately adopted, with variations, in what became paragraph 2 of Article 7 of the LOSC.[12] Another adjustment made to Article 4 was a separate provision contained in Article 16 of the LOSC requiring States to show certain types of baselines drawn for the purposes of measuring the breadth of the territorial sea on publicly available charts. Article 14 of the LOSC was equally an innovation, further clarifying that recourse to straight lines was just another method to draw baselines to suit certain conditions.

8. Article 7 of the LOSC is situated within Part II of the Convention titled "Territorial Sea and Contiguous Zone". Part II is divided into four sections, and Article 7 falls within Section 2 titled "Limits of the Territorial Sea". Relevant for present purposes is that it is immediately preceded by Articles 5 "Normal Baseline" and 6 "Reefs". The article provides as follows:

> *Article 7*
> *Straight baselines*
> 1. In localities where the coastline is deeply indented and cut into, or if there is a fringe of islands along the coast in its immediate vicinity, the method of straight baselines joining appropriate points may be employed in drawing the baseline from which the breadth of the territorial sea is measured.
>
> 2. Where because of the presence of a delta and other natural conditions the coastline is highly unstable, the appropriate points may be selected along the furthest seaward extent of the low-water line and,

11 Nandan and Rosenne (eds.), *United Nations Convention on the Law of the Sea: A Commentary* Vol. II, 97–98.

12 See discussion of the UNCLOS III negotiations in Nandan and Rosenne (eds.), *United Nations Convention on the Law of the Sea: A Commentary* Vol. II, 97–100; W. Michael Reisman and Gayle S. Westerman, *Straight Baselines in International Maritime Boundary Delimitation* (Macmillan, London: 1992) 57–62; J. Ashley Roach and Robert W. Smith, *Excessive Maritime Claims* 3rd (Martinus Nijhoff, Leiden/Boston: 2012) 124, n145.

notwithstanding subsequent regression of the low-water line, the straight baselines shall remain effective until changed by the coastal State in accordance with this Convention.

3. The drawing of straight baselines must not depart to any appreciable extent from the general direction of the coast, and the sea areas lying within the lines must be sufficiently closely linked to the land domain to be subject to the regime of internal waters.

4. Straight baselines shall not be drawn to and from low-tide elevations, unless lighthouses or similar installations which are permanently above sea level have been built on them or except in instances where the drawing of baselines to and from such elevations has received general international recognition.

5. Where the method of straight baselines is applicable under paragraph 1, account may be taken, in determining particular baselines, of economic interests peculiar to the region concerned, the reality and the importance of which are clearly evidenced by long usage.

6. The system of straight baselines may not be applied by a State in such a manner as to cut off the territorial sea of another State from the high seas or an exclusive economic zone.

9. The terms "straight baseline/s", or "straight line" are not limited to Article 7 and can also be found in Article 8 "Internal waters", Article 9 "Mouths of rivers", and Article 10 "Bays".

C Analysis of Article 7, LOSC

1 Text

10. A number of preliminary observations can be made with respect to Article 7. The first is that it retains many of the core elements found in Article 4 of the Convention on the Territorial Sea and the Contiguous Zone, which in turn were primarily based upon the ICJ's decision in the *Fisheries* case. This is particularly the case with paragraphs 1, 3, 4, 5, and 6 of Article 7 which are identical or nearly identical to equivalent paragraphs found in Article 4, even though the treaty background is distinct in either case.

11. The second observation is that Article 7 permits the coastal State to rely upon the method of straight baselines in three instances:

1. Where a coastline is deeply indented and cut into (Article 7(1) LOSC);
2. Where there is a fringe of islands along the coast in its immediate vicinity (Article 7(1) LOSC); or

3. Where because of the presence of a delta or other natural conditions the coastline is highly unstable (Article 7(2) LOSC).

12. These criteria are not cumulative and any one of these three geographic circumstances will be sufficient for the coastal State to become entitled to use the straight baseline method. In this respect the Committee recalls that Article 7(2) was added to the convention text during the LOSC negotiations and provides an additional basis upon which a coastal State can seek to draw straight baselines. Where straight baselines have been drawn consistently with Article 7(1), Article 7(5) also provides that account may be taken when drawing the baselines of economic interests peculiar to the region "the reality and importance of which are clearly evidenced by long usage".

13. The third observation is that the coastal State's entitlements to use the straight baseline method are subject to four controls as follows:

1. The drawing of straight baselines must not depart to any appreciable extent from the general direction of the coast (Article 7(3) LOSC);
2. The sea areas within the baselines must be sufficiently linked to the land domain to be subject to the regime of internal waters (Article 7(3) LOSC);
3. Straight baselines must not be drawn to and from low-tide elevations, except in the case:
   a. Where lighthouses or similar installations that are permanently above sea level have been built on the low-tide elevation, or
   b. Where the drawing of baselines to and from a particular low-tide elevation has received general international recognition (Article 7(4) LOSC);[13] and,
4. The drawing of straight baselines must not cut off the territorial sea of another State from the high seas or the exclusive economic zone (Article 7(6) LOSC).

14. In 1989 the United Nations Office for Ocean Affairs and the Law of the Sea (now the United Nations Division for Ocean Affairs and the Law of the Sea

13 This would extend to the recognition granted to such a feature by the ICJ or similar judicial body.

[UNDOALOS]) published a study on baselines (1989 UN Study) that explains several terms in Article 7:[14]

> "Straight baselines" are a system of straight lines joining specified or discrete points on the low-water line, usually known as straight baseline turning points. A "straight line" is mathematically the line of shortest distance between two points.
>
> "Delta" means a tract of alluvial land enclosed and traversed by the diverging mouths of a river.[15]

15. The 1989 UN Study also makes important observations with respect to how the relevant provisions of Article 7 could be interpreted. While observing that there may be "different views" on the matter, the Study notes that the "concept of straight baselines is designed to avoid the tedious application of rules dealing with the normal baselines and the mouths of rivers and bays, where their application would produce a complex pattern of territorial seas."[16] The 1989 UN Study highlights that an application of Articles 5 and 10 could in certain circumstances create enclaves and deep-pockets of "non-territorial sea" and that this "might create considerable difficulties for both the observance of the appropriate régime and surveillance."[17] It is then observed that:

> The spirit of article 7, in respect of indented coasts and fringing islands, will be preserved if straight baselines are drawn when the normal baseline and closing lines of bays and rivers would produce a complex pattern of territorial seas and when those complexities can be eliminated by the use of a system of straight baselines. It is not the purpose of straight baselines to increase the territorial sea unduly.[18]

16. The 1989 UN Study proceeds to provide some guidance on the interpretation of some of the critical terms found within Article 7. It is suggested that the

---

14 United Nations Office for Ocean Affairs and the Law of the Sea, *Baselines: An Examination of the Relevant Provisions of the United Nations Convention on the Law of the Sea* (United Nations, New York: 1989) (1989 UN Study); the UN study was subject to review by a Group of Technical Experts on Baselines who commented on a preliminary draft of the publication as prepared by the United Nations Office for Ocean Affairs and the Law of the Sea. This UN study is mentioned at this juncture for reasons of practicality.

15 1989 UN Study, Appendix I, 47; see also the definitions provided for these terms in Walker (ed.), *Definitions for the Law of the Sea: Terms Not Defined by the 1982 Convention*, 164, 306.

16 1989 UN Study, 18.

17 Ibid.

18 Ibid. 17–20.

term "deeply indented" found in Article 7(1) can be used in "either an absolute or a relative sense".[19] As to the characterisation of a fringe of islands, the UN Study observes that "[t]here is no uniformly identifiable objective test which will identify for everyone islands which constitute a fringe in the immediate vicinity. States should, however, be guided by the general spirit of article 7."[20] Two examples are given to illustrate where a fringe of islands is likely to exist. The first is one which relates to the circumstances of the *Fisheries* case and where the islands appear to form a unity with the mainland. The other is where the islands may be a distance from the coast and "form a screen which masks a large proportion of the coast from the sea."[21] As to the distance of the islands from the coast and being within the "immediate vicinity", the view was that a distance of 24 miles would be satisfactory.[22] It was also observed that the concept applies to the inner edge of the islands because the fringe may be of considerable width.[23]

17. The Committee considers the 1989 UN Study as a useful starting point for an analysis of the interpretation and application of Article 7. However, the Committee notes that since its publication there have been important developments in state practice and the decisions of international courts and tribunals. The 1989 UN Study will not therefore be strictly applied.

2 State Practice

18. A study undertaken by the Committee on state practice regarding straight baselines indicates that of the 150 coastal States,[24] 90 (including their nine dependencies) had drawn straight baselines along portions of their coasts. The full results are summarized in Appendix 1. Some coastal States which would otherwise be eligible to declare straight baselines under Article 7 (or the corresponding customary international law rule) have hitherto chosen not to do

19 Ibid. 20, at which there is an accompanying illustrative example.

20 Ibid.

21 Ibid.; an example of such islands is given as the Recherche Archipelago off the coast of Western Australia, Australia.

22 Ibid. 21; on a different but related point cf. *Maritime Delimitation in the Black Sea* (Romania v. Ukraine) Judgment [2009] ICJ Reports 61 [149] where Serpents' Island, 20 nautical miles from the Ukrainian coast, was not considered to be a part of Ukraine's coastal configuration.

23 1989 UN Study 21.

24 The Committee accepts that there are differing views as to the number of coastal States; the Committee takes no view on the status of the Palestinian Territories and Taiwan/Republic of China. Committee member Yee observed that "under the Constitution of the Republic of China, the Republic of China and the People's Republic of China claim the same territories".

so.[25] In this respect it needs to be recalled that under Article 7 coastal States "may" employ the method of straight baselines and that there is no requirement that they do so even when their coastal configurations meet the criteria identified in Article 7. This Report does not seek to provide an exhaustive analysis of all relevant state practice, or the legal grounds on which States may have predicated their recourse to straight (or closing) baselines, as typically that is not made publicly known. Rather, mention will be made of some particular examples of state practice in areas that have been the subject of debate.

19. The practice of the United States of America (US) in interpreting Article 7 is noted, including its diplomatic and other protests against the practice of other States which the US does not consider to have been consistent with Article 7 and customary international law. The Committee notes that the US is not a party to the LOSC, and is a party to the 1958 Territorial Sea Convention, but does take the view that the convention reflects customary international law. US diplomatic practice regarding baselines, and straight baselines in particular, provides insights into state practice which the Committee has found helpful. However, US state practice does not represent the international community and the US position on the interpretation of the LOSC and state practice is only one amongst those of many other States.

a *A Deeply Indented and Cut into Coastline (Article 7(1))*

20. Some coastal States accept that multiple indentations along the section of coast in question are necessary to satisfy Article 7(1). The US position, for example, is that three conditions must be met as follows:

1. In a locality where the coastline is deeply indented and cut into, there exist at least three deep indentations;
2. The deep indentations are in close proximity to each other; and
3. The depth of penetration of each deep indentation from the proposed straight baseline enclosing the indentation at its entrance to the sea is, as a rule, greater than half the length of that baseline segment.[26]

---

25 Greece and the USA are prominent States in this category: Victor Prescott and Clive H. Schofield, *The Maritime Political Boundaries of the World* 2nd (Martinus Nijhoff, Leiden/Boston: 2005), 163; Sophia Kopela, *Dependent Archipelagos in the Law of the Sea* (Martinus Nijhoff, Leiden/Boston: 2013) 73.

26 Roach and Smith, *Excessive Maritime Claims* 3rd, 61–2.

However, the US is distinctive in having identified such precise criteria on this issue. Canada and Denmark have each proclaimed straight baselines along their Arctic coasts with respect to Baffin Island and Ellesmere Island (Canada) and Greenland (Denmark) on the basis that the coasts are deeply indented and cut into.[27] The practice of a significant number of other States reflects a different approach. For example, there is state practice of straight baselines being drawn around a coastline that is generally smooth and without deep indentations, including those straight baselines drawn by Madagascar, by Norway around Jan Mayen, by Spain on its mainland,[28] and by Albania, Colombia, Costa Rica, Egypt, Guinea, Iran, Oman, Pakistan and Senegal.[29]

b *Fringe of Islands along the Coast (Article 7(1))*

21. The US position with respect to this criterion is that providing the islands in question meet the criteria under Article 121(1), then three further conditions must be met:

1. The most landward point of each island lies no more than 24 miles from the mainland coastline;
2. Each island to which a straight baseline is drawn is not more than 24 miles apart from the island from which the straight baseline is drawn; and
3. The islands, as a whole, mask at least 50% of the mainland coastline in any given locality.[30]

Again, the US is distinctive in having a precise position on this issue. Some States have drawn straight baselines to and from islands off their coasts without meeting these criteria. Relying upon the above criteria, the US has protested the straight baseline claims of China, Cuba, Djibouti, Ecuador, Honduras, Italy, Japan, Mexico, Oman, Portugal, South Korea and Thailand.[31] The US is also of the view that the straight baselines drawn by Mauritius to and from islands and rocks off its mainland are not consistent with these requirements.[32] In the

27 Jonathan I. Charney and Lewis M. Alexander (eds.), *International Maritime Boundaries* vol. 1 (Martinus Nijhoff, Dordrecht/Boston: 1993) 375.

28 Prescott and Schofield, *The Maritime Political Boundaries of the World* 2nd, 150.

29 Roach and Smith, *Excessive Maritime Claims* 3rd, 83–95 which have all been subject to protest by the US.

30 Ibid. 62–63.

31 Ibid. 98–107.

32 Department of State (USA), *Mauritius: Archipelagic and Other Maritime Claims and Boundaries* (Limits in the Sea No. 140) (Department of State, Washington: 2014) 5.

same vein, the straight baselines system of Vietnam relies on islands which are small, scattered and largely distant from the mainland coast and from each other.[33]

c *Highly Unstable Coastlines (Article 7(2))*

22. There is not a great deal of state practice giving precise effect to Article 7(2) which was intended for the Ganges-Brahmaputra River delta (Bangladesh).[34] In addition, Roach and Smith observe that other applicable deltas include the Mississippi River (USA), and the Nile River (Egypt).[35] Other relevant examples are those of the deltas of the Rhone (France)[36] and of the Ebro (Spain).[37] In 1990, Egypt established straight baselines along its Mediterranean coast which included the Nile River delta that empties into the Mediterranean Sea. In 1991 the US protested that claim, generally observing that the coastline was neither deeply indented nor cut into.[38] There is also some evidence of state practice amongst polar States regarding the drawing of straight baselines along and adjacent to ice-covered coasts in Antarctica and the Arctic but it is unclear whether that practice is based upon Article 7(2).[39]

23. Prior to the adoption of the LOSC, Bangladesh proclaimed a system of straight baselines in the Bay of Bengal on 13 April 1974 that followed the 10 fathom (approximately 18 metre) isobath. All the baselines were between 16 and 30 miles from the coastline to cater for the unstable nature of the Ganges-Brahmaputra River delta.[40] This is a combination subaerial and subaqueous

---

33 Roach and Smith, *Excessive Maritime Claims* 3rd, 99–100; Department of State (USA), *Straight Baselines: Vietnam* (Limits in the Sea No. 99) (Department of State, Washington: 1983) 6–10; e.g. Hon Hai is a small island situated 80.7 nm from the coast connected to other basepoints by straight baselines of 161 nm.

34 Kai Trümpler, "Article 7 Straight Baselines" in Proelss (ed.), *United Nations Convention on the Law of the Sea: A Commentary*, 65, 77.

35 Roach and Smith, *Excessive Maritime Claims* 3rd, 67.

36 Decree of 19 October 1967 as replaced by M.Z.N.117.2015.LOS of 12 November 2015 (UN Division for Ocean Affairs and the Law of the Sea, Office of Legal Affairs) (2008) Bulletin No. 66 *Law of the Sea* 28.

37 Royal Decree No. 2510/1977 of 5 August 1977.

38 Roach and Smith, *Excessive Maritime Claims* 3rd, 85, 89.

39 See discussion in Donald R. Rothwell, "Antarctic Baselines: Flexing the Law for Ice-Covered Coastlines" in Alex G. Oude Elferink and Donald R. Rothwell (eds.) *The Law of the Sea and Polar Maritime Delimitation and Jurisdiction* (Martinus Nijhoff, The Hague: 2001) 49–68; Tullio Scovazzi, "The Baseline of the Territorial Sea: The Practice of Arctic States" in Alex G. Oude Elferink and Donald R. Rothwell (eds.) *The Law of the Sea and Polar Maritime Delimitation and Jurisdiction* (Martinus Nijhoff, The Hague: 2001) 69–84.

40 Muhammad Nazmul Hoque, *The Legal and Scientific Assessment of Bangladesh's Baseline in the Context of Article 76 of the United Nations Convention on the Law of the Sea* (United

delta; the coastline is unstable as it both advances and retreats.[41] In 2015 Bangladesh undertook a revision of its baselines consisting of three segments respectively 12, 79 and 67 nm in length.[42] It can generally be observed that the first two of these segments follow the general direction of the coast while the third encloses the Meghna Estuary.

d *Length of Straight Baselines*

24. In the absence of definite criteria for the length of straight baselines in Article 7, there is considerable variance in state practice regarding the length of straight baseline segments. Finland and the US assert that baseline segments should not exceed 24 nautical miles (nm).[43] This is not consistent with the position that is found in state practice, which appears to reflect views expressed during UNCLOS I and UNCLOS III where strict limitations on the length of straight baselines were resisted. There are numerous instances of baseline segments which exceed 24 nm, particularly in Asia. In terms of historical trends, while the 1951 *Fisheries* case was influential with respect to the development of state practice concerning straight baselines, prior to 1958 only a few States had drawn straight baselines, including Iran (1934), Norway (1935), Ecuador (1948), Yugoslavia (1948), Saudi Arabia (1949) and Egypt (1951). However, in the 1960s and 1970s a number of ambitious claims were made, especially in South America and Asia, many of which continue to be asserted today. While recent practice amongst States drawing straight baselines suggests a more moderate approach, a number of longstanding and contemporary straight baseline claims have been considered by both publicists and other States to be excessive.[44]

25. Research undertaken by the Committee identified the following with respect to contemporary state practice regarding straight baselines, with complete details to be found in Appendix 1:

- 32 States have drawn in total 83 straight baselines between 40–50 nm in length;

Nations, New York: 2006) 74.

41 Ibid. 74–75.

42 S.R.O. No. 328-Law/2015/MOFA/UNCLOS/113/2/15 (4 November 2015), reproduced in M.Z.N. 118.2016 (LOS) Maritime Zone Notification (7 April 2016) at http://www.un.org/Depts/los/LEGISLATIONANDTREATIES/PDFFILES/mzn_s/mzn118.pdf.

43 Roach and Smith, *Excessive Maritime Claims* 3rd, 64, n26 giving the explanation for the US interpretation.

44 See Prescott and Schofield, *The Maritime Political Boundaries of the World* 2nd, Table 7.1, 654–655; Jonathan I. Charney and Lewis M. Alexander, *International Maritime Boundaries* vol. II (Martinus Nijhoff, Dordrecht/Boston: 1993) 1333.

- 29 States have drawn in total 52 straight baselines between 51–60 nm in length;
- 24 States have drawn in total 46 straight baselines between 61–70 nm in length;
- 15 States have drawn in total 25 straight baselines between 71–80 nm in length;
- 16 States have drawn in total 24 straight baselines between 81–90 nm in length;
- 8 States have drawn in total 9 straight baselines between 91–100 nm in length; and,
- 13 States have drawn in total 24 straight baselines in excess of 100 nm in length.[45]

e *Straight Baselines Drawn to and from Low-Tide Elevations (Article 7(4))*

26. Notwithstanding the potential for controversy over state practice in this area, other than in the case of Norway,[46] there is little apparent state practice giving effect to Article 7(4). The US has taken the position that "similar installations" are those that are permanent, substantial and actually used for safety of navigation and that "general international recognition" includes recognition by the major maritime users over a period of time.[47] Likewise, in 1989 the US protested straight baselines drawn by Sudan along shoals not more than 12 nautical miles from the mainland arguing these features were not low-tide elevations.[48]

f *Significance of State Practice*

27. Many publicists have commented upon the variations in state practice with respect to Article 7, which in turn have raised for consideration the significance of state practice as it relates to Article 7 and whether those variations have resulted in the development of a new rule of customary international law. In a detailed assessment of this issue in 2005, Churchill observed that:

> Although the amount of non-conforming state practice is substantial, it still represents no more than about a quarter of coastal States parties to the Convention. It is also quite diverse, in the sense that it does not

45 The data in Appendix 1 also includes the historic bay claims by Argentina, Libya, and Russia/USSR, the closing lines of which exceed 100 nm.

46 Prescott and Schofield, *The Maritime Political Boundaries of the World* 2nd, 160.

47 Roach and Smith, *Excessive Maritime Claims* 3rd, 66.

48 Ibid., 120, referring to the *Territorial Waters and Continental Shelf Act of 1970* (Sudan) [6(1)].

> point to any particular way in which straight baselines should be drawn: in reality, it seems to suggest no more than that a coastal State may draw straight baselines however it likes. All this, coupled with the fact that at least eight different States and the EU have protested to one or more baseline claims, leads to the conclusion that practice relating to the drawing of straight baselines does not amount (yet) either to an agreed interpretation of the Convention or a new rule of customary international law.[49]

Even if not leading to a customary rule, the aforesaid practice – of States which are parties to the LOSC and the 1958 Convention on the Territorial Sea and the Contiguous Zone – must be further reviewed. As a number of directly interested States have adopted a practice in respect of straight baselines that relies on a "flexible" interpretation of Article 7, it should be assessed as an element of interpretation of the treaty provisions. The criteria incorporated in Article 7 of the LOSC were drafted with such a degree of "fluidity" precisely because no agreement on "tighter" criteria was reached. Various States expressed the view that these criteria had to provide some room for adaptation to a broad range of circumstances. Not entirely surprisingly, the number of States which have protested relevant state practice in this regard, in proportion to the number of potentially interested States, is very small. The existence of a body of state practice that relies on the margin of appreciation of the indeterminate concepts embodied in Article 7 was acknowledged by O'Connell towards the end of UNCLOS III, when stating that:

> the attempt to restrict the straight baseline technique to coasts which are at least as complicated as that of Norway has failed. The concept of the "general direction of the coast" is a matter of appreciation, not of scientific discovery, and this necessarily requires that a considerable margin of appreciation be applied in favour of the coastal State.[50]

3 Case Law

28. Since adoption and eventual entry into force of the LOSC there have been a number of disputes determined by courts or arbitral tribunals in which

---

49 Robin R. Churchill, "The Impact of State Practice on the Jurisdictional Framework Contained in the LOS Convention" in Alex G. Oude Elferink (ed.), *Stability and Change in the Law of the Sea: The Role of the LOS Convention* (Martinus Nijhoff, Leiden: 2005) 91, 108; see also the more recent view of Yoshifumi Tanaka, *The International Law of the Sea* 2nd (Cambridge University Press, Cambridge: 2015) 51–52.

50 D.P. O'Connell, *The International Law of the Sea* Vol. I (Clarendon Press, Oxford: 1982) 214–215.

the status of Article 7 straight baselines has been considered. These cases have principally concerned maritime boundary disputes where the baselines from which maritime zones have been proclaimed have been relevant to the claims asserted by coastal States. However in those instances the principal issue for determination was what influence, if any, the straight baseline would have upon the delimitation of the maritime boundary and not the consistency of the straight baseline with the LOSC. In recent cases, international courts and tribunals have ignored straight baselines for the purpose of bilateral delimitation, instead selecting basepoints from the "physical geography"[51] or "natural coast".[52] An analysis of some of the principal cases highlights the following observations by courts and tribunals.

29. In the *Eritrea/Yemen Arbitration*,[53] the status of the Dahlaks, a "tightly knit group of islands and islets", and the capacity of the islands making up that group to be subject to straight baselines consistent with Article 7 of the LOSC was a matter of particular consideration.[54] While the Tribunal and both of the parties were in agreement that the Dahlaks were an appropriate island group for the establishment of a straight baseline system, ultimately the validity of the actual baselines proposed by the parties was not a matter the Tribunal was called upon to decide.[55] Brief reference was made to a feature known as "Negileh Rock" which lay beyond the Dahlaks and which on certain charts was shown as a reef and not above water at any tidal state.[56] The Tribunal directly referred to Article 7(4) and observed that "since Eritrea claims the

51 *Maritime Delimitation in the Black Sea* (Romania v. Ukraine) [2009] ICJ Reports 61, 108 [137] where the ICJ distinguished base points determined by a coastal State under LOSC Articles 7, 9, 10, 12, and 15 from the delimitation of maritime areas between States, where it was observed that the court "must, when delimiting the continental shelf and exclusive economic zone, select base points by reference to the physical geography of the relevant coasts". In this respect it needs to be recalled that Article 15 refers to the "nearest points on the baselines from which the breadth of the territorial seas of each of the two States is measured".

52 *Maritime Delimitation in the Caribbean Sea and the Pacific Ocean* (Costa Rica v. Nicaragua) [2018] ICJ Reports [100, 138, 143]; see also *Maritime Delimitation in the Black Sea* (Romania v. Ukraine) [2009] ICJ Reports 61, 108 [137] where the court observed that "the issue of determining the baseline for the purpose of measuring the breadth of the continental shelf and the exclusive economic zone and the issue of identifying base points for drawing an equidistance/median line for the purpose of delimiting the continental shelf and the exclusive economic zone between adjacent/ opposite States are two different issues".

53 *Eritrea v. Yemen* (Maritime Delimitation) Award of the Arbitral Tribunal in the Second Stage of the Proceedings (17 December 1999) (1999) XXII RIAA 335 (*Eritrea v. Yemen*).

54 *Eritrea v. Yemen* (1999) XXII RIAA 335 [139].

55 *Eritrea v. Yemen* (1999) XXII RIAA 335 [140–142].

56 *Eritrea v. Yemen* (1999) XXII RIAA 335 [143].

existence of a straight baseline system, that claim seems to foreclose any right to employ a reef that is not proud of the water at low-tide as a baseline of the territorial sea."[57]

30. In the *Qatar v. Bahrain* case[58] a number of matters arose before the ICJ with respect to maritime delimitation and related territorial questions. Qatar made an application instituting proceedings against Bahrain in respect of disputes between the two States relating to sovereignty over certain islands and shoals, and the delimitation of the maritime areas between the two States.[59] As to the method of straight baselines, Bahrain contended that it was a multi-island State characterised by a cluster of islands off the coast of its main islands and that as such it was a *de facto* archipelagic State.[60] Bahrain applied the method of straight baselines, maintaining that the external fringe should serve as the baseline for the territorial sea.[61] However, the ICJ observed that:

> ... the method of straight baselines, which is an exception to the normal rules for the determination of baselines, may only be applied if a number of conditions are met. This method must be applied restrictively. Such conditions are primarily that either the coastline is deeply indented and cut into, or that there is a fringe of islands along the coast in the immediate vicinity.[62]

Directly referring to Bahrain's claim that it was a "multi-island State", the Court went on to observe that such an assertion does not allow the State "to deviate from the normal rules for the determination of baselines unless the relevant conditions are met."[63] The Court rejected Bahrain's contention that the maritime features off the coast of its main islands could be assimilated to a fringe of islands, noting that the islands were relatively small and that they would only be a part of a "cluster of islands" or "island system" if Bahrain's main islands were included.[64]

31. On the basis of the Court's decision in the *Fisheries* case, and the subsequent reliance upon that judgment by the ILC in its Draft Articles and the

57 *Eritrea v. Yemen* (1999) XXII RIAA 335 [145].
58 *Maritime Delimitation and Territorial Questions between Qatar and Bahrain (Qatar v. Bahrain) (Judgment)* [2001] ICJ Rep. 40 (*Qatar v. Bahrain*).
59 *Qatar v. Bahrain (Judgment)* [2001] ICJ Rep. 40 [31].
60 *Qatar v. Bahrain (Judgment)* [2001] ICJ Rep. 40 [181].
61 *Qatar v. Bahrain (Judgment)* [2001] ICJ Rep. 40 [210–211].
62 *Qatar v. Bahrain (Judgment)* [2001] ICJ Rep. 40 [212].
63 *Qatar v. Bahrain (Judgment)* [2001] ICJ Rep. 40 [213].
64 *Qatar v. Bahrain (Judgment)* [2001] ICJ Rep. 40 [213–214].

accompanying commentaries, the principles that are now embodied in Article 7(1), 7(3) and 7(4) are reflective of customary international law.[65] In its more recent judgment in *Qatar v. Bahrain* the Court directly referred to Article 7(4) as reflecting customary international law.[66] While the customary nature of these provisions is doubtless, case law has yet to provide hard and fast rules as to the interpretation of the "indeterminate concepts" in Article 7. This has been acknowledged by the Court since the *Fisheries* case where, in referring to the "general direction of the coast", it stated that "however justified the rule in question may be, it is devoid of any mathematical precision."[67]

4 Commentary by Publicists

32. Article 7 of the LOSC and its predecessor, Article 4 of the Convention on the Territorial Sea and the Contiguous Zone, have been the subject of analysis by a great many law of the sea publicists.[68] Modern commentators, reflecting upon Article 7 of the LOSC, predominantly consider the following elements:
- Deeply indented and cut into coastline;
- Fringe of islands;
- General direction of the coast;
- Length of straight baselines.

A summary of some of the key observations follows.

a *A Deeply Indented and Cut into Coastline (Article 7(1))*

33. Reisman and Westerman assert that there must be more than one deep indentation along the coast, and observe that in the case where there is a single indentation along the coast then the closing line for a juridical bay would apply.[69] Recently, Tanaka has asserted that "There is no objective test that may identify deeply indented coasts".[70] Prescott and Schofield have noted that

65 *Fisheries* (United Kingdom v. Norway) [1951] ICJ Rep. 116, 127, 139.
66 *Qatar v. Bahrain (Judgment)* [2001] ICJ Rep. 40 [201].
67 *Fisheries* (United Kingdom v. Norway) [1951] ICJ Rep. 116, 141–142.
68 O'Connell, *The International Law of the Sea* Vol. I, 214–215; Hersch Lauterpacht, *The Development of International Law by the International Court* (Stevens, London: 1958) 192; Vaughan Lowe and Antonios Tzanakopoulos, "The Development of the Law of the Sea by the International Court of Justice" in Christian J. Tams and James Sloan (eds.), *The Development of International Law by the International Court of Justice* (Oxford University Press, Oxford: 2013) 177; Kopela, *Dependent Archipelagos in the Law of the Sea*, 74; Trümpler, "Article 7 Straight Baselines" 65, 82; Tullio Scovazzi, "Baselines" in *Max Planck Encyclopedia of Public International Law* (June 2007) opil.ouplaw.com [8].
69 Reisman and Westerman, *Straight Baselines in International Maritime Boundary Delimitation*, 81.
70 Tanaka, *The International Law of the Sea 2nd*, 50.

"there can be no doubt that the term "deeply indented" must have both an absolute and a relative meaning ... it is possible that "deeply indented" refers to horizontal penetration of the land and "cut into" refers to vertical incision."[71]

b *Fringe of Islands along the Coast (Article 7(1))*

34. Prescott and Schofield comment that "The reference to the fringe of islands being in the immediate vicinity of the coast must be construed to mean the landward edge of the fringe ... While the intent of the phrase ['immediate vicinity'] is clear enough, Article 7 fails to deliver a clear-cut, objective test by which to judge whether certain islands are close enough to a mainland in order to be considered in its immediate vicinity."[72] Reisman and Westerman are of the view that this requirement in Article 7(1) of the LOSC introduces three cumulative tests as follows. The first is a quantitative and spatially distributional test in that there must be a number of islands that are spatially related to each other so as to create a "fringe". The second is a spatial test with regard to the relation of the islands and coast in that they must be distributed "along" the coast. The third is a relational element as between the islands and coast in terms of their proximity. Tanaka, on the other hand, has doubted whether it is possible to "objectively identify the existence of a 'fringe of islands'."[73]

c *General Direction of the Coast (Article 7(3))*

35. The need for straight baselines to not depart from the general direction of the coast has been considered by Tanaka, who after reflecting on the *Fisheries* case[74] noted that the Court "seems to imply that "the general direction of the coast" provides the principle governing the baseline; and that the straight baseline method is a result of the application of this principle."[75] Prescott and Schofield are of the view that in light of the *Fisheries* decision, this requirement is one in which: "There is no reason why other countries should not treat the outer edge of a fringe of islands as the coastline from which departures of the straight baselines are measured, even if the fringe is not dovetailed into the mainland."[76]

---

71 Prescott and Schofield, *The Maritime Political Boundaries of the World* 2nd, 145.

72 Ibid., 147.

73 Tanaka, *The International Law of the Sea 2nd*, 50.

74 *Fisheries* (United Kingdom v. Norway) [1951] ICJ Rep. 116, 129–130.

75 Tanaka, *The International Law of the Sea 2nd*, 49.

76 Prescott and Schofield, *The Maritime Political Boundaries of the World* 2nd, 157; see also Scovazzi, "Baselines" [12]; Roach and Smith, *Excessive Maritime Claims* 3rd (2012) 64; and W. Michael Reisman, "Straight Baselines in International Law: a call for reconsideration" (1988) 82 *Proceedings of the American Society of International Law* 266.

d *Length of Straight Baselines*

36. The length of straight baselines has been the subject of extensive comment by some publicists, often in the context of particular controversies. Fitzmaurice observed, with respect to the views of the ICJ in *Fisheries* that "The Court did not say that the baseline must be moderate and reasonable in *length*, but rather that it must be so in its general character, and must be drawn in a reasonable *manner*. But length is nevertheless an element in assessing what is reasonable and moderate."[77] Churchill and Lowe assert that baseline length needs to be read against the overall provisions of Article 7 and that: "[i]t would seem, therefore, that there is in principle no restriction on the length of individual baselines, although obviously in practice the necessity for compliance with the general conditions set out above will be a restraining factor."[78] Tanaka, on the other hand, is of the view that "arguably length is an important element in assessing the validity of a straight baseline."[79] Kopela emphasises that the general conditions of Article 7 are "a "restraining factor" regarding the use of exorbitantly long lines",[80] Rothwell and Stephens give implicit support for straight baselines no longer than 24 nm in length,[81] while Trümpler proposes a limit of between 25 and 48 nm.[82]

III Straight Baselines and Bays

A *Relevant Historical Background*

37. The ILC considered the status of bays with respect to baselines and made provision for those circumstances in Article 7 of the Draft Articles. That provision sought to define a bay, including its relevant dimensions, and allowed for the drawing of a line across the mouth of the bay not exceeding 15 miles. Larger bays could have a closing line, including a combination of closing lines, drawn within the bay. These provisions did not apply in the case of "historic bays", a matter on which the ILA had commented in 1926 and 1928.[83] The ILC's recommendations formed the basis for what became Article 7 of the Convention on the Territorial Sea and the Contiguous Zone. Article 7 contained six sub-paragraphs

---

77 Sir Gerald Fitzmaurice, *The Law and Procedure of the International Court of Justice*, vol. 1 (Cambridge, Grotius: 1986) 239; on the significance of the *Fisheries* case to this point see Prescott and Schofield, *The Maritime Political Boundaries of the World* 2nd, 146; on this point see also Lewis M. Alexander, "Baseline Delimitations and Maritime Boundaries" (1982–1983) 23 *Virginia Journal of International Law* 503, 518.

78 Churchill and Lowe, *The law of the sea* 3rd, 37.

79 Tanaka, *The International Law of the Sea 2nd*, 50.

80 Kopela, *Dependent Archipelagos in the Law of the Sea*, 66.

81 Rothwell and Stephens, *The International Law of the Sea* 2nd, 46.

82 Trümpler, "Article 7 Straight Baselines", 75.

83 Prescott and Schofield, *The Maritime Political Boundaries of the World* 2nd, 115 referencing M.P. Stohl, *The international law of bays* (Martinus Nijhoff, The Hague: 1963) 306–307.

and retained the principal provisions of the ILC draft, though the entrance points of the bay were extended to 24 miles. Article 7, and its provisions for the drawing of closing lines within or across a bay, did not apply in the case of historic bays or where Article 4 straight baselines were drawn.

B *Article 10: LOSC Text*

38. Article 10 of the LOSC repeats the text of Article 7 with minor variations. All of the key components of the regime for baselines within a bay are retained.

> *Article 10*
> *Bays*
> 1. This article relates only to bays the coasts of which belong to a single State.
> 2. For the purposes of this Convention, a bay is a well-marked indentation whose penetration is in such proportion to the width of its mouth as to contain land-locked waters and constitute more than a mere curvature of the coast. An indentation shall not, however, be regarded as a bay unless its area is as large as, or larger than, that of a semi-circle whose diameter is a line drawn across the mouth of that indentation.
> 3. For the purposes of measurement, the area of an indentation is that lying between the low-water mark around the shore of the indentation and a line joining the low-water mark of its natural entrance points. Where, because of the presence of islands, an indentation has more than one mouth, the semi-circle shall be drawn on a line as long as the sum total of the lengths of the lines across the different mouths. Islands within an indentation shall be included as if they were part of the water area of the indentation.
> 4. If the distance between the low-water marks of the natural entrance points of a bay does not exceed 24 nautical miles, a closing line may be drawn between these two low-water marks, and the waters enclosed thereby shall be considered as internal waters.
> 5. Where the distance between the low-water marks of the natural entrance points of a bay exceeds 24 nautical miles, a straight baseline of 24 nautical miles shall be drawn within the bay in such a manner as to enclose the maximum area of water that is possible with a line of that length.
> 6. The foregoing provisions do not apply to so-called "historic bays", or in any case where the system of straight baselines provided for in article 7 is applied.

C *Analysis of Article 10*

1 Text

39. Article 10 provides a mechanism for the drawing of baselines within a juridical bay and uses two different terms to describe those lines. A "closing line" is drawn across a bay less than 24 nm, while a straight baseline is drawn in the case of a bay where the entrance exceeds 24 nm. Two types of bays are excluded from Article 10: a) bays shared by two or more States;[84] and b) historic bays.[85] Neither of these two exceptions are therefore assessed other than in instances where state practice relating to these bays is of more general application. Article 10(2) defines a juridical bay providing some general guidance as to size and indentation from the coast. A semi-circle test is applied on the basis of a semi-circle whose diameter is a line drawn across the mouth of the bay. The line is determined from the low-water mark of the natural entrance points of the bay. With respect to determining the entrance points of the bay, the *Virginia Commentaries* observes that: "Such points, however, are not always easy to determine because some bays have a number of such points and others possess smoothly curved entrances on which no single point is distinguishable."[86] Different outcomes arise if the distance between the natural entrance points is less than or greater than 24 nm. If less than 24 nm then a closing line may be drawn across those entrance points and the waters on the landward side of the line are considered internal waters. If greater than 24 nm then a straight baseline of 24 nm shall be drawn within the bay.

2 State Practice

40. Contemporary evidence of state practice suggests that adherence to the provisions of Article 10 remains varied in practice. While it is possible to identify examples of juridical bays that satisfy the definition in Article 10,[87]

84 Westerman asserts this provision was "necessary in order to prevent large bodies of water such as the Mediterranean or Baltic seas from technically becoming juridical bays under Article 7": Gayl Shaw Westerman, *The Juridical Bay* (Oxford University Press, Oxford: 1987) 79.

85 See generally on historic bays L.F.E. Goldie, "Historic Bays in international law: an impressionistic overview" (1984) 11 *Syracuse Journal of International Law and Commerce* 211–273; "Historic Bays: Memorandum by the Secretariat of the United Nations" (United Nations Conference on the Law of the Sea, 24 February–27 April 1958) UN Doc. A/CONF.13/1.

86 Nandan and Rosenne (eds.), *United Nations Convention on the Law of the Sea 1982: A Commentary* Vol. II, 117.

87 See, e.g., Department of State (USA), *Mauritius: Archipelagic and Other Maritime Claims and Boundaries*, 1, 6 – with the exception of Mathurn Bay, the six bay closing lines put forward by Mauritius in the 2005 Regulations to the *Maritime Zones Act 2005* satisfy the "semi-circle test" and do not rely upon closing lines in excess of 24 nm. Grenada's 28 bays equally satisfy both requirements: Department of State (USA), *Grenada: Archipelagic and*

several States have sought to draw a bay closing line across the entrances to gulfs and bays that exceed the length specified in Article 10. The state practice in the area is contested however because States have sought to justify their action on the basis of making an historic bay claim. Examples include Libya's claims with respect to the Gulf of Sidra, which have been subject to protest,[88] and the former USSR declaring a closing line of approximately 107 nm across Peter the Great Bay in 1957 which was also the subject of protest.[89] In 1966 Argentina drew closing lines across the mouths of the San Jorge and San Matias gulfs which were also subject to protest by the US on the basis that neither met the test as a juridical bay under the provisions of the Convention on the Territorial Sea and the Contiguous Zone.[90] Protests have also been lodged by the US with respect to the length of the closing lines drawn across bays by Mauritania,[91] Sudan[92] and Costa Rica.[93] The US has also objected to the use of straight baselines to delimit waters off the mainland coast of Portugal and the Azores on the grounds that the baselines relied upon "do not enclose juridical bays."[94] Closing lines drawn by Gabon in excess of 24 nm between Pointe Ngombe and Cap Lopes have also been questioned.[95]

41. Churchill and Lowe have identified New Zealand, Papua New Guinea, Samoa and Vanuatu as States whose domestic legislation conforms to the Article 10 definition of bays and the specifics of the semi-circle test.[96] It is

Other Maritime Claims and Boundaries (Limits in the Sea No. 135) (Department of State, Washington: 2014) 1, 3.

88 Roach and Smith, *Excessive Maritime Claims* 3rd, 46–47, 129.

89 Charney and Alexander, *International Maritime Boundaries* Vol. 1, 1137; Department of State (USA), *Straight Baselines: U.S.S.R.* (Limits in the Seas No. 107) (Department of State, Washington: 1987) 4–5.

90 Roach and Smith, *Excessive Maritime Claims* 3rd, 46–47, 129.

91 Ibid., 130.

92 Ibid.

93 Department of State (USA), *Straight Baselines Claim: Costa Rica* (Limits in the Seas No. 111) (Department of State, Washington: 1990) 1, 7 citing the Text of United States Protest Note to Costa Rica, 18 December 1989.

94 Department of State (USA), *United States Responses to Excessive National Maritime Claims* (Limits in the Seas No. 112) (Department of State, Washington: 1992) 1, 32 quoting a diplomatic note transmitted by the American Embassy at Lisbon, based on instructions found in 1986 State telegram 266998.

95 David A. Colston and Robert W. Smith, *International Maritime Boundaries* Vol. V (Martinus Nijhoff, Dordrecht/Boston: 2005) 3687.

96 Churchill and Lowe, *The Law of the Sea* 3rd, 54 citing *Territorial Sea and Exclusive Economic Zone Act 1977* (New Zealand) ss 2 and 6; *National Seas Act 1977* (Papua New Guinea) Schedule 1; *Territorial Sea Act 1971* (Samoa) No. 3, ss 2 and 6, *Maritime Zones Act No. 23 of 1981* (Vanuatu) ss 1 and 4 which has since been repealed by the *Maritime Zones Act No. 6 of 2010* (Vanuatu) ss 1 and 4 (the substantive provisions remains unchanged from the 1981 Act).

observed that references to bays in the domestic legislation of other LOSC State parties "either fail … to define a bay and/or fail … to prescribe the maximum limit of the closing line."[97] In spite of this inconsistency, Churchill and Lowe maintain that it is not possible to "conclude from this … that the practice of these States is necessarily contrary to the Conventions."[98] Churchill and Lowe argue that such a conclusion could only be based upon clear evidence of how these domestic provisions are applied in practice.[99] Writing in 1999, Churchill and Lowe noted that due to the limited evidence of relevant state practice it was impossible to reach a conclusion as to the degree of fidelity between State practice and Article 10.[100]

42. A more recent assessment of state practice by Prescott and Schofield (2005) reached the conclusion that "Article 10(2) presents most governments with few difficulties because they alone are responsible for interpreting this Article. They consider potential bays, apply the precise semi-circle test in the second sentence and if it is passed the bay is closed."[101] The practice of Australia and Mauritius is assessed by Prescott and Schofield as being consistent with the Article 10(2) test.[102] In the case of the UK, the Territorial Sea (Baselines) Order 2014 proclaims certain baselines adjacent to the UK, Channel Islands and Isle of Man in which the provisions of Article 10 are specifically endorsed.[103]

43. In some instances where Article 10 has been applied to bays that do not meet the definition of an Article 10 juridical bay, the normal baseline (as defined by the low-water line) has been identified by protesting States as an appropriate substitute.[104]

3 Case Law

44. The International Court of Justice in the *Land, Island and Maritime Frontier* case considered certain aspects of Article 10 and the regime of bays with respect to the Gulf of Fonseca, which the court accepted as an historic bay.[105]

97 Churchill and Lowe, *The Law of the Sea* 3rd, 54–55.

98 Ibid., 55.

99 Ibid.

100 Ibid.

101 Prescott and Schofield, *The Maritime Political Boundaries of the World* 2nd, 117.

102 Ibid.; more recently in 2014, the US Department of State also endorsed the six bay closing lines adopted by Mauritius: Department of State (USA), *Mauritius: Archipelagic and Other Maritime Claims and Boundaries*, 6.

103 *The Territorial Sea (Baselines) Order 2014* (2014 No. 1353) (UK) 'Explanatory Note'.

104 See, e.g., Department of State (USA), *Taiwan's Maritime Claims* (Limits in the Seas No. 127) (Department of State, Washington: 2005) 1, 12 referring to "a shallow indentation of the northwest coast that includes the mouth of the Tan-shui River leading to Taipei."

105 *Land, Maritime and Island Frontier Dispute* (El Salvador v. Honduras: Nicaragua intervening) (Judgment) [1992] ICJ Rep. 351, 588.

While the provisions of Article 10 do not apply to historic bays, the case's discussion of the effect of closing lines on the delimitation of surrounding maritime zones is equally applicable to juridical bays. The Court concluded that bay closing lines were effectively the Gulf's "ocean limit" and accordingly acted as the "baseline for whatever régime lies beyond it".[106] While the Court accepted El Salvador's submission that bay closing lines were acceptable as a line "depicting the ocean limit of the Gulf of Fonseca," it found that this limit must logically share the character of a baseline under international law.[107] Following on from this conclusion, the territorial seas of Honduras and El Salvador were to be calculated from the Gulf of Fonseca's closing lines, and not include waters enclosed by the bay closing lines.[108] Honduras accepted the court's findings by Executive Decree in 2000.[109]

45. In the 2017 *Croatia/Slovenia Arbitration* the tribunal determined the status of the Bay of Piran/Savudrija.[110] The bay was previously, until 25 June 1991, within the limits of Yugoslavia. Slovenia argued that "prior to the dissolution of the former Yugoslavia, the Bay enjoyed the status of a juridical bay consisting of internal waters"[111] under Article 7 of the Convention on the Territorial Sea and Contiguous Zone and Article 10 of the LOSC which "applied at the time Yugoslavia confirmed its straight baselines in the Adriatic."[112] It was also argued that the bay met the geographic and mathematical criteria required to "give rise to the entitlement of Yugoslavia to draw a closing line".[113] Croatia did not dispute that Yugoslavia may have been entitled to draw the closing line and thereby determine the bay as its internal waters, but argued that Yugoslavia never actually drew a closing line between the low-water marks of the natural entrance points of the bay and that the requirements of Article 7(4) of the Geneva Convention and Article 10(4) of the LOSC were never met,[114] since the provision requires that a closing line "may be drawn between these two

106 *Land, Maritime and Island Frontier Dispute* (El Salvador v. Honduras: Nicaragua intervening) (Judgment) [1992] ICJ Rep. 351, 604.

107 Ibid.

108 *Land, Maritime and Island Frontier Dispute* (El Salvador v. Honduras: Nicaragua intervening) (Judgment) [1992] ICJ Rep. 351, 607.

109 *Executive Decree No. PCM 007-2000* (Honduras) 21 March 2000, art. 1, B.

110 *In the Matter of an Arbitration under the Arbitration Agreement between the Government of the Republic of Croatia and the Government of the Republic of Slovenia, signed on 4 November 2009*, Final Award – 29 June 2017 (Croatia/Slovenia) (PCA Case No. 2012-04) (Croatia/Slovenia Award). Committee members Cleverly, Drenik, Miron and Vidas were participants in these proceedings as agents, counsel or advisors.

111 *Croatia/Slovenia Award*, 244 [775].

112 *Croatia/Slovenia Award*, 244 [778].

113 *Croatia/Slovenia Award*, 245 [779].

114 *Croatia/Slovenia Award*, 246 [785].

low-water marks, and the waters enclosed thereby shall be considered as internal waters". Croatia, therefore, referred to the requirement for the coastal State to determine the low-water marks of the natural entrance points of the bay in order for it to be able to actually draw the closing line between these, and thereby constitute the waters of the bay as its internal waters, rather than only being "entitled to do so" which in its view did not suffice to produce the effect under the relevant provision(s). However, the tribunal nonetheless concluded that the bay was Yugoslav internal waters and – rather than (the former) Yugoslavia – itself proceeded with determining the precise coordinates of low-water mark points needed for the closing line to be drawn.[115] The tribunal also considered that the bay's status as a juridical bay was not in doubt under the Convention on the Territorial Sea and Contiguous Zone and that there was no obligation at that time upon Yugoslavia to give publicity to closing lines of juridical bays.[116] It observed that "[t]he applicable Conventions do not subordinate the existence or the legality of juridical bays to such reproduction and it is not rare for States to incorporate bays or estuaries within their internal waters without publishing official maps with closing lines."[117]

46. The most prominent domestic courts that have considered and assessed the status of bays are those in the US in cases involving Louisiana, Mississippi, Alaska, Florida, Texas, Maine, and Rhode Island.[118]

4 Commentary by Publicists

47. Prescott and Schofield assess the application of Article 10 to single State bays. They observe, based on their analysis at the time (2005), that there are 25 "coastal indentations", other than estuaries, that coincide with the coastal termini of international boundaries,[119] and conclude that "[i]t does seem discriminatory that states with sovereignty over a bay can take advantage of

115 *Croatia/Slovenia Award*, 272 [880], where the Tribunal itself determined the coordinates of these points to be 45°31′49.3″N, 13°33′46.0″E and 45°30′19.2″N, 13°30′39.0″E, thereby enabling it to determine the exact position of the closing line and hence consider the waters landwards to be the internal waters rather than the territorial sea – thus precluding the application of Article 15 of the LOSC.

116 *Croatia/Slovenia Award*, 271 [877].

117 *Croatia/Slovenia Award*, 271 [878].

118 See e.g. *United States v. Louisiana* 394 US 11; *United States* v. *Alaska v. United States* 422 US 184; *United States v. Maine* 469 US 504; *United States v. California* 381 US 139; see the discussion in particular in M.W. Reed, *Shore and Sea Boundaries: the Development of International Maritime Boundary Principles through United States Practice* Vol. 3 (US Government Printing Office, Washington: 2000); and analysis in Prescott and Schofield, *The Maritime Political Boundaries of the World* 2nd, 118–121.

119 Prescott and Schofield, *The Maritime Political Boundaries of the World* 2nd, 113, Table 6.1.

Article 10 whereas two states with sovereignty over a bay of exactly the same proportions are prevented from agreeing to close it."[120] Westerman highlights the relationship between the delimitation of bays and expansionist policies, arguing that "many states have declared sovereignty over bays of increasing size as one strategy for maximising national control over waters previously considered high seas."[121]

48. A significant body of literature addresses the Article 10 conditions that define a juridical bay. The discussion which follows considers issues that publicists have considered in a more general context.[122]

a *"Natural Entrance Points" of an Indentation*

49. Churchill and Lowe have identified Article 10's ambiguous reference to a bay's "natural entrance points" as a likely source of difficulty in the "practical application" of the provision,[123] and assert that the identification of a bay's natural entrance points is a matter of degree.[124] On the other hand, Prescott and Schofield are of the view that in the case of a "classical bay shape with a narrow mouth between two headlands, the natural entrance points will be obvious".[125] In these instances, the points will possess a name such as cape, point, head or bluff leading to the selection of a "mathematical point" along the coast.[126] Prescott and Schofield are also of the view that "the selection of natural entrance points is the sole responsibility of the country concerned…."[127]

b *The Semi-Circle Test*

50. Writing in the context of Article 10's antecedent provision in the Convention on the Territorial Sea and the Contiguous Zone, O'Connell argued that the semi-circle test is an arbitrary means of defining a juridical bay.[128] O'Connell intimated that the provision fails to give effect to geographical variations that do not detract from an indentation's essential characteristic as a "bay".[129] Prescott and Schofield refer to the "simple principle of the semicircle

---

120 Ibid.
121 Westerman, *The Juridical Bay*, 5.
122 A detailed analysis of issues associated with bays appears in O'Connell, *The International Law of the Sea* Vol. 1, 389–416.
123 Churchill and Lowe, *The Law of the Sea* 3rd, 42.
124 Ibid.
125 Prescott and Schofield, *The Maritime Political Boundaries of the World* 2nd, 129.
126 Ibid.
127 Ibid.
128 O'Connell, *The International Law of the Sea* Vol. 1, 393.
129 Ibid.

test" found in the second sentence of Article 10(2),[130] and give emphasis to the linkage between Article 10(2) and Article 10(3) as giving effect to the principle outlined in Article 10(2). In their view, "[t]he three sentences in Paragraph 3 present no difficulties for most countries when the central authority has no aversion to creating internal waters and extending its territorial seas."[131]

IV Straight Baselines and Low-Tide Elevations

A *Relevant Historical Background*

51. The status of drying rocks and shoals was considered by the ILC and was reflected in Article 11 in the Draft Articles. At UNCLOS I the ILC draft text of Article 11 was not endorsed and in its place Article 11 of the Convention on the Territorial Sea and the Contiguous Zone addressed low-tide elevations.

B *Article 13: LOSC Text*

52. Article 13 of the LOSC repeats verbatim Article 11 of the Convention on the Territorial Sea and the Contiguous Zone. While there was some early debate at UNCLOS III with respect to the text of the article, consensus was reached for retention of the Geneva text as follows:

> *Article 13*
> *Low-tide elevations*
> 1. A low-tide elevation is a naturally formed area of land which is surrounded by and above water at low-tide but submerged at high tide. Where a low-tide elevation is situated wholly or partly at a distance not exceeding the breadth of the territorial sea from the mainland or an island, the low-water line on that elevation may be used as the baseline for measuring the breadth of the territorial sea.
> 2. Where a low-tide elevation is wholly situated at a distance exceeding the breadth of the territorial sea from the mainland or an island, it has no territorial sea of its own.

C *Analysis of Article 13*

1 Text

53. There are three dimensions to Article 13. The first is the definition of a low-tide elevation which has the following elements:

130 Prescott and Schofield, *The Maritime Political Boundaries of the World* 2nd, 121.
131 Ibid., 122.

- it is naturally formed;
- it is an area of land;
- it is surrounded by water;
- it is above water at low-tide; and
- it is submerged at high tide.

No reference is made to the composition of the feature other than that it is "naturally formed". The generic term "low-tide elevation" may therefore encompass a rock, a shoal or some other similar feature.[132] No connection is drawn between Article 13 and the Article 121 "Regime of Islands", though a feature which geologically is properly characterised as a rock may for the purposes of the law of the sea be properly characterised as either a "low-tide elevation" if it is submerged at high tide, or an Article 121(3) rock if it is above water at all times. The determining juridical characteristic is therefore whether the rock is or is not submerged at high tide. Importantly, no reference is made to the size or composition of the feature other than it being "an area of land".

54. The second dimension is the significance of a low-tide elevation for the purposes of the baseline. In this respect the location of the low-tide elevation is determinative as to its capacity for being used as a basepoint for measuring the breadth of the territorial sea. To that end, the low-tide elevation must wholly or partly fall within the breadth of the territorial sea as measured from the mainland or an island. If that requirement is met then the low-water line on the elevation may be used as a basepoint. An exception to this rule applies in the case of those low-tide elevations beyond the breadth of the territorial sea which have had a lighthouse or similar installation built upon them so that they are now permanently above sea level. In those instances straight baselines may be drawn to and from the low-tide elevation consistently with Articles 7(4) and 47. The other Article 7(4) exception is where the drawing of such baselines has received general international recognition.[133]

55. The third dimension relates to the maritime zone generated by a low-tide elevation. A low-tide elevation is not considered to be part of the coast and does not generate a distinctive territorial sea, but the low-water line may be used for measuring the breadth of the territorial sea if it falls within the territorial sea generated from the mainland or an island. Whether the low-tide elevation is utilised as a basepoint may depend on whether it is the most outer

---

132 These various features are assessed in *Territorial and Maritime Dispute* (Nicaragua v. Colombia) (Judgment) [2012] ICJ Rep. 624.

133 Note also that Article 47(4), LOSC addresses the drawing of archipelagic baselines to low-tide elevations.

lying low-tide elevation within the territorial sea of the mainland or an island. If the low-tide elevation is relied upon as a basepoint for the territorial sea, it can also be the basepoint from which other maritime zones are measured. Article 13(2) makes clear that if the low-tide elevation is situated at a distance which exceeds the breadth of the territorial sea from the mainland or an island, then it has no territorial sea of its own.

2 State Practice

56. It is possible to identify a number of coastal States whose relevant legislation and practice deviates from the LOSC principles regarding baselines associated with low-tide elevations, though it is difficult clearly to differentiate whether the state practice relates to Article 13 low-water line baselines or Article 7(4) straight baselines, partly arising from inaccurate charting. China has relied upon "eight low-tide elevations ... that cannot be used to determine the territorial sea because no part of any of these low-tide elevations are within 12 miles of the mainland or an island."[134] Furthermore, none of these elevations possess lighthouses or similar structures that would justify the drawing of straight baselines, nor have these baselines received general international recognition.[135] Saudi Arabian legislation relevant to basepoints is similarly inconsistent with Article 13, as it "appears to allow low-tide elevations wherever situated to generate a territorial sea."[136] States such as New Zealand and Trinidad and Tobago have created ambiguity with respect to how they characterise low-tide elevations for the purposes of measuring the breadth of the territorial sea by having enacted legislation equating low-tide elevations with an island.[137]

57. States including Japan and Mexico have implemented legislation that closely observes the provisions of Article 13.[138] Churchill and Lowe have noted

---

134 Department of State (USA), *Straight Baselines Claim: China*, 1, 6.

135 Ibid.; it is acknowledged that the circumstances as they existed in 1996 may have now altered.

136 Churchill and Lowe, *The Law of the Sea* 3rd, 55 citing Royal Decree concerning the *Territorial Waters of the Kingdom of Saudi Arabia* (Royal Decree No. 33 of 16 February 1958), arts. 1 and 5.

137 *Territorial Sea, Contiguous Zone, and Exclusive Economic Zone Act 1997 as amended by Act No. 146 of 1980* (New Zealand) s 5(2); *Territorial Sea Act 1969, No. 38 of 6 December 1969* (Trinidad and Tobago) art. 5(2).

138 UN Division for Ocean Affairs and the Law of the Sea, Office of Legal Affairs (2008) Bulletin No. 66 *Law of the Sea* 71ff extracting the *Enforcement Order of the Law on the Territorial Sea and the Contiguous Zone* (Japan) (Cabinet Order No. 210 of 1977, as amended by Cabinet Order No. 383 of 1993, Cabinet Order No. 206 of 1996 and Cabinet Order No. 434 of 2001), arts. 2(3) and 2(5) (which defines low-water elevations according to art. 13(1) of LOSC);

that "some States appear to accept the use of low-tide elevations as basepoints, regardless of whether lighthouses or similar installations have been built on them."[139]

3 Case Law

58. The International Court of Justice considered the issue of low-tide elevations in its 2001 judgment in the *Case Concerning Maritime Delimitation and Territorial Questions between Qatar and Bahrain (Qatar v. Bahrain)*,[140] where the ICJ determined that Article 13 reflected customary international law.[141] The dispute between Qatar and Bahrain rested on the issue of whether Fasht al Dibal (a low-tide elevation) could "be appropriated in accordance with the criteria which pertain to the acquisition of territory."[142] Qatar maintained that a territorial claim could not be made in relation to a low-tide elevation; Bahrain claimed the converse.[143] The Court confirmed that "[w]hen a low-tide elevation is situated in the overlapping area of the territorial sea of two States, …, both States in principle are entitled to use its low-water line for the measuring of the breadth of their territorial sea."[144] As both States would benefit from reliance upon the low-tide elevations for delimitation purposes, "the competing rights derived by both coastal States … would by necessity seem to neutralize each other."[145] Bahrain claimed that it held a superior title to the low-tide elevations "in the sea between Bahrain's main islands and the coast of the Qatar peninsula" and was thus able to exercise sovereign rights over these areas.[146] In support of this contention Bahrain claimed that the legal status of low-tide elevations is analogous to that of islands under the law of the sea.[147] The Court noted that "[i]nternational treaty law is silent on the question whether low-tide elevations can be considered … "territory" " and that "[t]he few existing

---

General Act of 31 December 1941 on National Property (Mexico) (as amended in January 1982), art. 29(II).

139 Churchill and Lowe, *The Law of the Sea* 3rd, 39–40 citing Department of State (USA), *Straight Baselines: Saudi Arabia* (Limits in the Seas No. 20) (Department of State, Washington: 1970) 1; Department of State (USA), *Straight Baselines: Syria* (Limits in the Seas No. 53) (Department of State, Washington: 1973) 1.

140 *Case Concerning Maritime Delimitation and Territorial Questions between Qatar and Bahrain (Qatar v. Bahrain) (Merits)* [2001] ICJ Rep. 40 (Qatar v. Bahrain).

141 *Qatar v. Bahrain* [2001] ICJ Rep. 40, 100 [201].

142 *Qatar v. Bahrain* [2001] ICJ Rep. 40, 100 [200].

143 Ibid.

144 *Qatar v. Bahrain* [2001] ICJ Rep. 40, 101 [202].

145 Ibid.

146 *Qatar v. Bahrain* [2001] ICJ Rep. 40, 101 [203].

147 Ibid.

rules [in the law of the sea] do not justify a general assumption that low-tide elevations are territory in the same sense as islands".[148] The Court rejected Bahrain's submission that a low-tide elevation is susceptible of a claim to territorial sovereignty, supporting this finding with a reference to the rule in Article 13(2) that low-tide elevations situated beyond the limits of a State's territorial sea do not themselves generate a territorial sea.[149] On this basis the Court concluded that neither Bahrain nor Qatar was able to rely upon the low-water line of the low-tide elevations "in the zone of overlapping claims" for the purposes of drawing the equidistance line between the two States.[150]

59. The ICJ also assessed Article 13 in its 2012 judgment in *Territorial and Maritime Dispute* (Nicaragua v. Colombia)[151] and confirmed that low-tide elevations within 12 nautical miles of an Article 121(3) rock could be used for the purpose of delimiting the territorial sea.[152] In that context Article 13(1) makes no distinction regarding the territorial sea generated from the mainland, an island, or a low-tide elevation.

60. In the *South China Sea* case before an Annex VII LOSC Tribunal, there was extensive discussion regarding the characterisation and entitlements of low-tide elevations, and the important distinctions between these features and islands. In that respect, the Tribunal observed that Article 13 "operates in parallel" with the definition of an island in Article 121.[153] As to the characterisation of a low-tide elevation, the Tribunal noted that "the status of a feature is to be determined on the basis of its natural condition",[154] and that notwithstanding human modification of the feature "[a] low-tide elevation will remain a low-tide elevation under the Convention, regardless of the scale of the island or installation built atop it."[155] Commenting on the fact that a number of such features in the South China Sea had been subject to significant human modification, the Tribunal indicated that in characterising a feature its status would "be ascertained on the basis of its earlier, natural condition, prior to the onset of significant human modification."[156] The Tribunal also commented on the use of the term "high tide" in Article 13 which becomes a determining factor in distinguishing between a low-tide elevation submerged at high tide, and an

148 *Qatar v. Bahrain* [2001] ICJ Rep. 40, 101–2 [205–206].
149 *Qatar v. Bahrain* [2001] ICJ Rep. 40, 102 [207].
150 *Qatar v. Bahrain* [2001] ICJ Rep. 40, 102–3 [209].
151 *Territorial and Maritime Dispute* (Nicaragua v. Colombia) (Judgment) [2012] ICJ Rep. 624.
152 Ibid., 693 [182–183].
153 2016 *South China Sea Arbitration* [304].
154 2016 *South China Sea Arbitration* [305].
155 Ibid.
156 2016 *South China Sea Arbitration* [306]; see also [511].

Article 121 island or rock. It was concluded that "high tide" was not a technical term and could be subject to varying interpretations and accordingly there was nothing in the LOSC or in customary international law requiring that any particular high tide datum be applied.[157] The Tribunal also reaffirmed the position of the ICJ that a low-tide elevation cannot be appropriated, distinguishing between a low-tide elevation located within the territorial sea and as a result falling within the territorial sea legal regime, and a low-tide elevation beyond the territorial sea which subject to its location may fall within the continental shelf regime.[158] As to the entitlements of a low-tide elevation the Tribunal observed that while Article 13(2) only made direct reference to low-tide elevations falling beyond the territorial sea not generating a territorial sea of their own, it followed that low-tide elevations not entitled to a territorial sea were likewise not entitled to a continental shelf or exclusive economic zone.[159]

4 Commentary by Publicists

61. Prescott and Schofield have commented on the location of the low-tide elevation within the confines of the territorial sea. They have observed that "[a] strict interpretation of the phrase means that to be used as a baseline, a low-tide elevation must lie within, or at least partially within, the territorial sea generated from the normal baseline of the mainland or an island."[160] Accordingly, in their view "[l]ow-tide elevations that lie outside the territorial sea generated from the mainland or an island cannot be used to generate a further area of territorial sea."[161] Churchill and Lowe provide further support for the principle that "it is not possible to "leapfrog" from one low-tide elevation

157 2016 *South China Sea Arbitration* [311].

158 2016 *South China Sea Arbitration* [309].

159 2016 *South China Sea Arbitration* [308] where it was commented: "Article 13(2) does not expressly state that a low-tide elevation is not entitled to an exclusive economic zone or continental shelf. Nevertheless the Tribunal considers that this restriction is necessarily implied in the Convention. It follows automatically from the operation of Articles 57 and 76, which measure the breadth of the exclusive economic zone and continental shelf from the baseline for the territorial sea. Ipso facto, if a low-tide elevation is not entitled to a territorial sea, it is not entitled to an exclusive economic zone or continental shelf." However, a low-tide elevation may be located within the continental shelf of a coastal State and as a result fall within the continental shelf regime; this was the finding of the Tribunal with respect to Mischief Reef and Second Thomas Shoal which were found to be low-tide elevations located with the continental shelf of the Philippines: 2016 *South China Sea Arbitration* [647].

160 Prescott and Schofield, *The Maritime Political Boundaries of the World* 2nd, 107.

161 Ibid., 108.

to another."[162] Sir Gerald Fitzmaurice reached a similar conclusion on this issue.[163]

V Combination of Methods in Drawing Baselines

A *Relevant Historical Background*

62. Article 14 of the LOSC has no predecessor in either the work of the ILC or the deliberations at UNCLOS I. At UNCLOS III a proposal was made in 1973 by China for a provision recognising the capacity of a coastal State to "reasonably define the breadth and limits of its territorial sea" with respect to a variety of relevant factors. This eventually formed the basis for deliberation around the capacity of a coastal State to rely upon a series of methods for the determination of baselines.

B *Article 14: LOSC Text*

63. Originally this provision was subsumed within what became Article 7 of the LOSC, but UNCLOS III elected to create an independent article that follows all of the relevant articles dealing with baselines. It provides as follows:

> *Article 14*
> *Combination of methods for determining baselines*
> The coastal State may determine baselines in turn by any of the methods provided for in the foregoing articles to suit different conditions.

C *Analysis of Article 14*

1 Text

64. While Article 14 is short, it provides to a coastal State reassurance as to how it can go about determining its baselines. To that end the following points can be made. First, the coastal State "may" determine baselines in this manner. This removes doubt as to whether a coastal State must rely upon a combination of baseline techniques and confirms that depending on particular circumstances a coastal State may determine its baselines solely in reliance upon the Article 5 normal baseline method, or on the Article 7 straight baseline method. Second, the baselines can be determined by any of the methods provided for in the "foregoing articles". Here the use of the words "in turn" is of significance. The *Virginia Commentaries* observes in this respect that:

---

162 Churchill and Lowe, *The Law of the Sea* 3rd, 48, with reference to art. 13(2).

163 Gerald Fitzmaurice, "Some Results of the Geneva Conference on the Law of the Sea: Part 1 – The Territorial Sea and Contiguous Zone and Related Topics" (1959) 8 *International and Comparative Law Quarterly* 73, 87.

> The expression "in turn" is rendered *en fonction des différentes situations* and in similar terms in other languages. The English expression must therefore be assumed to mean something along the lines of "according to the circumstances" or "to suit different conditions".[164]

This view is reinforced by the chapeau and its title "Combination of Methods for determining baselines". It is also confirmed by the text of the article where it refers to the coastal State adopting these approaches to "suit different conditions" thereby explicitly acknowledging that States will encounter multiple coastal and maritime variables as they assess how to determine their baselines.

2 State Practice

65. General acceptance of the principle that States may exercise discretion when selecting a "baseline methodology" is possibly best evidenced by the variety of methods employed by coastal States. States that have adopted legislation and decrees allowing for a combination of methods include Argentina,[165] Brazil,[166] Japan,[167] and Uruguay.[168] In the case of Mauritius, Article 4(2) of the Mauritian *Maritime Zone Act 2005 (No 2)* specifies that the State may rely upon "straight archipelagic baselines…, normal baselines…, the seaward low-water line of reefs…, straight baselines [or] a combination of [these] methods" to delimit its maritime zones.[169] In the case of Mexico, Article 26 of its Federal Act Relating to the Sea provides that "[t]he limits of the territorial sea [of Mexico] shall be measured from baselines, either normal or straight, or a combination of the two."[170]

66. It is also possible to point to examples in state practice where States have sought to validate the methods employed in drawing baselines which have then formed the basis for the delimitation of maritime boundaries between those States. The 1993 Treaty between Cape Verde and Senegal is an example of this approach which expressly validates the baselines drawn by each State

164 Nandan and Rosenne (eds.), *United Nations Convention on the Law of the Sea 1982: A Commentary* Vol. II, 130–131.

165 Article 1, Act No. 23.968 of 14 August 1991 (Argentina).

166 Article 2, Decree No. 8.400 of 4 February 2015 (Brazil).

167 Article 2, Law on the Territorial Sea and the Contiguous Zone (Law No. 30 of 1977, as amended by Law No. 73 of 1996) (Japan).

168 Article 14, Act 17.033 of 20 November 1998 establishing the boundaries of the territorial sea, the adjacent zone, the exclusive economic zone, and the continental shelf (Uruguay).

169 UN Division for Ocean Affairs and the Law of the Sea, Office of Legal Affairs (2006) Bulletin No. 62 *Law of the Sea* 52ff extracting the *Maritime Zone Act 2005 (No. 2)* (Mauritius) 28 February 2005, art. 4.

170 Article 26, *Federal Act relating to the Sea* (Mexico) 8 January 1986.

and upon which their respective maritime boundaries have been delimited as being "drawn in conformity" with the LOSC.[171] The 1982 Agreement on Historic Waters between Vietnam and Kampuchea (Cambodia) is also illustrative of this approach where the straight baselines of both States are relied upon to form an integrated single straight baseline system notwithstanding significant international criticism that has been levelled against the legitimacy of those baselines.[172] Similar language is used in the 2003 Treaty on the Delimitation of the Maritime Frontier between Mauritania and Cape Verde.[173]

3 Case Law

67. No international court or tribunal has had occasion to consider the application of Article 14.

4 Commentary by Publicists

68. Symmons has claimed that the purpose of Article 14 is "self-evident and straightforward",[174] while Churchill and Lowe note that while it is not possible to prescribe a single method for the calculation of baselines, it is necessary that the rules are applied consistently.[175]

VI Archipelagic Baselines

A *Relevant Historical Background*

69. The first formal consideration of whether a distinctive status should be assigned the waters that comprise an archipelago took place in the 1920s when the ILA (1924 and 1926), the American Institute of International Law (1925), and the *Institut de droit international* (1927 and 1928) gave some preliminary consideration to the matter.[176] In preparation for the 1930 Hague Codification Conference, active consideration was given to the status of the territorial sea of an archipelago, however no agreement was possible during the Hague Conference on this issue.[177] Academic debate continued during the 1930s; however it was the emergence of Indonesia and the Philippines as independent

---

171 Article 2, *Treaty on the Delimitation of the Maritime Frontier between the Republic of Cape Verde and the Republic of Senegal* (1994) 26 *Law of the Sea Bulletin* 45; see also Charney and Alexander, *International Maritime Boundaries* vol. III (1998) 2287.

172 Charney and Alexander, *International Maritime Boundaries* vol. III, 2360.

173 Colson and Smith, *International Maritime Boundaries* vol. V, 3703, art. 2.

174 Clive R. Symmons, "Article 14 Combination of methods for determining baselines" in Proelss (ed.), *United Nations Convention on the Law of the Sea: A Commentary* , 147, 149.

175 Churchill and Lowe, *The Law of the Sea* 3rd, 32–33.

176 D.P. O'Connell, "Mid-Ocean Archipelagos in International Law" (1971) 45 *British Year Book of International Law* 1, 5–7.

177 Ibid. 8–10.

States that introduced for the first time significant state practice in the area which is detailed in the First Report (2014).

B *United Nations Conferences on the Law of the Sea: I, II, III*

70. UNCLOS I did not directly address what was at that time referred to as a "mid-ocean archipelago". This in part reflected the inability of the ILC to agree upon any precise recommendation on the matter.[178] At the 1960 Second United Nations Conference on the Law of the Sea (UNCLOS II), notwithstanding efforts by the Philippines to generate some debate as to the breadth of the territorial sea as it related to certain historic waters, there was no active consideration of archipelagic waters.[179] With a decision having been made to include the topic of "Archipelagos" on the agenda of UNCLOS III, in 1973 during sessions of the Seabed Committee, Fiji, Indonesia, Mauritius, and the Philippines sought to advance debate by introducing proposals which outlined the principles for an archipelagic regime.[180] By 1976 agreement had been reached that the archipelagic regime would focus on mid-ocean archipelagos, and not those archipelagos associated with a continental State. UNCLOS III ultimately decided to deal with the question of archipelagos in Part IV of the final convention text.

C *LOSC Text: Article 47*

71. Part IV of the LOSC titled "Archipelagic States" encompasses nine articles and brings together the principal articles of the convention dedicated to the specific law of the sea issues that arise with respect to archipelagos. Part IV, however, both directly and indirectly cross-refers to other provisions in the LOSC and as such no effort is made to create a special regime for archipelagic States outside of the general law of the sea. Nevertheless, Part IV does create a distinctive regime applicable to the island States that make up certain archipelagos, especially with respect to archipelagic baselines and archipelagic navigation.

72. An "archipelagic State" is entitled to draw straight archipelagic baselines consistent with Article 47(1). An "archipelagic State" is defined in Article 46(a) as "a State that is constituted wholly by one or more archipelagos and may

178 ILC "Articles concerning the Law of the Sea with commentaries" 270 where in discussing draft Article 10 'Islands' the ILC noted that: "The Commission had intended to follow up this article with a provision concerning groups of islands. Like The Hague Conference … the Commission was unable to overcome the difficulties involved."

179 O'Connell, "Mid-Ocean Archipelagos in International Law", 22.

180 R.P. Anand, *Origin and Development of the Law of the Sea* (Martinus Nijhoff, The Hague/Boston: 1983) 203.

include other islands". Such a State must therefore not only meet the criteria of a State under international law, but it needs to also meet the geographic criteria of being a State principally comprised of one or more archipelagos. Article 46(b) provides further definition for the meaning of an archipelago, including reference to the term meaning "a group of islands, including parts of islands".

73. An archipelagic State may draw archipelagic baselines which join the outermost points of the outermost islands and drying reefs of the archipelago in the manner provided for under Article 47, which provides as follows:

> *Article 47*
> *Archipelagic baselines*
>
> 1. An archipelagic State may draw straight archipelagic baselines joining the outermost points of the outermost islands and drying reefs of the archipelago provided that within such baselines are included the main islands and an area in which the ratio of the area of the water to the area of the land, including atolls, is between 1 to 1 and 9 to 1.
>
> 2. The length of such baselines shall not exceed 100 nautical miles, except that up to 3 per cent of the total number of baselines enclosing any archipelago may exceed that length, up to a maximum length of 125 nautical miles.
>
> 3. The drawing of such baselines shall not depart to any appreciable extent from the general configuration of the archipelago.
>
> 4. Such baselines shall not be drawn to and from low-tide elevations, unless lighthouses or similar installations which are permanently above sea level have been built on them or where a low-tide elevation is situated wholly or partly at a distance not exceeding the breadth of the territorial sea from the nearest island.
>
> 5. The system of such baselines shall not be applied by an archipelagic State in such a manner as to cut off from the high seas or the exclusive economic zone the territorial sea of another State.
>
> 6. If a part of the archipelagic waters of an archipelagic State lies between two parts of an immediately adjacent neighbouring State, existing rights and all other legitimate interests which the latter State has traditionally exercised in such waters and all rights stipulated by agreement between those States shall continue and be respected.
>
> 7. For the purpose of computing the ratio of water to land under paragraph l, land areas may include waters lying within the fringing reefs of islands and atolls, including that part of a steep-sided oceanic plateau which is enclosed or nearly enclosed by a chain of limestone islands and drying reefs lying on the perimeter of the plateau.

8. The baselines drawn in accordance with this article shall be shown on charts of a scale or scales adequate for ascertaining their position. Alternatively, lists of geographical coordinates of points, specifying the geodetic datum, may be substituted.

9. The archipelagic State shall give due publicity to such charts or lists of geographical coordinates and shall deposit a copy of each such chart or list with the Secretary-General of the United Nations.

D Analysis of Article 47

1 Text

74. The core elements of the straight archipelagic baseline provisions in Article 47 set out five tests which the baselines must satisfy.[181] In 1989 the UN Study identified those five tests as being:[182]

1. That the baselines include the main islands;[183]
2. That the baselines must enclose an area of sea at least as large as the area of enclosed land but must not be more than nine times that land area;[184]
3. No segment of baseline may exceed 125 nautical miles in length;[185]
4. Not more than 3 per cent of baseline segments may exceed 100 nautical miles;[186] and
5. That the baselines must not depart to any appreciable extent from the general configuration of the archipelago.[187]

75. These requirements make clear that the archipelagic baselines are to enclose the main islands of the archipelago and may extend to the outermost points and drying reefs of the archipelago, thereby thwarting any attempt to enclose small separate clusters of islands that do not include one of the main islands of the archipelago. In addition, the water-to-land ratio requirement ensures that the archipelagic State is one in which there is a focus upon the

181 J.R.V. Prescott, "Straight and Archipelagic Baselines" in Gerald Blake (ed.), *Maritime Boundaries and Ocean Resources* (Croom Helm, Beckenham: 1987) 38, 46 observed that "Three of the five tests are incapable of consistent objective interpretation".

182 1989 UN Study, 35.

183 Article 47(1), LOSC.

184 Article 47(1), LOSC; that is, the water to land ratio is between 1:1 and 9:1.

185 Article 47(2), LOSC.

186 Article 47(2), LOSC.

187 1989 UN Study, 35.

ocean spaces which connect the islands, rather than a State which is dominated by large island land masses. For example, Cuba does not qualify as an archipelagic State entitled to draw archipelagic baselines because of the size of its main islands compared to the size of its accompanying islands and the consequence this has for the water to land ratio. The Bahamas does qualify because of the presence of several main islands and adjoining smaller islands including atolls resulting in an estimated water to land ratio of 6.8 to 1.[188]

76. In its 1989 commentary to Article 47, the UN Office for Ocean Affairs and the Law of the Sea made reference to the 3 per cent rule embedded in Article 47(2) and how the capacity of an archipelagic State to draw baselines in excess of 100 nautical miles will be contingent upon the total number of baselines enclosing the archipelago. In this respect it was noted that: "Since there is no restriction on the number of segments a country can draw, and since the more segments used the closer the system is likely to be to the general configuration of the archipelago, it will usually be possible to adjust the number of segments to secure the necessary number of very long baselines."[189] Reference was also made to Article 47(7) and the means by which an archipelagic State can calculate the area of water to land and be able to include in the calculations certain waters. With respect to those waters which are "enclosed or nearly enclosed by a chain of limestone islands and drying reefs" on the perimeter of a steep-sided oceanic plateau, there "might be difficulties in deciding whether particular formations could be properly judged to nearly enclose a specific plateau."[190]

2 State Practice

77. Since the conclusion of UNCLOS III and adoption of the LOSC, 22 States have sought to claim archipelagic State status.[191] Those States claiming such status under the LOSC and which have declared archipelagic baselines in reliance upon Article 47 of the LOSC, are identified in Appendix 3. On the basis of available information with respect to archipelagic State claims, the following observations can be made. The water to land ratio of between 9:1 to 1:1 is

---

188 Department of State (United States), *Bahamas: Archipelagic and Other Maritime Claims and Boundaries* (Limits in the Sea No. 128) (Department of State, Washington: 2014) 2.

189 1989 UN Study, 35.

190 Ibid., 36. This is an issue that has been relevant for the Bahamas and Mauritius.

191 An extensive review of state practice amongst archipelagic States can be found in Kevin Baumert and Brian Melchior, "The Practice of Archipelagic States: A Study of Studies" (2015) 46 *Ocean Development and International Law* 60–80; an earlier study detailing state practice up to 1991 can be found in Barbara Kwiatkowska and Etty R. Argoes, *Archipelagic State Regime in Light of the 1982 UNCLOS and State Practice* (ICLOS/UNPAD, Bandung: 1991).

met by the vast majority of archipelagic States. In 1977 Cape Verde proclaimed archipelagic baselines which resulted in a water to land ratio that exceeded the limits set down in Article 47(1).[192] The US protested this claim in 1980, and in 1992 Cape Verde modified its straight archipelagic baselines in a manner that is consistent with the LOSC.[193] The Seychelles has enclosed four separate groups of islands within straight archipelagic baselines, three of which exceed the 9:1 ratio. However, if reliance was placed upon Article 47(7) and the relevant calculations were done on the basis of land areas including waters lying within fringing reefs of islands and atolls, then only one of the four separate groups is non-compliant.[194] When applying the land to water ratio test, the Bahamas counts oceanic plateaus in apparent reliance upon Article 47(7).[195] The US has also identified a deficiency in the straight archipelagic baselines drawn by Papua New Guinea which do not terminate on the island of New Guinea but rather at sea, and as such are not in accordance with Article 47(1), which requires that baselines join "the outermost points of the outermost islands."[196] The Seychelles has also drawn baselines to and from open water points in a manner inconsistent with Article 47(4).[197] Mauritius has proclaimed two straight archipelagic baseline systems around outlying archipelagos (Saint Brandon and Chagos), and in the case of the main island of Mauritius used a combination of the normal baseline, straight baselines, and river and bay closing lines.[198]

78. Some States have had their claims of being an Article 46 archipelagic State recognised under Part IV of the LOSC challenged. The claim of the Dominican Republic has been challenged on the grounds that archipelagic straight baselines have been drawn to and from certain low-tide elevations that do not meet the Article 47(4) exemption. In 2007 following its declaration

---

192 The Cape Verde claim enclosed an area of water of 50,546 km^2, while the land area was 4,031 km^2 resulting in an approximate ratio of 12.5:1.

193 See Roach and Smith, *Excessive Maritime Claims* 3rd, 209.

194 Department of State (United States), *Seychelles: Archipelagic and Other Maritime Claims and Boundaries* (Limits in the Seas No. 132) (Department of State, Washington: 2014) 3.

195 Prescott and Schofield, *The Maritime Political Boundaries of the World* 2nd, 177.

196 Department of State (United States), *Papua New Guinea: Archipelagic and Other Maritime Claims and Boundaries* (Limits in the Sea No. 138) (Department of State, Washington: 2014) 3–4.

197 Department of State (United States), *Seychelles: Archipelagic and Other Maritime Claims and Boundaries*, 4.

198 Department of State (USA), *Mauritius: Archipelagic and Other Maritime Claims and Boundaries*, 4–5.

as an archipelagic State,[199] the United Kingdom (UK) and the US issued a joint demarche indicating that they did not accept the Dominican Republic's claim and in particular contesting the reliance upon certain low-tide elevations as basepoints.[200] The US is of the view that the water-to-land ratio under the proclaimed straight archipelagic baselines is 1.03:1 which if modified to take into account the baselines drawn to non-eligible low-tide elevations would not fall within the Article 47(1) water-to-land ratio range.[201] The archipelagic claim by Comoros has been subject to criticism because of the drawing of Article 47(1) straight archipelagic baselines to and from Banc Vailheu, a submerged feature that the US asserts is neither an island, a drying reef, or a feature that qualifies under the Article 47(4) low-tide elevation exception.[202]

79. It would appear on the basis of existing state practice that the 125 nm baseline length constraint is not a significant issue for the great majority of archipelagic States.[203] The US has questioned the claim of the Maldives, where three of its 37 straight archipelagic baselines are in the 100–125 nm range, thereby exceeding the three per cent limit found in Article 47(2).[204] Papua New Guinea has a straight archipelagic baseline segment that is 174.78 nm in

199 Law No. 66–07 of 22 May 2007 (Dominican Republic); see Sophia Kopela, "2007 Archipelagic Legislation of the Dominican Republic: An Assessment" (2009) 24 *International Journal of Marine and Coastal Law* 501.

200 "Text of a Joint Declaration Undertaken by the United Kingdom of Great Britain and Northern Ireland and the United States of America in relation to the Law of the Dominican Republic Number 66-07 of 22 May 2007, Done on 18 October 2007" (2008) 66 *Law of the Sea Bulletin* 98–99.

201 Department of State (United States), *Dominican Republic: Archipelagic and Other Maritime Claims* (Limits in the Seas No. 130) (Department of State, Washington: 2014) 2–3.

202 Department of State (United States), *Comoros: Archipelagic and Other Maritime Claims and Boundaries* (Limits in the Seas No. 134) (Department of State, Washington: 2014) 2; the drawing of archipelagic straight baselines to and from the islands of Mayotte is also contentious as those islands are claimed and administered by France; ibid. p. 3.

203 This is reflected in a survey of the studies undertaken by the US Department of State as part of the Limits in the Seas series; see Department of State (United States), *The Bahamas: Archipelagic and Other Maritime Claims and Boundaries* (Limits in the Seas No. 128) (Department of State, Washington: 2014) 2–3.

204 Cape Verde adjusted the length of two of its straight archipelagic baselines in 1992 in response to a United States protest to achieve compliance with this provision: Roach and Smith, *Excessive Maritime Claims* 3rd, 216; the Philippines in 2009 adjusted its archipelagic baseline in the Gulf of Moro from 140 nm to 122 nm; see M.N.Z. 69.2009 LOS of 21 April 2009, Deposit of the list of geographical coordinates of points as contained in Republic Act No. 9522: An Act to Amend Certain Provisions of Republic Act No. 3046, as Amended by Republic Act No. 5446, to Define the Archipelagic Baselines of the Philippines, and for Other Purposes at http://www.un.org/Depts/los/LEGISLATIONANDTREATIES/PDFFILES/mzn_s/mzn69.pdf.

length and is inconsistent with the Article 47(2) limit of 125 nm.[205] There is also evidence of States having adjusted their claims in response to protest.[206]

80. Some archipelagic States have adjusted their archipelagic baselines from time to time, partly as a result of the changing circumstances of the territory that makes up their State. Indonesia, one of the largest archipelagic States, modified its original 1960 baselines with Act no. 6/1996 on Indonesian Waters. The changes that were made in regard to the baselines/basepoints around the Celebes Sea included Pulau Sipadan and Pulau Ligitan within the Indonesian archipelagic baselines system.[207] A further baseline designation occurred in 2008 under PP no. 37/2008 (19 May 2008), which revised the baseline system in the Sulawesi Sea, in the vicinity of Timor, and off the south coast of Java. Changes to Indonesia's archipelagic baseline on the south coast of Java were made in order to accommodate the three per cent requirement of Article 47(2), with the effect that one long baseline has now been divided into three shorter ones. In this instance the new baseline configuration has been shifted slightly landwards, only minimally impacting upon Indonesia's archipelagic waters and territorial sea claims.[208]

3 Case Law

81. There has to date been little case law interpreting Article 47, or even Part IV of the LOSC.[209] However in *Qatar v. Bahrain* the ICJ did make some observations with respect to the interpretation of Article 47. In that case Bahrain had contended that it was a *de facto* archipelago and that it was entitled to declare itself an archipelagic State under Part IV of the LOSC and accordingly to draw baselines consistent with Article 47.[210] While the ICJ took the view

---

205 Department of State (United States), *Papua New Guinea: Archipelagic and Other Maritime Claims and Boundaries* (Limits in the Seas No. 138) (Department of State, Washington: 2014) 3–4.

206 See Roach and Smith, *Excessive Maritime Claims* 3rd, 209.

207 This adjustment was required following the decision of the ICJ in the case of *Sovereignty Over Pulau Ligitan and Pulau Sipadan* (Indonesia/Malaysia) [2002] ICJ Rep. 625 which determined that sovereignty over the islands rested with Malaysia.

208 Clive Schofield and I. Made Andi Arsana, "Closing the loop: Indonesia's revised archipelagic baselines system" (2009) 1 (2) *Australian Journal of Maritime and Ocean Affairs* 57, 61–2.

209 *In the Matter of the Duzgit Interity Arbitration* (Award of 5 September 2016) (Malta/São Tomé and Príncipe) PCA Case N° 2014-07, 15 [51] the tribunal observed that "São Tomé is an archipelagic State within the meaning of Article 46" and proceeded to assess the matter on that basis. A similar position was taken in *In the Matter of an Arbitration between Barbados and Trinidad and Tobago* (11 April 2006) 9 [44] where Trinidad and Tobago's status as an archipelagic State was not challenged.

210 *Qatar v. Bahrain* [2001] ICJ Rep. 40 [180–183].

that it was not required to take a position on the issue of Bahrain's status as an archipelagic State as it had not formally made such a claim,[211] the Court did observe that "in such a situation the method of straight baselines is applicable only if the State has declared itself to be an archipelagic State under Part IV of the 1982 Convention on the Law of the Sea, which is not true of Bahrain in this case".[212] The Court had also declared that the fact that a State may consider itself to be a *de facto* archipelagic State does not allow it to deviate from the normal rules with respect to baselines.[213] In his dissenting opinion though not on this point, Judge *ad hoc* Torres Bernárdez observed that there is "no such thing in conventional or general international law as a "secret archipelagic State" appearing in or disappearing from general international judicial proceedings or international relations in general."[214]

82. In the *South China Sea* case before an Annex VII LOSC Tribunal, discussion arose regarding Article 47 in the context of the use of archipelagic baselines with respect to offshore archipelagos. This issue arose because the Tribunal took the view that statements made by China could have been interpreted to suggest that the Spratly Islands in the South China Sea may be enclosed by a system of archipelagic baselines. The Tribunal observed that the use of archipelagic baselines is "strictly controlled by the Convention" and that their use is limited to archipelagic States,[215] and that as China was principally a mainland Asian State it did not meet the definition of an archipelagic State. Notwithstanding that the Philippines is an archipelagic State, the Tribunal was also of the view that the Philippines could not declare archipelagic baselines around the Spratly Islands as the ratio of water to land would "greatly exceed 9:1 under any conceivable system of baselines."[216]

4 Commentary by Publicists

83. Churchill and Lowe have identified seven conditions for the drawing of archipelagic baselines. They classify two as "precise and mathematical" and

211 *Qatar v. Bahrain* [2001] ICJ Rep. 40 [183].

212 *Qatar v. Bahrain* [2001] ICJ Rep. 40 [214]; given the context the Court may have mistakenly referred to 'straight' rather than 'archipelagic' baselines.

213 *Qatar v. Bahrain* [2001] ICJ Rep. 40, 103 [213].

214 *Qatar v. Bahrain* [2001] ICJ Rep. 40, 280 [56] Dissenting Opinion of Judge Torres Bernárdez.

215 2016 *South China Sea Arbitration* [573].

216 2016 *South China Sea Arbitration* [574]. The Tribunal also made observations regarding the relationship between Articles 7 and 47 which is considered more fully in para. 91 below.

the remainder as "more general and less precise".[217] Rothwell and Stephens identify five core elements associated with the Article 47 archipelagic baseline provisions, observing that "These requirements, whilst technical in nature, sit comfortably alongside the definitions of an archipelagic state and archipelago found in Article 46 and provide objective criteria that conform with the geography of the major archipelagic states engaged in UNCLOS III negotiations."[218] Prescott and Schofield argue that "[i]n contrast to the provisions for straight baselines, those relating to archipelagic baselines are technically robust, leave little room for interpretation and represent a clear attempt to provide rational tests by which to determine the validity or otherwise of a particular archipelagic baseline system."[219] Roach and Smith observe that "[u]ntil an archipelagic State claims archipelagic status, the normal baseline is the low-water line around each island."[220] They subsequently observe that notwithstanding the provisions of Part IV, several continental States with offshore groups of islands that may be described as archipelagos but which do not meet the juridical definition in Article 46 of the LOSC, have sought to enclose "islands with straight baselines in a manner simulating an archipelago."[221]

VII Distinctions among Islands, Rocks, and Low-Tide Elevations

84. The distinction among islands, rocks and low-tide elevations has gained increased significance in the law of the sea as a result of the conclusion of the LOSC and the prominence given in Part VIII to the "Regime of Islands". The important distinction between an Article 121(2) island, an Article 121(3) rock, and low-tide elevations was highlighted by the *South China Sea* case before an Annex VII LOSC Tribunal.[222] The Committee notes the distinction made among these features by the Tribunal, but takes no view on how the Tribunal interpreted and applied Article 121.

---

217 Churchill and Lowe, *The Law of the Sea* 3rd, 123. They also observe that "many of" the general and less precise conditions "parallel the conditions governing the drawing of straight baselines". Ibid.

218 Rothwell and Stephens, *The International Law of the Sea* 2nd, 194.

219 Prescott and Schofield, *The Maritime Political Boundaries of the World* 2nd (2005) 171–172; cf. an earlier comment by Prescott who observed that: "Three of the five tests are incapable of consistent objective interpretation": Prescott, "Straight and Archipelagic Baselines" 46.

220 Roach and Smith, *Excessive Maritime Claims* 3rd, 23.

221 Ibid., 208, where reference is made to the practice of Canada, Denmark, Ecuador, Portugal, Sudan and the UK.

222 2016 *South China Sea Arbitration* [473–553].

85. The LOSC makes clear that both islands and Article 121 (3) rocks have a minimum entitlement to a territorial sea, and as such the baseline provisions of the LOSC apply and accordingly straight baselines may, subject to the provisions of the LOSC, be drawn from an island or a rock. As an Article 121(3) rock is also an island, being a naturally formed area of land that is permanently above water at high tide, a low-tide elevation that falls within the territorial sea generated by an Article 121(3) rock could be utilised for the purposes of a baseline. A low-tide elevation, as properly classified under Article 13(1) of the LOSC, may only be used as a basepoint for delimiting the territorial sea if located within the territorial sea of the mainland or an island. No distinction should be made, therefore, as to whether a low-tide elevation falls within the territorial sea of an island or an Article 121(3) rock. The case of an Article 121(3) rock with an adjoining low-tide elevation has parallels with the case of an island having a fringing reef, where under Article 6 the baseline is drawn from the seaward low-water line of the reef.

86. With respect to Article 47 straight archipelagic baselines, baselines are to be drawn from islands and drying reefs of the archipelago.[223] Baselines are not to be drawn by an archipelagic State to or from low-tide elevations unless the feature falls within the territorial sea, or a lighthouse or similar installation that is permanently above sea level has been built on the feature.[224] Consistent with the drawing of straight baselines the Committee is also of the view that an Article 121(3) rock would be considered to be an "island" for the purposes of Article 47 and accordingly could be relied upon for the drawing of straight archipelagic baselines, subject to the other controlling elements of Article 47 being applied. This approach is also reflected in state practice, such as the case of Jamaica. Symmons has observed:

> It seems clear that mere 'rocks' within the definition of Art. 121(3) may qualify as basepoints in the capacity of being 'islands', as they are above water at high tide (just as they may also be appropriate linking points under Art. 7(1)). Thus, for example, in the Jamaican archipelagic claim, several of its southern critically-placed archipelagic basepoints consists of small rocks, such as Blower Rock.[225]

223 Article 47(1), LOSC.

224 Article 47(4), LOSC.

225 Clive R. Symmons, "Article 47 Archipelagic Baselines" in Proelss (ed.), *United Nations Convention on the Law of the Sea: A Commentary*, 352, 362–363; see Department of State (USA), *Jamaica's Maritime Claims and Boundaries* (Limits in the Seas No. 125) (Department of State, Washington: 2004) 3–4.

Rocks have also been relied upon in the drawing of archipelagic baselines by the Bahamas,[226] Grenada,[227] Mauritius,[228] Papua New Guinea,[229] and Trinidad and Tobago.[230]

VIII Distinct Island Issues

87. The LOSC in Article 121 makes a distinction between islands and rocks, with rocks being a sub-set of islands. This distinction is also relevant with respect to the islands that comprise an archipelago and make up an Article 46 archipelagic State. However, it is also possible to classify islands in other ways based upon geographic concepts. While other classifications of islands are not found in the LOSC or customary international law, applying additional classifications to certain islands assists in understanding straight and archipelagic baselines in other contexts. For these purposes, the Committee will use the terms "Oceanic Islands" and "Offshore Archipelago" to consider some additional distinct baseline issues as they apply to islands.

A *Oceanic Islands*

88. The situation of oceanic islands raises some distinctive issues. For these purposes an "oceanic island" is a single island which meets the criteria for an island under Article 121 of the LOSC and is not part of an archipelago. These islands generate the full suite of maritime zones as recognised in Article 121(2). There are two types of such islands:

- An oceanic island State – an example is Nauru; and
- An oceanic island that is separate from the mainland State of which it forms a part, and may be located adjacent to the coastal State and fall within the EEZ of the State or in another ocean or sea – examples include Ascension Island (UK), Bouvet Island (Norway), Campbell Island (New Zealand), Guam (USA), Macquarie Island (Australia), Marion Island (South Africa), and Wrangel Island (Russia).

---

226 Department of State (USA), *The Bahamas Archipelagic and Other Maritime Claims and Boundaries*.

227 Department of State (USA), *Grenada: Archipelagic and Other Maritime Claims and Boundaries* (Limits in the Seas No. 135) (Department of State, Washington: 2014).

228 Department of State (USA), *Mauritius: Archipelagic and Other Maritime Claims and Boundaries*.

229 Department of State (USA), *Papua New Guinea: Archipelagic and Other Maritime Claims and Boundaries*.

230 Department of State (USA), *Trinidad and Tobago: Archipelagic and Other Maritime Claims and Boundaries* (Limits in the Seas No. 131) (Department of State, Washington: 2014).

Provided straight baselines can be drawn around oceanic islands consistently with Article 7, then such baselines would be permissible.[231]

B *Offshore Archipelagos*

89. Offshore archipelagos and the capacity of coastal States to draw straight baselines around such islands pursuant to Article 7 or Article 47 have proven contentious in state practice. Offshore archipelagos can take two forms:[232]

- An offshore coastal archipelago located geographically adjacent to the continental state within the territorial sea or the EEZ – an example is the Åland Islands [Finland]);[233] or
- An offshore outlying archipelago located at a considerable distance from the continental state – an example is the Hawaiian Islands (USA).

States that are comprised of islands, and that are not Article 46 archipelagic States may also have offshore archipelagos.[234] Straight baselines around and between islands that comprise offshore coastal archipelagos are permissible provided that, mutatis mutandis, the geographical circumstances of those islands allow for the application of Article 7 and other related provisions. This stems from the principle of entitlement of islands to maritime zones in the same terms as other land territory as reflected in Article 121.

90. A recent study by Roach has identified the following offshore archipelagos enclosed by straight baselines: Azores (Portugal), Canary Islands (Spain), Co Co and Preparis (Myanmar), Diaoyu Dao/Senkakus (China), Falklands/Malvinas (UK/Argentina), Faroes (Denmark), Galapagos (Ecuador), Guadeloupe (France), Hainan, Paracels (China), Kerguelen Islands (France), Loyalty Islands (France), Svalbard (Norway), and Turks and Caicos (UK).[235] A number of States have protested some of these claims, including Bangladesh,

---

231 Australia has drawn straight baselines around the west coast of Macquarie Island; see "Australian Maritime Projection around Macquarie Island – Lambert Project" (Geoscience Australia) available at https://ecat.ga.gov.au/geonetwork/srv/eng/search#!a05f7892-eeed-7506-e044-00144fdd4fa6.

232 Kopela, *Dependent Archipelagos in the Law of the Sea* uses the term 'Dependent Archipelago', however, the Committee has not endorsed that characterization.

233 The islands that comprise an offshore coastal archipelago would in most instances fall within the ambit of an Article 7(1) "fringe of islands" subject to their geographic proximity from the mainland.

234 Small clusters of offshore islands, some of which are called archipelagos, lie offshore the main islands of Japan and New Zealand.

235 J. Ashley Roach, "Offshore Archipelagos Enclosed by Straight Baselines: an Excessive Claim?" (2018) 49 *Ocean Development and International Law* 176, 180–181; all of these are offshore outlying archipelagos excepting the Co Co and Preparis (Myanmar), and Hainan (China).

Belgium, Germany, Philippines, Senegal, Spain, Sweden, UK, US, Vietnam and the EC.[236]

91. In the *South China Sea* case before an Annex VII LOSC Tribunal, discussion arose regarding whether it would be permissible for China to enclose the Spratly Islands by a system of straight or archipelagic baselines "surrounding the high tide features of the group, and accorded an entitlement to maritime zones as a single unit".[237] China had not formally drawn a system of archipelagic baselines, nor made a claim that it was an archipelagic State. Nevertheless, the Tribunal made several observations that are relevant to this analysis including:

> The use of archipelagic baselines (a baseline surrounding an archipelago as a whole) is strictly controlled by the Convention, where Article 47(1) limits their use to "archipelagic states". Archipelagic States are defined in Article 46 as States "constituted wholly by one or more archipelagos and may include other islands." The Philippines is an archipelagic State (being constituted wholly by an archipelago), is entitled to employ archipelagic baselines, and does so in promulgating the baselines for its territorial sea.[238]

The Tribunal then considered the application of Article 7 straight baselines, and observed that "the Tribunal is aware of the practice of some States in employing straight baselines with respect to offshore archipelagos to approximate the effect of archipelagic baselines."[239] Two views were expressed on this matter: one technical and the other relating to the overall application of the LOSC. The Tribunal made clear that Article 7 straight baselines could not be drawn in the case of an offshore archipelago where the relevant conditions did not exist.[240] The Tribunal then went on to observe:

> Although the Convention does not expressly preclude the use of straight baselines in other circumstances, the Tribunal considers that the grant of permission in Article 7 concerning straight baselines generally, together with the conditional permission in Articles 46 and 47 for certain States to draw archipelagic baselines, excludes the possibility of employing

236 Ibid.

237 2016 *South China Sea Arbitration* [573]; this question was discussed in the context of statements made by China indicating that it claimed a territorial sea, EEZ and continental shelf "based on the Nansha Islands as a whole." ibid. [571].

238 2016 *South China Sea Arbitration* [573].

239 2016 *South China Sea Arbitration* [575].

240 Ibid.

> straight baselines in other circumstances, in particular with respect to offshore archipelagos not meeting the criteria for archipelagic baselines. Any other interpretation would effectively render the conditions in Articles 7 and 47 meaningless.

92. Through this assessment and review of the specific and general provisions of the LOSC with respect to the drawing of straight and archipelagic baselines the Tribunal made clear that a restrictive approach should be taken towards the drawing of such baselines in the case of offshore archipelagos.

IX Settlement of Disputes with Respect to Straight and Archipelagic Baselines

93. The LOSC contains both general and compulsory procedures for the settlement of disputes in Part XV. Disputes arising with respect to straight and archipelagic baselines fall within the subject matter jurisdiction of these LOSC mechanisms as they relate to the interpretation or application of the convention. An exception would arise with respect to matters relating to the customary international law of the sea that fell outside of the scope of the convention. However, given the extent of the provisions in the LOSC relating to straight and archipelagic baselines it would be difficult for a State to assert that any new customary international law regarding baselines did not relate to the interpretation or application of the convention. The general provisions for the settlement of disputes in the LOSC mirror those found in Article 33 of the Charter of the United Nations and emphasise peaceful means and reference to other general, regional or bilateral agreements.[241] Where a dispute arises the parties are to proceed expeditiously to an exchange of views regarding the settlement of the dispute by negotiation or other peaceful means.[242] The compulsory procedures for dispute settlement under Part XV provide for recourse to the International Tribunal for the Law of the Sea, the International Court of Justice, an Annex VII Arbitral Tribunal, or an Annex VIII Special Arbitral Tribunal.[243] Subject to declarations made by the parties, default jurisdiction rests with an Annex VII Arbitral Tribunal.[244]

94. When straight or archipelagic baselines have been contested in dispute resolution proceedings under Part XV, Section 2, or separately before international courts or tribunals via other routes, those baselines have – with the

241 Articles 280, 282, LOSC.

242 Article 283, LOSC.

243 Article 287, LOSC.

244 Article 287(5), LOSC.

exception of the landmark *Fisheries* case (UK v. Norway) – not been the principal subject matter of the dispute. The status of baselines has predominantly arisen in maritime boundary delimitation cases where increasingly the view of courts and tribunals has been to use their own base points. The Committee can therefore observe that it is exceptionally rare for a case where the principal dispute relates to straight or archipelagic baselines to have arisen before an international court or tribunal. In addition, as occurred in *Qatar v. Bahrain* and *South China Sea*, the legality of baselines is the subject of analysis in the context of a larger dispute between the parties.

95. The practice of States with respect to disputes regarding straight or archipelagic baselines predominantly relies upon diplomatic means, rather than the formal means for dispute settlement found in the LOSC or general international law. The US is the most active individual State in this regard and relies upon diplomatic protest, and the actual physical exercise of its asserted freedoms of navigation by government vessels, to challenge straight and archipelagic baselines claims that it does not consider to be in conformity with the law of the sea. The US has also joined with States that are parties to the LOSC to protest against straight or archipelagic baseline claims not considered to be in conformity with the convention, as occurred with the joint UK/US demarche of October 18, 2007 with respect to the archipelagic baseline claim of the Dominican Republic.[245] The Committee also observes that not all diplomatic protests are publicly available and some States may resolve these matters by bilateral exchanges at a diplomatic or Ministerial level.

X Final Observations and Conclusions

96. In light of the analysis and review of the relevant provisions of the LOSC, state practice, relevant jurisprudence, and the views of commentators and publicists, the Committee will now make some final observations and conclusions.[246]

245 Department of State (United States), *Dominican Republic: Archipelagic and Other Maritime Claims*, Annex 4.

246 Committee member Yee made the following comments on this Report: "First, I take issue with the very much raw data approach to the assessment of protests and other State practice data that the draft final report more or less takes. Second, I take issue with the position that continental States cannot claim archipelagic waters under customary international law. I believe there is sufficient material to support the view that they can. The continental States' argument seems to be take the view that the whole Part IV does not apply to their outlying archipelagos. Thirdly, I object to citing the South China Sea arbitration uncritically, taking it as sacred, although the awards did not provide any analysis on many of the relevant issues, simply making conclusory statements. We are an academic entity; simply citing to unsupported conclusory statements as proven is inappropriate".

A Straight Baselines and Diplomatic Protests

97. The legality and validity of straight and archipelagic baselines are subject to their conformity with the LOSC and customary international law. However, as long as the legality and validity of the baselines has not been assessed by an international court or tribunal, the opposability of those baselines largely depends upon an absence of protest from other States. Thus, a survey of protests is very important for the purposes of assessing state practice concerning straight baselines. In this respect, the First Report (2014) indicated as follows:

> 30. For the purposes of this Report it is not possible to provide an exhaustive analysis of all relevant state practice. Nor is it possible to discuss the legal grounds on which States may have predicated their recourse to straight (or closing) baselines, as typically that is not made publicly known. Rather mention will be made of some particular examples of state practice in areas that have been the subject to debate.

The report goes on to indicate:

> 41. Not entirely surprisingly, the number of States which have protested relevant state practice in this regard, in proportion to the number of potentially interested States, is very small.

In this regard, the First Report placed reliance upon Churchill who in 2005 observed: "at least eight different States and the EU have protested to one or more baseline claims….".[247]

98. Since the First Report the straight baseline claims of 88 States were identified. A detailed search for protests thereof uncovered additional objections as set out in Appendix 1. It lists a total of 82 protests or other forms of objection. It shows that the straight baseline claims of 39 States (almost 50% of the total SBL claims) – all but Iran being parties to the LOSC – have been objected to by 21 States and the EU/EC (only two of which – Iran and the US – are not party to the LOSC). Appendix 2 consolidates the data in Appendix 1, distinguishing between States whose straight baseline claims are less than 40 miles, those States whose straight baseline claims are not greater than 50 miles, and those States whose straight baselines claims are greater than 50 miles.

247 Robin R. Churchill, "The Impact of State Practice on the Jurisdictional Framework Contained in the LOS Convention", 108.

99. The Committee has been cautious not to place too much weight on diplomatic protests for a number of reasons. First, while details of US diplomatic protests are publicly available, as noted above that may not be the case with the diplomatic protests of other States. Second, diplomatic protests raise issues of characterisation requiring detailed assessment of the actual language in a note verbale or equivalent in order to be able to make a precise assessment as to the subject matter of the dispute and whether it relates to an interpretation or application of the LOSC. Nevertheless, the Committee has sought to take into account, where appropriate, diplomatic protests that are publicly available as evidence of state practice and the views of certain states regarding either the development of customary international law or the interpretation of the LOSC.

B *Straight Baselines*

100. The Committee observes that a majority of coastal States – 90 of 150 – have sought to proclaim straight baselines in reliance upon Article 7 of the LOSC. However, the data in Appendix 1 highlights that state practice is variable, which also reflects the variables in coastal geography that impact upon the interpretation of Article 7. The Committee's analysis of Article 7 has identified a number of constraints in its application. The controls that apply to the interpretation of Article 7 are consistent with judicial interpretation. However, the evolution of Article 7 via the judgment in *Fisheries*, work of the ILC, debates at the 1958 Geneva Conference, the resulting text of Article 4 of the Convention on the Territorial Sea and the Contiguous Zone, and the debates in and outcome of UNCLOS III, make clear that notwithstanding a number of proposals for specific limitations to be placed upon the straight baseline regime, they were rejected in favour of the current text, which incorporates certain indeterminate concepts to be concretised in light of specific circumstances. In this respect the Committee recalls the comments of J.P.A. François in his capacity as Expert to the Secretariat of the 1958 Geneva Conference when he observed with respect to the work of the ILC and straight baselines:

> The Commission was criticized for not having drafted some of the articles as precisely as might be desired. Such expressions as "where circumstances necessitate", "to any appreciable extent", "sufficiently closely linked", "adequate grounds", "reasonable measures", "unjustifiable interference" and others are, it is said, out of place. The Commission cannot regard these objections as fully justified. It is true that the articles ought to be drafted in the clearest possible language. Perhaps the Commission's texts can still be improved in this respect. Nevertheless, it should

> be remembered that these expressions all occur in national legislation. In the opinion of the International Law Commission, a codification of international law can no more do without these expressions than can national law. Any attempt to codify international law without using such expressions will prove vain. In contentious cases, the meaning will have to be decided by an impartial authority, to which disputes regarding the interpretation of these expressions in specific cases are to be submitted.[248]

In the absence of objective criteria, a succession of indeterminate concepts have been used throughout the history of the straight baselines regime and this needs to be borne in mind when interpreting Article 7. Such an approach is also consistent with acknowledging that there is also a margin by which coastal States can seek legitimately to interpret the drawing of straight baselines so as to reflect their distinctive circumstances.

101. The Committee also acknowledges that interpretations of Article 7 that are arguably not seen as consistent with the LOSC have been the subject of protest, principally by the US but also by the European Union and other States. As noted above, the Committee also accepts that there may be other instances of diplomatic protests having been lodged with respect to state practice and Article 7 that have not been publicly released. The Committee also notes that a small number of significant maritime States have lodged Declarations under Article 310 expressing their views with respect to the drawing of straight baselines not in accordance with the LOSC. Diplomatic protest will have an impact on the development of treaty interpretation at variance with the LOSC. In this respect the Committee acknowledges that the general rules of treaty interpretation as provided for in Article 31 of the Vienna Convention on the Law of Treaties[249] are applicable and that it is legitimate to take into account state practice of parties to the LOSC with respect to the interpretation of Article 7, which incorporates "indeterminate concepts" that stem from the negotiations in UNCLOS I and UNCLOS III. The weight accorded to that state practice must be assessed against whether it reflects the "agreement of the parties regarding its interpretation."[250]

---

248 *United Nations Conference on the Law of the Sea, Volume III: First Committee (Territorial Sea and Contiguous Zone)*, 21st mtg, 69 [15], UN Doc. A/CONFC.13/C.1/L.10 (1958); François was an ILC member from 1949–1961 and Special Rapporteur for the "Law of the sea – regime of the high seas" (1950–1954, 1956) and "Law of the sea – regime of the Territorial Sea" (1952–1956).

249 1155 UNTS 331 (VCLT).

250 Article 31(3)(b), VCLT.

102. The Committee notes that a number of publicists have been critical of the Article 7 straight baseline regime. Reisman and Westerman, writing in 1992, were firmly of the view that the regime of straight baselines requires a form of reconceptualization.[251] In 2005, Prescott and Schofield, for example commented that "[a] survey of the approximately 70 straight baselines drawn around the world demonstrates that the rules established in 1958 and 1982 to govern their delimitation have been bent out of shape. That should surprise no analyst. The terms of Article 7 are so imprecise that it would be possible for most countries to draw straight baselines along some or all of their coastlines. Nor would such countries need to invent new interpretations of terms in Article 7, because existing baselines provide all the justifications in terms of state practice and precedents that any could need."[252] More recently, Tanaka wrote in 2015 that "the rules governing straight baselines are so abstract that the application of the rules to particular coasts is to a large extent subject to the discretion of coastal States."[253] In 2013, Kopela claimed that "expanding tendencies need to be assessed by taking into consideration the purpose of straight baselines", which is not an easy task since such purpose and objective was not spelt out in Article 7.[254]

103. As to the general status of Article 7 and its interpretation, the Committee notes its observations in paragraphs 10–36. It endorses the observations of Churchill[255] that there is no agreed single interpretation of Article 7 or a new rule of customary international law, and also notes the 2016 comments by the Annex VII LOSC Tribunal in *South China Sea* rejecting the formation of a new rule of customary international law regarding baselines especially with respect to the relationship between Articles 7 and 47.[256] Notwithstanding significant evidence of variations in state practice, the Committee's analysis demonstrates that many straight baselines when considered in their distinct geographic settings are in general conformity with Article 7 consistent with the indeterminate concepts that it contains. There is also evidence that following protests over practice not considered to be in conformity with Article 7, some States have modified their straight baselines so as to be in conformity with the LOSC.

251 Reisman and Westerman, *Straight Baselines in International Maritime Boundary Delimitation*, 73–74.

252 Prescott and Schofield, *The Maritime Political Boundaries of the World* 2nd, 160.

253 Tanaka, *The International Law of the Sea* 2nd, 51.

254 Kopela, *Dependent Archipelagos in the Law of the Sea*, 73–74.

255 Churchill, "The Impact of State Practice on the Jurisdictional Framework Contained in the LOS Convention" 108.

256 2016 *South China Sea Arbitration* [576].

104. With respect to some of the specific provisions of Article 7, the Committee observes that the terms "deeply indented and cut into" are criteria that are not subject to absolute precision in their interpretation. While they have traditionally been understood in the context of the geographical circumstances of the Norwegian coastline considered in the *Fisheries* case, the Committee notes that the Court referred to a consideration of "all the geographical factors involved."[257] This supports the view that a variety of geographical factors can be taken into account in order to determine whether the particular coastline in question is one that is deeply indented and cut into, which may involve the application of a proportionality test.[258]

105. The Committee is of the view that the Article 7(1) reference to a "fringe of islands" can be applied flexibly so as to take into account multiple different island configurations that may be located offshore a mainland. Each island must meet the criteria set by Article 121. There is no provision in the LOSC, consistency in state practice, or assessment by international courts and tribunals as to the distance between a fringe of islands and the mainland; rather the proximity of the islands to the coast is controlled by the general criteria within Article 7. As emphasised by the Annex VII LOSC Tribunal in *South China Sea* a clear distinction exists between Article 7 straight baselines being drawn to and from and between islands, and Article 47 straight archipelagic baselines, and coastal States need to be mindful of this limitation. Artificial islands or low-tide elevations without a lighthouse or similar installation cannot be utilised for the purpose of drawing Article 7 straight baselines to and from the mainland, or between the islands that comprise the "fringe".

106. The Committee is of the view that Article 7(2) is to be read independently, and not cumulatively, with Article 7(1) and notes the historic basis for this provision is separate and distinct from the criteria outlined in Article 7(1). However, while Articles 7(1) and 7(2) are separate and distinct, each needs to be read cumulatively with Articles 7(3)–(6). The Committee also notes the potential difficulties that may arise from a strict application of Article 7(3) to the circumstances outlined in Article 7(2) in that a highly unstable coastline may be one in which determining the general direction of the coast may present significant challenges. In that respect, the Committee notes that the "general direction" criterion in Article 7(3), recognised by the Court in *Fisheries*

257 *Fisheries* (United Kingdom v. Norway) [1951] ICJ Rep. 116, 141.

258 *Fisheries* (United Kingdom v. Norway) [1951] ICJ Rep. 116, 141 which was applied in the case of the Lakesfjord and Porsangerfjord.

as devoid of any mathematical precision,[259] is qualified by the words "to any appreciable extent" which would permit a margin of appreciation for a coastal State seeking to draw straight baselines along a highly unstable coastline.

107. The Committee has carefully assessed whether it is possible to specify limits on the length of straight baselines. The only judicially approved straight baselines were those of Norway which in 1951 in *Fisheries* the ICJ approved in toto. The Court did not in its opinion identify the longest segments that it was approving. A later analysis stated that the longest Norwegian straight baseline considered in that decision was segment 45–46 at 40.0 nm long (the longer segment, 20–21, 43.6 nm, enclosed a body of water that the Court found to be historic waters). The Committee has noted that the court in *Fisheries* endorsed a Norwegian straight baseline 40 nm in length. Given that remains the longest judicially endorsed straight baseline it is appropriate to consider that a straight baseline of 40 nm, subject to other relevant criteria, is consistent with Article 7.

108. Publicists have proposed various length limits, however, there is no consensus on this point. Appendix 1, which reflects claims made till mid-2018, includes the data currently available for all (Article 7) straight baseline segments, including those longer than 40 nm (many of the lengths have been calculated to hundredths of a nautical mile based on modern satellite imagery). The data presently available indicates that of the 90 States (including their dependencies) that have drawn straight baseline segments, 41 have no segments longer than 40 nm, while 49 have one or more segments longer than 40 nm. This analysis is located in Appendix 2. The Committee observes that the state practice is variable and concludes that it is not possible to assert that state practice has crystallized around the permissible length of a straight baseline.

109. Having carefully assessed the history and background to the development of Article 7, state practice, the decisions of international courts and tribunals, and the views of commentators and publicists, the Committee has not proposed limits on the length of Article 7 straight baselines. Nevertheless, Article 7 straight baselines cannot be of unlimited length and several controlling factors need to be taken into account including the cumulative criteria of Article 7 of which the configuration of the coastline, including the location of any fringing islands, prevail. In reaching this conclusion the Committee notes the emphasis placed upon proportionality in the *Fisheries* case, and that according to the Court in *Qatar v. Bahrain* the regime should be "applied restrictively". Noting those observations, the Committee observes that the

259 *Fisheries* (United Kingdom v. Norway) [1951] ICJ Rep. 116, 142.

longer the length of a straight baseline the more difficult it will be for that baseline to comply with Article 7. The Committee also notes that the LOSC sets the presumptive outer limit for a straight archipelagic baseline as 100 nm and permits only a small percentage of straight archipelagic baselines up to a limit of 125 nm.

C *Internal Waters and Straight Baselines*

110. With respect to Article 8(2), the Committee assessed this provision in its Second Report (2016) where the absence of extensive state practice was noted. As such it can be observed that the recognition of the right of innocent passage within waters enclosed by Article 7 straight baselines that previously were not considered internal waters is not contentious. Notwithstanding the characterisation by publicists such as Smith that Article 8(2) seeks to "preserve" a right of innocent passage within waters newly enclosed by Article 7 straight baselines, Article 8(2) does not require that the right of innocent passage have been previously accepted. Rather, Article 8(2) addresses waters that were previously not considered to be internal waters. Therefore, whether the coastal State had or had not previously acknowledged the right of innocent passage within those waters is not determinative to the enjoyment of the right following the establishment of Article 7 straight baselines. Other factors may need to be taken into account including the breadth of the territorial sea prior to and following establishment of a straight baseline.

D *Bays and Straight Baselines*

111. The Committee observes that the status of a juridical bay in the modern law of the sea within which a straight/closing line may be drawn has a long history as reflected in both the Convention on the Territorial Sea and the Contiguous Zone and the LOSC. The ICJ in the *Land, Island and Maritime Frontier* case considered the provisions of Article 10 to reflect "general customary law". The Committee acknowledges that a particular difficulty that arises with Article 10 is the multiple criteria a coastal State must apply in order to determine that the indentation along the coast is a juridical bay. Given the ambiguity that exists with those criteria it is unsurprising that there exist some variations in state practice and that the drawing of straight/closing lines has been the subject of protest, especially by the US. While the Committee acknowledges that Article 10 could be redrafted with greater precision there would not appear to be much incentive for doing so given the general customary international law status of the provision. In that respect, the Committee accepts that Article 10(4) closing lines bear similarities to Article 7 straight baselines in that account must be taken of coastal irregularities such that

coastal States enjoy some margin of appreciation in its interpretation. The Committee does note, however, that Article 10(4) makes clear that a bay closing line is to be no greater than 24 nm in length and that no variation from this is permissible. The Committee also notes that Article 10 does not apply to multi-state bays or to historic bays, both of which are addressed under general international law. Decisions of international courts and tribunals have considered multi-state bays in the *Land, Island and Maritime Frontier* case and in *Croatia/Slovenia*.

E *Low-Tide Elevations and Straight Baselines*

112. The Committee notes that Article 13 permits a coastal State to rely on the low-water line on a low-tide elevation as the baseline from which the territorial sea is measured if the low-tide elevation is situated wholly or partly at a distance not exceeding the breadth of the territorial sea from the mainland or an island. There is also a direct linkage between Article 13 and Articles 7(4) and 47(4), which some coastal States have relied upon to engage in ambiguous conduct as to which of these provisions they have utilized when they rely upon certain low-tide elevations to measure the breadth of their territorial sea or to draw straight baselines. While Article 13 identifies the essential characteristics of a low-tide elevation there remains the potential for coastal State discretion in characterising a feature as a low-tide elevation. Nevertheless, the Committee notes the approach of the Annex VII LOSC Arbitral Tribunal in *South China Sea* that a low-tide elevation is to be determined on the basis of its natural condition and a strict approach must be taken to distinguish between a low-tide elevation in its natural condition, and a feature that as a result of state intervention has acquired the characteristics of an artificial island. The Committee notes its previous views on determining the relevant vertical datum and its application to Article 5 and low-tide elevations,[260] and the flexible approach taken by the Annex VII LOSC Arbitral Tribunal in *South China Sea* on that matter.

F *Combination of Methods in Drawing Baselines*

113. In view of the different methods that Part II, Section 2 of the LOSC permits coastal States to rely upon when determining their baselines, the Committee observes that Article 14 provides certainty that a combination of methods may be utilised according to different geographical and maritime circumstances. This is appropriate and reaffirms the significance associated

260 International Law Association, *Baselines under the International Law of the Sea* (Sofia Conference 2012) p. 25.

with the declaration of baselines for the identification of internal waters and maritime zones including the territorial sea. However, while Article 14 reaffirms coastal State discretion, the Committee emphasises that the baselines methodology selected by a coastal State must be appropriate and adapted to the particular coastline under consideration.

G *Archipelagic Baselines*

114. The Committee notes that Part IV of the LOSC was carefully drafted during UNCLOS III to reflect the aspirations of those States that were pressing for recognition under the law of the sea of archipelagic State status. That the technical provisions of Article 47 were only finalised following extensive consultations with the principal aspiring archipelagic States has resulted in substantive compliance by the great majority of those States claiming archipelagic State status since the entry into force of the LOSC. The Committee observes that variations in state practice which appear to depart from Article 47 have either been relatively minor, or subject to protest by other States, which in some instances has resulted in an adjustment of state practice and consistency with the LOSC.

115. Part IV of the LOSC has given greater status to the "archipelagic State" and has raised issues as to whether a State must declare itself as such to be able to draw straight archipelagic baselines consistent with Article 47. The ICJ in *Qatar v. Bahrain* has suggested that for a State to enjoy entitlements under Part IV of the LOSC, including the drawing of Article 47 archipelagic baselines, then the making of such a declaration is necessary. The Committee notes in particular the significance of the relationship between Articles 46 and 47 which has been reinforced by the decision in *Qatar v. Bahrain* with the emphasis upon the connection in Articles 46 and 47 between an "archipelagic State" and a State able to draw straight archipelagic baselines consistent with Article 47. This distinction was also alluded to by the Annex VII LOSC Arbitral Tribunal in *South China Sea*. The Committee also notes the requirement under Article 47(9) that an archipelagic State is to give due publicity to charts or geographical coordinates referring to straight archipelagic baselines. While observing that there are some variations in state practice, albeit amongst a small group of only 22 States claiming archipelagic State status, consistent with the distinctive rights and entitlements enjoyed under Part IV and emerging state practice it is desirable that States relying upon Part IV should proclaim themselves as archipelagic States. Such action would resolve any ambiguity as to the status of the state for the purposes of the LOSC, and also provide greater certainty for other States, including adjoining coastal States and flag States whose vessels navigate through the waters of the archipelagic State. Where the status

of a declared archipelagic State is disputed, the rights and entitlements of that State consistent with Part IV, and its maritime claims proclaimed from straight archipelagic baselines, may not be recognised by the protesting State A State party to the LOSC that contests the status of an archipelagic State may avail itself of Part XV mechanisms for the peaceful settlement of international disputes.

116. The Committee notes that compared to Article 7 of the LOSC, there is little room for widely varying interpretation of the more technical provisions of Article 47. With respect to the 3 per cent straight archipelagic baseline requirement in Article 47(2), the Committee notes that this provision should be applied to each set of archipelagic baselines drawn by an archipelagic State around each archipelago that comprises the archipelagic State. On the other hand, terms such as "appreciable extent", and "general configuration" found within Article 47 are more indeterminate and provide the archipelagic State with some capacity to apply those provisions consistently with its particular geographic circumstances. In this respect the Committee observes that some archipelagic States have sought to draw more than one set of complete archipelagic baselines so as to enclose distinct archipelagos that may be geographically separate. These states include Kiribati, Marshall Islands, Mauritius, Seychelles, and the Solomon Islands.[261] Such practice is consistent with Articles 46 and 47 providing other controls on straight archipelagic baselines are met.

117. The Committee notes that straight archipelagic baselines are to enclose the "main islands". This term is not defined in Article 47(1), though the island must meet the Article 121 criteria. The Committee notes that, consistent with the widely varying geographic circumstances of archipelagic States, the term "main islands" should be interpreted flexibly to encompass the larger geographic islands, the more heavily populated islands, and the more economically significant islands. The main islands of an archipelagic State may therefore be of varying geographic size.

118. The archipelagic State within its archipelagic waters may also under Article 50 draw closing lines so as to delimit internal waters in accordance with Articles 9, 10 and 11. This allowance for archipelagic States is limited in scope and applies only in the case of mouths of rivers, bays, and ports. Some archipelagic States have sought to draw Article 50 closing lines.[262] With the exception

261 See Appendix 3.

262 Kevin Baumert and Brian Melchior, "The Practice of Archipelagic States: A Study of Studies" 60, 71 who refer to the practice of Antigua and Barbuda, Fiji, Grenada, Mauritius, Saint Vincent and the Grenadines, and Tuvalu.

of a claim made by the Dominican Republic,[263] the Committee is not aware that state practice in this area, albeit very limited, is contentious.

119. In the case of oceanic islands (as the Committee has used that term in paragraph 88) either comprising a single State, or being part of the territory of a coastal State, the Committee observes that straight baselines may be drawn around the coast of those islands provided such baselines are in accordance with Article 7. In the case of offshore archipelagos (as the Committee has used that term in paragraph 89) the Committee distinguishes between two types: the offshore coastal archipelago, and the offshore outlying archipelago. An offshore coastal archipelago may be capable of being enclosed by Article 7 straight baselines subject to the controls set by Article 7 being met. The Committee is of the view that subject to the size and the maritime features of the islands comprising an offshore archipelago, it may be possible to draw Article 7 straight baselines around an individual island located within an archipelago consistently with the LOSC where that island is not otherwise part of an archipelagic State. In nearly all cases known to the Committee, this would only be possible where the coastline of the island is "deeply indented and cut into".

120. The Committee notes that in the case of offshore outlying archipelagos, consistent with *Qatar v. Bahrain* and *South China Sea*, a State is unable to proclaim archipelagic baselines unless it meets the criteria of being an archipelagic State. This may include a State made up of groups of islands that comprise an archipelago such that each group can be enclosed by separate straight archipelagic baselines as is the case with Kiribati, the Marshall Islands, the Seychelles, and the Solomon Islands. The Committee confirms that a continental State – that is a State that has territory located on a continent – is unable to proclaim Article 47 straight archipelagic baselines as the State would be constituted other than by archipelagos and islands.[264]

H *Final Observations*

121. The Committee has sought to review and assess baselines under the international law of the sea consistent with its mandate. While the LOSC provided a firm basis for the study much of the Committee's work focussed on

263 See "Text of a Joint Declaration Undertaken by the United Kingdom of Great Britain and Northern Ireland and the United States of America in relation to the Law of the Dominican Republic Number 66-07 of 22 May 2007, Done on 18 October 2007" (2008) 66 *Law of the Sea Bulletin* 98–99.

264 Committee member Yee notes there is sufficient material to support the view that continental States can claim archipelagic waters under customary international law, citing Chinese Society of International Law "The South China Sea Arbitration Awards: A Critical Study" (2018) 17 *Chinese Journal of International Law* 207, 475–552.

assessing state practice and decisions of international courts and tribunals. Given the significant impact both have upon this area of the law of the sea it can be anticipated that the interpretation and application of the law will continue to evolve.

122. The Committee acknowledges the research assistance provided to the Rapporteur by students at the ANU College of Law, Australian National University. The Committee also acknowledges the ILA (American Branch), ILA (Singapore Branch), American Society of International Law, and the Centre for International Law at the National University of Singapore for hosting inter-sessional meetings. This brings the Committee's work to a conclusion.

B *Dissenting Report by Sienho Yee*

I respectfully dissent. First, the Committee's raw data approach to assessing State practice is wrong. General international law requires a careful examination of State conduct and the underlying reasons, with due regard to specially affected States' positions. The Report (para. 98) found 21 States objecting to some straight baselines, without considering that those 21 (already minor among over 192 existing States) apparently include at least 18 neighbors protesting against each other apparently for overlapping territorial and/or maritime claims. Thus, Lowe and Tzanakopoulos (Report, n.68, 190) found that "state practice has tended [...] to consider straight baselines almost as an open alternative to "normal" baselines, in the face of rather limited objection". Second, the regime of continental States' outlying archipelagos as units is already established under customary international law. The UNCLOS text and *travaux préparatoires* show that Part IV does not apply to such archipelagos. State practice and the accompanying *opinio juris* support that regime. An overwhelming majority of geographically eligible continental States (at least 17 out of some 20) have claimed such a regime with special baselines, to sporadic, limited objections (Chinese Society of IL, *The South China Sea Arbitration Awards: A Critical Study* (https://doi.org/10.1093/chinesejil/jmy012, paras. 585–587). Third, I object to citing to the South China Sea Arbitration awards uncritically, because of the many serious errors including those regarding jurisdiction and the tribunal's making conclusory statements without examining State practice, as demonstrated in the *Critical Study* as well as in earlier papers by others (2016–17). The Committee's closing its eyes to this side of the story is regrettable.

C *Appendix 1*

Straight Baseline Segments[265]

State	Law and Date of Claim[266]	Source of Analysis[267]	Segment >40 nm[268]	Length (nm) >40 nm
Albania[a] *US Protested*[269]	Decree No. 4650, April 15, 1970, as amended Decree No. 7366, March 24, 1990	LIS 7 LIS 116	— —	— —
Algeria[a]	Decree No. 84-181, Aug. 4, 1984	van de Poll/ Schofield	—	—
Angola[a]	Portuguese Decree No. 47,771, June 27, 1969	LIS 28	—	—

265 Updated to 1 June 2018.

266 UN, Law of the Sea Bulletin ("LOSB"), http://www.un.org/Depts/los/doalos_publications/los_bult.htm; UN, Law of the Sea Information Circular ("LOSIC"), http://www.un.org/Depts/los/LEGISLATIONANDTREATIES/losics.htm; Maritime Zone Notifications ("M.Z.N."), http://www.un.org/Depts/los/LEGISLATIONANDTREATIES/depositpublicity.htm.

267 U.S. Department of State, Limits in the Seas ("LIS"), http://www.state.gov/e/oes/ocns/opa/c16065.htm; Sophia Kopela, *Dependent Archipelagos in the Law of the Sea* (Leiden/Boston: Martinus Nijhoff 2013); Donat Pharand, *Canada's Arctic Waters in International Law* (Cambridge: Cambridge 2008); J. Ashley Roach, "China's Straight Baseline Claim: Senkaku (Diaoyu) Islands" *ASIL Insight* (2013) vol. 17, issue 7 (Feb. 13 2013) http://www.asil.org/insights/volume/17/issue/7/china%E2%80%99s-straight-baseline-claim-senkaku-diaoyu-islands; Coalter Lathrop, Robert van de Poll, Clive Schofield, Brian Melchior, Niels Andersen unpublished calculations; G. Francalanci & T. Scovazzi (eds), *Lines in the Sea* (Martinus Nijhoff, Dordrecht/Boston/London: 1994). G.H. Blake and D. Topalović, *The Maritime Boundaries of the Adriatic Sea* (IBRU, Maritime Briefing, Volume 1 Number 8, 1996); M. Grbec, *The Extention of Coastal State Jurisdiction in Enclosed or Semi-Enclosed Seas, A Mediterranean and Adriatic Perspective* (Routledge, Oxford/New York: 2014). Van de Poll calculations to hundredths of nm are all geodetics.

268 "—" indicates no segment longer than 40 nm. "n/a" indicates not applicable with just enabling legislation or low water line (LWL) only.

269 See J. Ashley Roach and Robert W. Smith, Excessive Maritime Claims 3rd (Martinus Nijhoff, Leiden/Boston: 2012) 74–82 for a table listing these protests.

Straight Baseline Segments (*cont.*)

State	Law and Date of Claim	Source of Analysis	Segment >40 nm	Length (nm) >40 nm
Argentina[a] *US Protested*	Law No. 17,094, Jan. 19, 1967	LIS 44 Bay closing lines	 Golfo San Matias Golfo San Jorge	 65 123
	Law No. 23,968, Aug. 14, 1991, Annex I, http://www.un.org/Depts/los/LEGISLATIONANDTREATIES/PDFFILES/ARG_1991_23968.pdf;	van de Poll	1–2 (Golfo Rio da Prata) 23–24 (Golfo San Matias) 48–49 (Golfo San Jorge)	59.51 63.17 130.84
Malvinas So. Georgia Isl.	http://www.un.org/Depts/los/LEGISLATIONANDTREATIES/PDFFILES/DEPOSIT/arg_mzn10_1996.pdf	Kopela 277 van de Poll	— —	— —
Australia[a]	Proclamation, Feb. 4, 1983	Kopela 121, 127	—	—
Bangladesh[a]	Declaration, April 13, 1974	Lathrop	6–7 7–8	47 52
	Notification, 4 November 2015; repeals 1974 declaration. bgd_mzn118.pdf	van de Poll	1–2 2–3 3–4 4–5	— 79.85 66.81 LWL
Barbados[a]	Act No. 26, 1976 [enabling legislation] Territorial Waters Act, No. 1977-26(1) [enabling legislation]	—	n/a	n/a
Belize[a]	Marine Areas Act, 1992 Section 4(3)(a) & schedule	van de Poll	—	—
Brazil[a]	Decree Law No. 1098, March 27, 1970; Law 8617, Jan. 4, 1993, LOSB No. 23, at 17 [enabling legislation] LOSB No. 55, at 25–28 (cords. & map) (2004), repealed	—		

Straight Baseline Segments (*cont.*)

State	Law and Date of Claim	Source of Analysis	Segment >40 nm	Length (nm) >40 nm
	by Decree No. 8,400 of	van de Poll	1 to 2	52.92
	4 February 2015, LOSB 87,		2 to 3	41.72
	http://www.un.org/Depts/los/		3 to 4	188.66
	LEGISLATIONANDTREATIES/		6 to 7	68.22
	STATEFILES/BRA.htm		7 to 8	82.23
			8 to 9	111.03
			10 to 11	56.43
			71 to 72	66.61
			79 to 80	66.98
			80 to 81	53.26
			81 to 82	74.26
			85 to 86	90.38
			86 to 87	54.84
Bulgaria[a]	Decree No. 514, Oct. 10, 1951 [Varna and Bourgas Bays] Act of July 8, 1987, LOSB No. 13, at 9 (repealed)			
	Maritime Space, Inland Waterways and Ports Act, Jan. 28, 2000, LOSB No. 49, at 20–22	van de Poll/ Schofield	—	—
Burma (Myanmar)[a]	Decree, Nov. 15, 1968	LIS 14	Araran:	
			d–e	42.5
			e–f	57.0
	Map at Kopela 268		Martaban:	222.3
			a–b	80.8
			Tenasserim:	71.1
			b–c	—
US & UK Protested	Law No. 3, April 9, 1977 LOSIC No. 9, at 42		f–g	
Bangladesh Protested	Law No. 8/2008, Dec. 5, 2008, LOSB No. 69, at 69–73 (Preparis and CoCo Islands)	Kopela 136	—	
Cambodia	Council of State Decree, July 31, 1982	Lathrop	2–3	53

Straight Baseline Segments (*cont.*)

State	Law and Date of Claim	Source of Analysis	Segment >40 nm	Length (nm) >40 nm
Cameroon[a]	Decree 62-DF-216, June 1962	van de Poll/	—	—
US Protested	Decree 71-DF-416, Aug. 1971	Schofield		
Canada[a]	Order-in-Council P.C.	Pharand 155	Newfoundland	
	1967-2025,		Notre Dame	49
US Protested	Oct. 26, 1967 (Labrador,		Placentia Bays	45
	Newfoundland & Nova Scotia)			
US Protested	Order-in-Council P.C. 1969-1109, May 29, 1969 (Vancouver & Queen Charlotte Island)			
	Order-in-Council P.C. 1972-966, May 9, 1972 (Labrador, Newfoundland, Nova Scotia, Vancouver Isl., Queen Charlotte Isl.)			
EC & US	Order-in-Council P.C.	Pharand	Arctic	
Protested	1985-2739,	156–157		46
	Sept. 10, 1985 (Arctic)			51.3
				77.2
				69.2
				99.5
				92.2
Chile[a]	Decree No. 416, July 14, 1977	LIS 80	3–4	67.071
	LOSIC No. 13, at 33		6–7	55.879
			10–11	43.389
			11–12	64.958
			18–19	44.025
			20–21	59.671
			57–58	54.805
			60–61	47.086
			65–66	45.978
		LIS 80 Add.	—	—

Straight Baseline Segments (*cont.*)

State	Law and Date of Claim	Source of Analysis	Segment >40 nm	Length (nm) >40 nm
China[a]	Declaration, Sept. 4, 1958 Law, Feb. 25, 1992, LOSB No. 21, at 24–27	LIS 43	hypothetical	—
US & Vietnam Protested	Declaration, May 15, 1996 (coordinates) LOSIC No. 9, at 18; LOSB No. 32, at 37–40	LIS 117	Mainland	
			6–7	84.1
			7–8	71.8
			8–9	121.7
			10–11	100.2
			11–12	62.5
			14–15	84.2
			17–18	69.3
			18–19	73.2
			20–21	50.3
			22–23	83.6
			23–24	48.3
			26–27	43.8
			27–28	84.6
			28–29	71.3
			29–30	66.8
			31–32	107.8
			33–34	83.7
Xisha/Paracels			7–8	75.8
			14–15	78.8
			22–23	41.5
Diaoyu/ Senkaku *Japan & US Protested*	Statement of Sept. 10, 2012, LOSB No. 80, at 30–31	ASIL Insight 17-1, Feb. 13, 2013	—	—
Colombia *US Protested*	Decree No. 1436, June 13, 1984	LIS 103	Caribbean	
			5–6	75.4
			13–14	51.8
			14–15	81.6

Straight Baseline Segments (*cont.*)

State	Law and Date of Claim	Source of Analysis	Segment >40 nm	Length (nm) >40 nm
			Pacific	
			3–4	42.4
			4–5	76.8
			5–6	81.6
	Decree No. 1946, Sept. 9, 2013, Annex 8 to Nicaragua ICJ application [enabling legislation for Western Caribbean islands]. No coordinates available. Inferred from map of contiguous zone.	van de Poll	—	—
Congo, Dem. Rep.[a]	Law No. 09/002, May 7, 2009 LOSB No. 70, at 44	Lathrop	—	—
Costa Rica[a] *US Protested*	Law No. 18581-RE, Nov. 21, 1988 (Pacific Ocean)	LIS 111	9–10 11–12	88.0 47.0
Cote d'Ivoire[a]	Law No. 77-926, Nov. 17, 1977 [enabling legislation]	—	n/a	n/a
Croatia[a]	The Maritime Code, March, 1994, http://www.un.org/depts/los/LEGISLATIONANDTREATIES/PDFFILES/HRV_1994_Code.pdf, Art. 7, 19.	Blake, Topalović 10–12	—	—
Yugoslavia[a] [former; Croatia successor State]	Law No. 876, Dec. 8, 1948 Law, May 22, 1965	LIS 6	—	—
Cyprus[a]	Note Ref 2001/254, May 3, 1993 LOSIC No. 9, at 22 LOSB No. 24, at 6–9	Lathrop	—	—
Denmark[a]	Royal Ordinance No. 437, Dec. 21, 1966, modified by Royal Ordinance No. 189, April 19, 1978 Executive Order No. 242, Apr. 21, 1999, LOSB No. 40, at 18–28	LIS 19 rev.	—	—

Straight Baseline Segments (*cont.*)

State	Law and Date of Claim	Source of Analysis	Segment >40 nm	Length (nm) >40 nm
	Executive Order No. 680, July 18, 2003, LOSB No. 53, at 44–53 (coords. & map)	van de Poll	—	—
Denmark	Decree No. 156, April 24, 1963	LIS 13	2–3	44.0
Faroe Isl.			10–11	60.8
US Protested	Decree No. 128, April 1, 1976			
	Decree No. 598, Jan. 1, 1977			
	Executive Order No. 306, May 16, 2002; LOSB No. 53, at 53 (map showing 12 pts); LOSB No. 68, at 15–16 (map not showing turning pts)	van de Poll	4–5 (w. side) 9–10 (e. side)	44.0 61.29
Denmark Greenland	Executive Order No. 629, Jan. 1, 1977			
	Executive Order No. 176, May 14, 1980			
	Royal Decree No. 1004, Oct. 15, 2004, LOSB No. 56, at 126–132 (## 1–190 [mainland])	Andersen van de Poll	3–4	75.39
			19–20	42.08
			23–24	69.57
			30–31	47.90
			33–34	66.40
			40–41	62.68
			46–47	61.62
			49–50	60.98
			50–51	76.59
			59–60	43.95
			71–72	61.76
			88–89	43.08
			109–110	44.63
			125–126	54.41
			147–148	44.43
			149–150	40.05
			158–159	48.18
			161–162	42.38
			164–165	53.50

Straight Baseline Segments (*cont.*)

State	Law and Date of Claim	Source of Analysis	Segment >40 nm	Length (nm) >40 nm
			165–166	48.58
			170–171	48.71
			173–174	73.59
			174–175	41.55
			180–181	65.09
			182–183	40.78
			183–184	45.41
Djibouti[a]	Law No. 52/AN/78, Jan. 9, 1979			
US Protested	Decree No. 85–048 PR/PM, May 5, 1985, LOSB No. 39, at 21–22	LIS 113	—	—
Dominica[a]	Act No. 26, Aug. 25, 1981 [enabling legislation]	—	n/a	n/a
Dominican Republic[a]	Law No. 186, Sept. 6, 1967 Act No. 573, April 1, 1977	LIS 5	Escocesa bay	45.0
US & UK Protested	In 2007 claimed archipelagic status	LIS 130		
Ecuador[a] *UK Protested*	Legislative Decree Feb. 21, 1951 (Galapagos) (inferred) Decree Law No. 1542, Nov. 10, 1966			
US Protested *Spain, Sweden & Belgium protested*	Decree No. 959-A, July 13, 1971, reaffirmed in Declaration VI accompanying its instrument of accession to the LOS Convention on Sept. 12, 2012	LIS 42	Mainland	
			1–2	81
			2–3	136
			3–4	56
			4–5	72
Galapagos *US & Germany Protested*		Kopela 279	Galapagos	
			6–7	95
			7–8	54
			8–9	77
			9–10	48
			10–11	51
			11–12	66
			13–6	124

Straight Baseline Segments (*cont.*)

State	Law and Date of Claim	Source of Analysis	Segment >40 nm	Length (nm) >40 nm
Egypt[a]	Decree January 15, 1951	LIS 22	—	—
US Protested	Decree No. 27, Jan. 9, 1990, LOSB No. 16, at 3–11	LIS 116	—	—
Estonia[a]	Decision No. 62, March 10, 1993, LOSB No. 25, at 55–59 (replaces 1985 USSR SBL in LIS 109)	van de Poll/ Schofield	—	—
Fiji[a]				
Rotuma	Legal Notice No. 118, Nov. 1981, LOSB No. 66, at 66–67; PAS 43–44	van de Poll	—	—
	Legal Notice 83, Oct. 31, 2012 (transforming WGS 72 to ITRS2005)	LOSB 87		
Ceva-i-ra Rotuma archipelago	Legal Notice 82, Oct. 31, 2012	van de Poll	105–140 70–104	LWL
Finland[a]	Decree No. 464, Aug. 18, 1956	LIS 48	—	—
	Act 981/95, July 30, 1995, LOSIC No. 9, at 26, LOSB No. 29, at 56–61 (coords. & map)	van de Poll	—	—
France[a]	Mainland France and Corsica,	LIS 37	—	—
	Decree No. 2015-958 of 31 July 2015, LOSB 89 See generally <Limitesmaritimes.gouv.fr> for details on all French maritime spaces	van de Poll	—	—
French Departments and Dependencies:[a]				
Fr. Guiana	Decree No° 2015-1611, Dec. 8, 2015	van de Poll	—	—

Straight Baseline Segments (*cont.*)

State	Law and Date of Claim	Source of Analysis	Segment >40 nm	Length (nm) >40 nm
La Réunion	Decree No. 2014-1309, Oct. 30, 2014, MZN.109.2014, LOSB No. 86	van de Poll	—	—
Antilles françaises	Decree No. 2017-1511, Oct. 30, 2017	Kopela 124, van de Poll	—	—
Mayotte	Decree No. 2013-1177, Dec. 17, 2013, MZN.101.2013; LOSB No. 84	van de Poll	—	—
New Caledonia	Decree No. 2002-827, May 3, 2002, LOSB No. 53, at 58–66	Kopela 134, van de Poll	—	—
St. Pierre & Miquelon	Decree No. 2015-1528, Nov. 24, 2015	van de Poll/ Schofield	—	—
Fr. Southern & Antarctic Lands	Decree No. 2013-1175, Dec. 17, 2013, MZN.101.2013 (Saint-Paul Isl.), LOSB No. 84	van de Poll		
	Crozet Archipelago, Decree 2015-551 of 18 May 2015 (SBL & LWL)		—	—
	Kerguelen Isl., Decree No. 78-112, Jan. 11, 1978, replaced by		—	—
	Decree No. 2015-635 of 5 June	Kopela 117	—	—
	2015, LOSB 89 (SBL & LWL)	van de Poll	—	—
Fr. Polynesia	Decree No. 2012-1068, Sept. 18, 2012, LOSB 82, at 20–50	van de Poll	—	—
Wallis & Futuna	Decree No. 2013-1176, Dec. 17, 2013, MZN.101.2013, LOSB No. 84	van de Poll	—	—
Gabon[a]	Decree No. 02066/PR/ MHCUCDM, Dec. 4, 1992, LOSIC No. 11, at 41, LOSB No. 42, at 168–169, LOSB No. 50, at 65–67	van de Poll	D–E	66.83
Germany[a]	Notice to Mariners No. 2, Jan. 1969 [former GDR]	LIS 52	—	—

Straight Baseline Segments (*cont.*)

State	Law and Date of Claim	Source of Analysis	Segment >40 nm	Length (nm) >40 nm
Germany, Fed. Rep.	1970 Charts (replaced by:) Proclamation November 11, 1994, LOSB 27, at 55, 60–61	LIS 38 van de Poll	—	—
Guinea[a]	Decree No. 224/PRG/64, June 6, 1964	LIS 40	one	ca. 120
US Protested	Decree No. 336/PRG/80, July 30, 1980 (low water line) Decree D/2014/092/PRG/SGG of 11 April 2014, amended by Decree D/2015/122/PRG/SGG of 19 June 2015 (36 points; # 25–36 missing; DOALOS requested – SBL segments + LWL)	van de Poll		
Guinea-Bissau[a]	Decree Law No. 47,771, June 27, 1967 Decision No. 14/74, Dec. 31, 1974 Law No. 3/78, May 19, 1978	LIS 30	—	—
Senegal Protested	Act No. 2/85, May 17, 1985, LOSB No. 7, at 23	Kopela 79, 279	1–2	42.6
Haiti[a]	Decree, April 6, 1972	LIS 51	E–F	93.89
		van de Poll	I–J	111.64
Honduras[a] *El Salvador, Guatemala, Nicaragua & US Protested*	Exec. Decree No. PCM 007-2000, March 21, 2000, LOSIC No. 12, at 52, LOSB No. 43, at 96–100; LOSB No. 50, at 25–26	LIS 124 van de Poll	12–13 13–14 14–15	54.91 42.85 62.71
Iceland[a]	Regulations, March 19, 1952			
	Regulations, March 11, 1961	LIS 34 rev.	1–2	56.75
			9–10	57.70
			29–30	70.30
			31–32	74.10
			32–33	40.30
	Regulations, Sept. 9, 1972			

Straight Baseline Segments (*cont.*)

State	Law and Date of Claim	Source of Analysis	Segment >40 nm	Length (nm) >40 nm
	Law No. 41, June 1, 1979,	van de Poll	1–2	57.21
	http://www.un.org/Depts/los/		9–10	57.13
	LEGISLATIONANDTREATIES/		29–30	69.27
	PDFFILES/ISL_1979_Law.pdf		31–32	73.54
India[a]	Notifications of India, May 11,	Kopela 137	102–103	84.7
Pakistan	2009 and Nov. 20, 2009, LOSB		103–104	57
Protested	No. 71, at 31 (Andaman and		104–105	83
	Nicobar Isl.),			
	LOSB No. 72, at 80 (corr.)			
	(Lakshadweep Islands)		125–126	113.7
			127–128	109
Iran	Act, April 12, 1959			
US Protested	Decree No. 2/250–67, July 21, 1973			
US, EC, Qatar, Protested	Marine Areas Act, May 2, 1993	LIS 114	Group A	
		van de Poll	1–2	49.68
			2–3	61.26
			3–4	101.53
			4–5	113.36
			5–6	41.21
			Group B	
			7–8	43.07
			Group C	
			17–18	55.37
			23–24	45.68
Iraq[a]	Note to UN March 16, 2011, LOSB No. 77, at 15–17	Lathrop	—	—
Ireland[a]	Statutory Instrument No. 173 Act Jan. 1, 1960	LIS 3	—	—
Italy[a]	Decree No. 816, Apr. 26, 1977,	*Lines in the*	Gulf of Taranto	60.8
US Protested	LOSIC No. 9, at 31	*Sea* 88; van		
	UN: Baselines: National	de Poll		
	Legislation with Illustrative			
	Maps, pp. 201–206			

Straight Baseline Segments (*cont.*)

State	Law and Date of Claim	Source of Analysis	Segment >40 nm	Length (nm) >40 nm
Japan[a]	Enforcement Order No. 210 of	LIS 120	H–I (20–21)	51.99
	1977 as amended in 1993 and		D–A (28–29)	41.46
US Protested	1996		B–C (30–31)	54.27
	LOSIC No. 9, at 40; LOSIC No.		F–A (34–35)	41.72
	10, at 37; LOSIC No. 11, at 45		D–E (38–39)	55.81
	LOSB No. 35, at 76–90		I–J (43–44)	46.19
	Replaced in 2001		A–B (77–78)	57.21
			J–K (86–87)	62.27
			Q–R (93–94)	60.06
			S–T (95–96)	60.63
			T–U (96–97)	57.31
			A–B (128–129)	52.06
			C–D (131–132)	62.15
			F–G (135–136)	43.25
			G–H (136–137)	50.36
			I–J (138–139)	58.21
			R–S (146–147)	48.73
			S–T (147–148)	48.99
			T–U (148–149)	41.41
			U–V (149–150)	53.27
			AA–BB	40.37
			(170–171)	52.00
	Amended by Cabinet Order No.	van de Poll	2i–2j	54.25
	434 of 2001,		4c–4d	55.81
	LOSB No. 66, at 71–81		5c–5d	46.19
			5j–5k	52.05
			11a–11b	62.15
			12c–12d	80.84
			12h–12i	

Straight Baseline Segments (*cont.*)

State	Law and Date of Claim	Source of Analysis	Segment >40 nm	Length (nm) >40 nm
Kenya[a]	Territorial Waters Act, May 16, 1972 Presidential Proc. Feb. 29, 1979			
Somalia considers SBLs do not conform to article 7 UNCLOS	Presidential Proc. June 9, 2005, LOSIC No. 23, at 20, LOSB No. 61, at 96–97 CLCS Map 1 at http://www.un.org/depts/los/clcs_new/submissions_files/ken35_09/ken2009_map1.pdf	Lathrop van de Poll	Mwamba Haasani-Mwamba wa Punju Leopard Reef-Jumba la Mtwana	45.76 45.76
Korea, Rep. of[a]	Decree No. 9162, Sept 20, 1978, as amended by Decrees No. 13463, Sept. 7, 1991;	LIS 82	7–8 13–14 17–18	46.09 60.30 46.09
US Protested	No. 15133 July 31, 1996, LOSB No. 33, at 50–51.	LIS 121	7–8 13–14 17–18	46.1 60.3 Not id.
	Decree No. 17803 Dec. 18, 2002 LOSB No. 51, at 88–92 (cords. & map) (no significant change with 3 segments > 40 nm)	van de Poll	7–8 13–14 17–18	46.09 61.78 53.91
Latvia[a]	Regulation No. 779, Aug. 17, 2010, LOSB No. 76, at 15–27	Lathrop	—	—
Libya *US Protested*	Foreign Ministry *note verbale* MQ/40/5/1/3345, Oct. 1973			
	Decision No. 104, June 20, 2005, LOSB No. 59, at 15–18	van de Poll/ Schofield	17–18 (Gulf of Sidra)	300.27
Lithuania[a]	Act on the State Boundary, June 25, 1992, LOSB No. 25, at 75			
	Resolution No. 1597, Dec. 6, 2004 LOSB No. 61, at 17–21	Lathrop	n/a LWL	n/a LWL

Straight Baseline Segments (*cont.*)

State	Law and Date of Claim	Source of Analysis	Segment >40 nm	Length (nm) >40 nm
Madagascar[a]	Decree No. 63–131, Feb. 27, 1963	LIS 15	3–4	60.70
	Act No. 99–028, Feb. 3, 2000, LOSIC No. 17, at 59 (map), LOSB No. 51, at 93–94 (map) (coordinates not changed)	van de Poll	4–5	58.60
			5–6	87.50
			6–7	123.57
			8–9	70.66
			9–10	48.81
			13–14	45.63
			14–15	43.22
			16–17	61.13
			22–23	44.63
			24–25	54.02
			26–27	69.46
			30–31	65.40
			36–37	117.47
			38–1	62.62
Malaysia[a]	Ordinance No. 7, Aug. 1969 [enabling legislation]			
	Baselines of Maritime Zones Act 2006, May 1, 2007 [enabling legislation]			
	Inferred from joint submission to CLCS by Malaysia and Vietnam.	van de Poll/ Schofield	Sarawak	
			1–2	ca.54.57
			2–3	ca.79.65
	No official map illustrating baselines for peninsular Malaysia yet available		4–5	ca.112.05
			5–6	ca.88.39
			Sabah	
			12–13	ca.65.41
			14–15	ca.100.40

Straight Baseline Segments (*cont.*)

State	Law and Date of Claim	Source of Analysis	Segment >40 nm	Length (nm) >40 nm
Malta[a]	Act No. XXXII, Dec. 7, 1971, as amended in 1975, 1978, 1981, 2002 [enabling legislation]			
	Sketch map No. 2 in Malta Memorial vol. III, ICJ Proceedings Libya/Malta vol. V (no coordinates)	van de Poll	—	—
Mauritania[a]	Law 67-023, Jan. 21, 1967	LIS 8	Blanc-Timiris	87.62
	Law 78,043, Feb. 28, 1978	van de Poll		
US Protested	Law 88-120, Aug. 31, 1988, LOSB No. 13, at 36 (SBL unchanged)			
Mauritius[a]	Territorial Seas Act, April 16, 1970	LIS 41	—	—
	Maritime Zones Act 2005, No. 2, Feb. 28, 2005; Prime Minister Regulations 2005, Aug. 5, 2005	LIS 140	Archipelagic and straight	—
Mexico[a]	Decree, Aug. 28, 1968	LIS 4	—	—
US Protested	[Gulf of California]			
	Decree, Jan. 8, 1986 reiterates claim w/o list of coordinates [Gulf of California]	van de Poll	—	—
Montenegro[a]	Maritime and Inland Navigation Law, 12/98, 1998.	Blake, Topalović 10–12, Grbec	—	—
Mozambique[a]	Decree Law 47,771, June 27, 1967	LIS 29	4–5	41.0
			18–19	60.4
			25–26	45.5
			27–28	44.6
	Law 4/96, Jan. 4. 1996, Gazette, Jan. 4, 1996, at 10–15 (in Portuguese) (coords.) same as 1967.	van de Poll	4–5	40.74
			18–19	59.80
			25–26	45.72
			27–28	44.54

Straight Baseline Segments (*cont.*)

State	Law and Date of Claim	Source of Analysis	Segment >40 nm	Length (nm) >40 nm
Nauru[a]	Sea Boundaries Act, Aug. 12, 1997, Proclamation, LOSIC No. 10, at 31 map), LOSB No. 41, at 21–23, 44 (coords. and map)	Melchoir	—	—
Netherlands[a]	Territorial Sea (Demarcation) Act, Jan. 9, 1985, LOSB No. 6, at 16–18	Melchoir	—	—
Netherlands Antilles	Territorial Sea Act, Jan. 9, 1985, LOSB No. 7, at 68–71	Melchoir	—	—
Nicaragua[a] *Costa Rica, Colombia & US Protested*	Decree No. 33-2013, Aug. 27, 2013, LOSB No. 83, at 35–36	Lathrop van de Poll	4–5 6–7 8–9	72.33 43.54 83.33
Norway[a]	Royal Decree, July 12, 1935 Royal Decree, July 18, 1952 Royal Decree June 14, 2002; LOSIC No. 16, at 34–35 LOSIC No. 19, at 57–58 LOSB No. 49, at 51–55	Melchior	NM19–NM20 NM49–NM50 NM65–NM66 NM94–NM95	44 45.5 44.5 42
Norwegian Dependencies:				
Jan Mayen[a]	Royal Decree, June 30, 1955 Royal decree Aug. 30, 2002 LOSIC No. 16, at 37; LOSIC No. 19, at 61; LOSB No. 50, at 22–24; LOSB No. 54, at 81–88, 96	Melchoir	—	—
Svalbard[a]	Royal Decree, July 18, 1952 Royal Decree June 1, 2001 LOSIC No. 14, at 35; LOSIC No. 19, at 59–60; LOSIC No. 21, at 13; LOSB No. 46, at 72–80; LOSB No. 49, at 79–80; LOSB No. 54, at 41–80, 94–95	LIS 39 Kopela 134, 274	— —	— —

Straight Baseline Segments (*cont.*)

State	Law and Date of Claim	Source of Analysis	Segment >40 nm	Length (nm) >40 nm
Bouvet Isl.	Royal Decree, Feb. 25, 2005 LOSB No. 60, at 49–55	Melchior	—	—
Oman[a] *Iran & US Protested*	Royal Decree 38/82, June 1, 1982, LOSB No. 1, at 35–37	LIS 113	—	—
Pakistan[a] *India & US Protested*	S.R.O. 714(I) 96, Aug. 29, 1996 LOSIC No. 10, at 39 LOSB No. 34, at 45	LIS 118 van de Poll	c–d d–e f–g g–h	81.70 40.19 85.22 70.81
Peru	Law No. 28621, Nov. 3, 2005, LOSB No. 64, at 15–33; as amended by Law No. 29687, May 19, 2011	Lathrop	0–1[270] 31–32 42–43	52 41 51
Portugal[a]	Decree-Law No. 47,771, June 27, 1967 (mainland), repealed by Decree Law No. 495/85, Nov. 29, 1985 (Table I) UN, Baselines: National Legislation with Illustrative Maps (1989), pp. 260–266 (Tables I–V and map)	LIS 27 van de Poll	— 1–2: Ver-o-Mar – mouth of Vouga River (North jetty) 3–4: Cabo Mondego (Pedra da Nau) – Farilhoes(Pedra Grande) Farilhoes (Pedra Grande)	— 46.20 51.45

270 Peru's 2011 law amending its 2005 law added the Peruvian "half" of the closing line across the Gulf of Guayquil, here referred to as line 0–1.

Straight Baseline Segments (*cont.*)

State	Law and Date of Claim	Source of Analysis	Segment >40 nm	Length (nm) >40 nm
			10–11: Cabo de Sines – Cabo de Sao Vicente (Pedra do Gigante)	54.11
			12–13: Ponta de Sagres – Cabo de Santa Maria (Barreta Isl.)	51.28
Azores *US Protested*	Decree Law No. 495/85, Nov. 29, 1985, LOSIC No. 9, at 47 (Madeira Table II) & Azores (Tables III–V)	Kopela 131, 284 van de Poll	Azores: Ilhéu da Vila – Ponta da Candelaria	62.08
Romania[a]	Act, Aug. 7, 1990, LOSB No. 19, at 9, 20	Lathrop	—	—
Russian Federation [former Soviet Union/USSR[a]] *US Protested*	Decree, Feb. 7, 1984, http://www.un.org/Depts/los/LEGISLATIONANDTREATIES/PDFFILES/RUS_1984_Declaration.pdf, pp. 1–10 (continental coastline and islands of the Pacific Ocean, the Sea of Japan, the Sea of Okhotsk and the Bering Sea), 12 (Sakhalin Island), 12–16 (Kurils), 16 (Komandorski Islands). Peter the Great Bay #1–2	LIS 107 van de Poll	1–2	106.74
			36–37	41.09
			38–39	60.67
			68–69	45.41
			105–106	71.66
			106–107	103.84
			108–109	81.49
			112–113	62.37
			113–114	43.90
			114–115	44.09
			115–116	75.4

Straight Baseline Segments (*cont.*)

State	Law and Date of Claim	Source of Analysis	Segment >40 nm	Length (nm) >40 nm
US Protested	Decree, Jan. 15, 1985, http://www.un.org/Depts/los/LEGISLATIONANDTREATIES/PDFFILES/RUS_1985_Declaration.pdf, pp. 1–35 (Arctic)	LIS 109 van de Pol	Black Sea Arctic	None
			25–26	84.40
			32–33	43.59
			162–163	62.50
			169–170	43.70
			173–174	65.70
			174–175	44.11
			185–186	40.56
			188–189	40.56
			194–195	60.08
			349–350	41.87
			383–384	42.29
Samoa	Maritime Zones Order 21 April 2014, LOSB 88 http://www.un.org/Depts/los/LEGISLATIONANDTREATIES/PDFFILES/WSM_2015_MaritimeZ.pdf	van de Poll	—	—
Saudi Arabia[a]	Royal Decree No. 33, Feb. 16, 1958	LIS 20	—	—
Iran, Egypt, UAE Protested	Council of Ministers Resolution No. 15, Jan. 11, 2010 and Royal Decree No. M/4 Jan. 26, 2010, LOSB No. 72, at 81–86 (coords. & map)	van de Poll	RS96–RS97	47.75
Senegal[a]	Decree 72-765, July 5, 1972	LIS 54	—	—
US Protested	Decree 90-670, June 18, 1990, LOSB No. 20, at 23–25	van de Poll	—	—

Straight Baseline Segments (*cont.*)

State	Law and Date of Claim	Source of Analysis	Segment >40 nm	Length (nm) >40 nm
Slovenia[a]	Maritime Code, March 23, 2001, http://www.un.org/depts/los/LEGISLATIONANDTREATIES/PDFFILES/SVN_2001_maritimecode.pdf , Art. 13/2 (bays). See also http://www.un.org/depts/los/LEGISLATIONANDTREATIES/PDFFILES/communications/NV016_SVN.pdf (coords. & maps)	Blake, Topalović 10–12	—	—
South Africa[a]	Maritime Zones Act No. 15 of 1994 LOSB No. 32, at 81 (segment #s added)	van de Poll	39–40 48–49 50–51 53–54	44.03 41.16 71.45 40.56
Spain[a] (mainland)	Act 20/1967, Apr. 1967 [enabling legislation] Decree No. 627/1976, Mar. 5, 1977	—	n/a	n/a
	Decree No. 2510/1977, Aug. 5, 1977; UN, Baselines: National Legislation with Illustrative Maps, pp. 281–293	van de Poll	Puerto de Sangunto – Pensiccola Punta de la Ensenada – Punta Grieta (Algranza)	51.09 43.35
Balearic Isl.			—	—

Straight Baseline Segments (*cont.*)

State	Law and Date of Claim	Source of Analysis	Segment >40 nm	Length (nm) >40 nm
Canary Islands	Law 44/2010, Dec. 30, 2010 See Kopela 127, 128, 282 (sketch maps)	van de Poll (based on Kopela sketch map)	Gran Canaria – Tenerife	55.60
			Tenerife – Hierro	72.94
			Hierro – Palma	61.73
			Palma – Tenerife	88.49
			Tenerife – Gran Canaria	44.82
			Gran Canaria – Lanzarotte	98.93
			Lanzarotte – Fuerteventura	51.44
			Fuerteventura – Gran Canaria	68.63
Sudan[a] *US Protested*	Act No. 106, Dec. 31, 1970 [enabling legislation]	—	n/a	n/a
Egypt Protested	Decree No. 148 (2017), March 2, 2017, LOSB No. 94, pp. 15–16, 20–23 (2017)	van de Poll	6–7	52.14
			7–8	67.97
			9–10	70.01
			10–11	69.22
Sweden[a]	Royal Notice No. 375, July 1, 1966 (amended in 1978, 1979 – no change in SBL)	LIS 47	—	—
Syria	Legislative Decree No. 304, Dec. 28, 1963	LIS 53	—	—
	Law No. 28, Nov. 8, 2003 [enabling legislation], LOSB No. 55, at 14–20	—	n/a	n/a

Straight Baseline Segments (*cont.*)

State	Law and Date of Claim	Source of Analysis	Segment >40 nm	Length (nm) >40 nm
Taiwan[271]	Notice to Mariners No. 19, Mar. 22, 1999	LIS 127, van de Poll	T8–T9	109.06
			T13–T14	74.20
			T14–T15	42.44
			T15–T16	45.32
			T17–T18	44.21
			T18–T19	48.04
			T19–T20	62.23
	ROC Amended Decree of Nov. 18, 2009	Melchoir	T7–T8	110.5
			T13–T14	73.5
			T14–T15	43.0
			T15–T16	45.3
			T17–T18	44.2
			T18–T19	47.7
			T19–T20	62.5
Tanzania[a]	Notice No. 209, Aug. 24, 1973 Territorial Sea & Exclusive Economic Zone Act of 1989, Oct. 1989			
	Note to UN Aug. 2, 2012, LOSB No. 80, at 32–33	Lathrop, van de Poll	VITO–ZANZ	69.58
			LATH–MAFI	44.25
			MFSE–NJOV	49.22
			SONM–LIND	45.95
			LIND–MSI2	45.26
Thailand[a] *US Protested*	Announcement June 12, 1970, replaced by Announcement pub. Aug. 18, 1993	LIS 31	A–B	59.15
		LIS 122	Area 4: 1–2	81.4
		Kopela 269	Area 4: 2–3	98.4
EU & US Protested	Announcement Aug. 11, 1992, LOSB No. 23, at 29–31 Announcement Aug. 17, 1992, LOSB No. 25, at 83–84		Area 4: 3–4	65.3

271 This table expresses no opinion on whether Taiwan is an entity referred to in the international law of the sea. Taiwan's maritime claims as at 2005 were analyzed in Department of State (USA), *Taiwan's Maritime Claims* (Limits in the Seas No. 127) (Department of State, Washington: 2005) and J. Ashley Roach, "An International Law Analysis of Taiwan's Maritime Claims" (2005) 2 *Taiwan International Law Quarterly* 249–321.

Straight Baseline Segments (*cont.*)

State	Law and Date of Claim	Source of Analysis	Segment >40 nm	Length (nm) >40 nm
Tunisia[a]	Decree No. 73-527, Nov. 3, 1973 LOSIC No. 9, at 53 [European datum 1950]	Melchoir, van de Poll	6k–7 (closing Gulf of Gabes)	45.21
Ukraine[a]	List of geographic coordinates, Nov. 11, 1992, LOSB No. 36, at 49–52	Melchoir	—	—
United Arab Emirates *Saudi Arabia Protested*	Federal Law No. 19, Oct. 1993 Decision 5/2009, Jan. 14, 2009 LOSB No. 69, at 78–80	Lathrop	—	—
United Kingdom[a]	Order in Council, Sept. 25, 1964 Territorial Waters (Amendment) Order 1979 redefining points 1–27 between Cape Wrath and the Mull of Kintyre	LIS 23, van de Poll	1–2	40.25 40.06
	Territorial Sea (Baselines) Order 2014 (Statutory Instrument 2014 No. 1353), May 27, 2014, defining points 1–28 between Cape Wrath and Laggan	van de Poll	1–2	40.039
U.K. Overseas Territories:				
Turks& Caicos	Statutory Instrument 1989 No. 1996 Turks and Caicos Islands (Territorial Sea) Amendment Order 1998, No. 1260, Statutory Instrument 1989 No. 1993	Kopela 133, 281	—	—
Falkland Isl.	Statutory Instrument 1989 No. 1995	van de Poll, Kopela 123, 276	12–13	41.23
So. Georgia Isl.	Statutory Instrument 1989 No. 1995	van de Poll	—	—

Straight Baseline Segments (*cont.*)

State	Law and Date of Claim	Source of Analysis	Segment >40 nm	Length (nm) >40 nm
Uruguay[a]	Law No. 17.033, Nov. 20, 1998, Annexes I and II, LOSIC No. 10, at 44, LOSB No. 41, at 51–52	LIS 123 van de Poll	1–2	59.92
Venezuela	Decree, July 10, 1956			
US Protested	Decree, July 10, 1968	LIS 21	A–B	98.9
Vietnam[a]	Statement, Nov. 12, 1982,	LIS 99	A1–A2	99.24
China, US,	LOSB No. 1, at 74–75	van de Poll	A2–A3	105.19
France, Germany,			A5–A6	161.33
Singapore,			A6–A7	161.84
Thailand			A8–A9	60.24
Protested			A9–A10	89.47
			A10–A11	149.00
US Protested	Law No. 18/2012/QH13, June 21, 2012		—	None new
Yemen[a]	Act No. 45 of 1977, Jan. 15, 1978 [enabling legislation]	—	n/a	n/a
	Law No. 26 (2014), LOSB 88, http://www.un.org/Depts/los/LEGISLATIONANDTREATIES/STATEFILES/YEM.htm (SBL & LWL)	van de Poll	—	—

[a] Party to LOS Convention

Appendix 1 Data Summary

Total number of coastal States = 150 (not including Cook Islands, Niue, Palestine and Taiwan)

Total number of coastal States with dependencies (overseas territories, departments) = 6

- Denmark, with 2 dependencies
- France, with 10 dependencies
- Netherlands, with one dependency
- Norway, with 3 dependencies
- Spain, with one dependency
- UK, with 3 dependencies

Total States with all SBL segments < 40 nm = 42
Total States with one or more SBL segments > 40 nm = 49 (+ Taiwan)
Total States claiming SBL segments = 91 (including their 9 dependencies)
Total States with only enabling legislation = 3
State whose legislation remains to be analyzed: Guinea (2015)
Total number of SBL segments worldwide > 40 nm = 264 (+ Taiwan (7)):
Total number of SBL segments worldwide between 40–50 nm = 83

> Brazil, Burma, Canada (3), Chile (4), China (4), Colombia, Costa Rica, Cuba, Denmark (16), Dominican Republic, Ecuador, Guinea-Bissau, Honduras, Iceland, Iran (4), Kenya (2), Madagascar (4), Mozambique (3), Nicaragua, Norway (4), Pakistan, Peru, Portugal, ROK, Saudi Arabia, Spain (3), South Africa (2), Tanzania (4), Tunisia, UK (2), Russian Federation (11) + Taiwan (4) (32 States)

Total number of SBL segments worldwide between 51–60 nm = 52

> Argentina, Brazil (4), Burma, , Canada, Chile (3), China, Colombia, Cuba (4), Denmark (3), Ecuador (3), Honduras, Iceland (2), India, Iran, Italy, Japan (4), Madagascar (3), Malaysia, Mozambique, Peru, Portugal (3), ROK, Spain (3), Sudan, Thailand, Uruguay, Russian Federation (2), Vietnam (29 States)

Total number of SBL segments worldwide between 61–70 nm = 46

> Argentina (2), Bangladesh, Brazil (3), Canada, Chile (2), China (5), Cuba, Ecuador, Denmark (8), Gabon, Honduras, Iceland, Iran, Japan, Madagascar (3), Malaysia, Pakistan, Portugal, ROK, Spain (2), Sudan (3), Tanzania, Thailand, Russian Federation (3) + Taiwan (24 States)

Total number of SBL segments worldwide between 71–80 nm = 25

> Bangladesh, Brazil, Burma (2), Canada, China (5), Colombia (2), Denmark (3), Ecuador (2), Iceland, Japan, Malaysia, Nicaragua, South Africa, Spain, Russian Federation (2) + Taiwan (15 States)

Total number of SBL segments worldwide between 81–90 nm = 24

> Brazil (2), China (4), Colombia (2), Costa Rica, Ecuador, India (2), Japan, Madagascar, Malaysia, Mauritania, Nicaragua, Pakistan (2), Spain, Thailand, Russian Federation (2), Vietnam (16 States)

Total number of SBL segments worldwide between 91–100 nm = 9

Canada (2), Ecuador, Haiti, Malaysia, Spain, Thailand, Venezuela, Vietnam (8 States)

Total number of SBL segments worldwide between 101–110 nm = 8

China (2), India, Iran, Malaysia, Russian Federation (2), Vietnam + Taiwan (6 States)

Total number of SBL segments worldwide between 111–120 nm = 6

Brazil, Haiti, India, Iran, Madagascar, Malaysia (6 States)

Total number of SBL segments worldwide between 121–130 nm = 3

China, Ecuador, Madagascar (3 States)

Total number of SBL segments worldwide between 131–140 nm = 2

Argentina, Ecuador (2 States)

Total number of SBL segments worldwide between 141–150 nm = 1

Vietnam

Total number of SBL segments worldwide between 151–160 nm = 0
Total number of SBL segments worldwide between 161–170 nm = 2

Vietnam (2)

Total number of SBL segments worldwide between 171–180 nm = 0
Total number of SBL segments worldwide between 181–190 nm = 1

Brazil

Total number of SBL segments worldwide between 191–200 nm = 0
Total number of SBL segments worldwide between 201–210 nm = 0
Total number of SBL segments worldwide between 211–220 nm = 0
Total number of SBL segments worldwide between 221–230 nm = 1

Burma (222.3 nm)

Total number of SBL segments worldwide >300 nm = 1

Libya (300.27 nm)

D Appendix 2

Straight Baselines State Practice

States	Dep	SB <40nm	SB 40–50nm	SB >50nm	Protests
1. Albania		X			
2. Algeria		X			
3. Angola		X			
4. Argentina		X		X – 3	USA
5. Australia		X			
6. Bangladesh		X		X – 2	
7. Barbados					
8. Belize		X			
9. Brazil			X – 1	X – 12	
10. Bulgaria		X			
11. Cambodia				X – 1	
12. Cameroon		X			
13. Canada			X – 3	X – 5	EC, USA
14. Chile			X – 4	X – 5	
15. China		X	X – 3	X – 17	Vietnam, USA
16. Colombia		X	X – 1	X – 5	USA
17. Congo, Dem Rep		X			
18. Costa Rica			X – 1	X – 1	USA
19. Cote d'Ivoire					
20. Croatia		X			
21. Cuba				X – 5	USA
22. Cyprus		X			
23. Denmark	2		X – 11	X – 13	USA (Faroe Is)
24. Djibouti		X			
25. Dominica					

Straight Baselines State Practice (*cont.*)

States		Dep	SB <40nm	SB 40–50nm	SB >50nm	Protests
26.	Dominican Republic (AS)					UK, USA
27.	Ecuador			X – 1	X – 10	Belgium, Germany, Spain, Sweden, UK, USA
28.	Egypt		X			
29.	Estonia		X			
30.	Fiji (AS)		X			
31.	Finland		X			
32.	France	10	X			
33.	Gabon				X -1	
34.	Germany		X			
35.	Guinea					USA
36.	Guinea-Bissau			X – 1		Senegal
37.	Haiti				X – 2	
38.	Honduras			X – 1	X – 2	El Salvador, Guatemala, Nicaragua, USA
39.	Iceland				X – 4	
40.	India				X – 5	Pakistan
41.	Iran			X – 4	X – 4	EC, Qatar, USA
42.	Iraq		X			
43.	Ireland		X			
44.	Italy				X – 1	USA
45.	Japan			X – 9	X – 20	USA
46.	Kenya			X – 2		Somalia
47.	Korea, Rep			X – 1	X – 2	USA
48.	Latvia		X			
49.	Libya				X -1	USA
50.	Lithuania					
51.	Madagascar			X – 4	X – 11	
52.	Malaysia				X – 6	
53.	Malta		X			
54.	Mauritania				X – 1	
55.	Mauritius (AS)		X			

Straight Baselines State Practice (*cont.*)

States		Dep	SB <40nm	SB 40–50nm	SB >50nm	Protests
56.	Mexico		X			
57.	Montenegro		X			
58.	Mozambique			X – 3	X – 1	
59.	Myanmar		X	X -1	X – 4	Bangladesh, UK, USA
60.	Nauru		X			
61.	Netherlands	1	X			
62.	Nicaragua			X – 1	X – 2	Colombia, Costa Rica, USA
63.	Norway	3		X – 4		
64.	Oman		X			
65.	Pakistan			X – 1	X – 3	India, USA
66.	Peru			X – 1	X – 2	
67.	Portugal			X – 1	X – 4	USA
68.	Romania		X			
69.	Russian Federation			X – 11	X – 11	USA
70.	Samoa		X			
71.	Saudi Arabia			X – 1		Egypt, Iran, UAE
72.	Senegal		X			
73.	Slovenia		X			
74.	Somalia		X			
75.	South Africa			X – 3	X – 1	
76.	Spain	1		X – 2	X – 8	
77.	Sudan				X – 4	Egypt, USA
78.	Sweden		X			
79.	Syria					
80.	Taiwan*			X – 5	X – 3	
81.	Tanzania			X – 4	X – 1	
82.	Thailand				X – 4	EU, USA
83.	Tunisia			X – 1		
84.	UAE		X			
85.	UK	3		X – 2		
86.	Ukraine		X			
87.	Uruguay				X – 1	
88.	Venezuela				X – 1	USA

Straight Baselines State Practice (*cont.*)

States	Dep	SB <40nm	SB 40–50nm	SB >50nm	Protests
89. Vietnam				X – 7	China, France, Germany, Singapore, Thailand, USA
90. Yemen		X			
Totals		41	29–88	41–197	

Key: Dep – Dependencies; SB – Straight Baselines; AS – Archipelagic State

* This table expresses no opinion on whether Taiwan is an entity referred to in the international law of the sea.

E *Appendix 3*

Archipelagic States[272]

No	State	Legislation/ Proclamation	Date	No	Ratio	% ABL >100nm	ABL <125nm	Art. 47 Compliant
1	Antigua and Barbuda	Maritime Areas Act 1982 (Act No. 18)	01/09/1982	1	7.91:1	0/22: 0%	Yes	Yes

272 Rothwell and Stephens, *The International Law of the Sea* 2nd (2016) 198–199 based on data from Roach and Smith, *Excessive Maritime Claims* 3rd (2012) 206–208, as updated by Department of State (United States), *Limits in the Sea* No. 98, 101, 125, 126, 128, 129, 130, 131, 132, 133, 134, 135, 136, 137, 138, 139, 140, 141, 142; United Nations, *Law of the Sea Bulletin* No. 86, 87, 91.

Archipelagic States (*cont.*)

No	State	Legislation/ Proclamation	Date	No	Ratio	% ABL >100nm	ABL <125nm	Art. 47 Compliant
2	The Bahamas	The Archipelagic Waters and Maritime Jurisdiction 1993; modified by The Archipelagic Waters and Maritime Jurisdiction (Archipelagic Baselines) Order 2008	04/01/1996; 08/12/2008	1	6.86:1	2/95: 2.11%	Yes	Yes
3	Cape Verde	Decree Law No. 60/IV 92	21/12/1982	1	8.92:1	0/25: 0%	Yes	Yes
4	Comoros	Law No. 82-005 (1982); Presidential Decree No. 10-092 (2010)	06/05/1982; 13/08/2010	1	5.99:1	0/13: 0%	Yes	Yes
5	Dominican Republic	Act 66-07 (2007)	22/05/2007	1	1.03:1 (cf. UK, US)	0/20: 0%	Yes	Yes (cf. UK, US)
6	Fiji	Marine Spaces Act 1978; Marine Spaces (Archipelagic Baselines and Exclusive Economic Zone) Order, Legal Notice No. 117 of 1981	01/12/1981	2	4.00:1 0.88:1	1/68:0.01% 0/35:0%	Yes	Yes

Archipelagic States (*cont.*)

No	State	Legislation/ Proclamation	Date	No	Ratio	% ABL >100nm	ABL <125nm	Art. 47 Compliant
7	Grenada	Territorial Sea and Maritime Boundaries Act 1989; Statutory Rules and Orders No. 31 of 1992	25/04/1989; 16/12/1992	1	1.61:1	0/23: 0%	Yes	Yes
8	Indonesia	List of geographical coordinates of points of archipelagic baselines, Government Regulation No. 38 of 2002 (as amended by Government Regulation No. 37 of 2008)	19/05/2008	1	1.61:1	5/197: 2.6%	Yes	Yes
9	Jamaica	The Maritime Areas Act, 1996; Exclusive Economic Zone (Baselines) Regulation (1992)	12/10/1982	1	2.00:1	0/28: 0%	Yes	Yes
10	Kiribati	Maritime Zones (Declaration) Act 2011; Baselines around the Archipelagos of Kiribati Regulations 2014	01/07/2011; 04/11/2014	2	9.31:1 8.04:1	0/58 0/55	Yes	No

Archipelagic States (*cont.*)

No	State	Legislation/ Proclamation	Date	No	Ratio	% ABL >100nm	ABL <125nm	Art. 47 Compliant
11	Maldives	Maritime Zones Act No. 6/96	27/06/1996	1	2.63: 1	3/37: 8.1%	Yes	No
12	Marshall Islands	Republic of the Marshall Islands Maritime Zones Declaration Act 2016; Baselines and Maritime Zones Outer Limits Declaration 2016	18/03/2016; 18/04/2016	2	9.27:1 8.45:1	0/22:0% 1/42:0.02%	Yes	No
13	Mauritius	Maritime Zones Act 2005; Maritime Zones (Baselines and Delineating Lines) Regulations 2005	05/08/2005	2	2.84:1 7.5:1	0/3: 0% 0/32: 0%	Yes	Yes
14	Papua New Guinea	National Sea Act 1977; Offshore Seas Proclamation 1978; Declaration of the baselines by method of coordinates of base points for purposes of the location of archipelagic baselines 2002	25/07/2002	1	1.22:1	1/74: 1.35%	No: 1 × 174.78 nm	No

Archipelagic States (*cont.*)

No	State	Legislation/ Proclamation	Date	No	Ratio	% ABL >100nm	ABL <125nm	Art. 47 Compliant
15	Philippines	Republic Act No. 3046 (1961); Republic Act No. 9522 (2009)	10/03/2009	1	1.98:1	3/101: 2.97%	Yes	Yes
16	Saint Vincent and the Grenadines	Archipelagic Closing Lines and Baselines of Saint Vincent and the Grenadines (Notice No. 60/2014)	01/04/2014	1	3.81:1	0/33: 0%	Yes	Yes
17	Sao Tome and Principe	Law No. 1/98	31/03/1998	1	4.03:1	0/14: 0%	Yes	Yes
18	Seychelles	Maritime Zones Act 1999; Maritime Zones (Baselines) Order, 2008 (as amended)	06/11/2008	4	10.5:1 239:1 44.5:1 5.15:1	0/45:0% 0/48:0% 0/29:0% 0/35:0%	Yes	No
19	Solomon Islands	The Delimitation of Marine Waters Act (No. 32 of 1978); Declaration of Archipelagos of Solomon Islands, 1979	31/08/1979	5	4.06:1 4.44:1 29.9:1 7.03:1 3.57:1	1/37: 1.2% 0/10: 0% 0/13: 0% 0/15: 0% 0/8: 0%	Yes	No

Archipelagic States (*cont.*)

No	State	Legislation/ Proclamation	Date	No	Ratio	% ABL >100nm	ABL <125nm	Art. 47 Compliant
20	Trinidad and Tobago	Archipelagic Waters and Exclusive Economic Zone Act (No. 24 of 1986)	11/11/1986	1	1.39:1	0/11: 0%	Yes	Yes
21	Tuvalu	Tuvalu Maritime Areas Act 2012; Declaration of Archipelagic Baselines 2012	04/05/2012 22/11/2012	1	7.58:1	0/60:0%	Yes	Yes
22	Vanuatu	Maritime Zones Act (No. 6 of 2010); Amendments of the Schedule of the Maritime Act (29 July 2009)	18/06/2009	1	5.83: 1	0/59:0%	Yes	Yes

Key
No – number of archipelagic straight baseline systems used to enclose islands and parts of islands of the archipelagic State
Ratio – whether the straight baseline systems are consistent with the area of water to land ratio of 9:1 to 1:1 in Article 47(1)
SBL <125nm – whether all of the archipelagic baselines are less than the maximum length of 125nm

F *Resolution 1/2018: Committee on Baselines under the International Law of the Sea*

The 78th Conference of the International Law Association, held in Sydney, Australia, 19–24 August 2018:

HAVING CONSIDERED the Report of the Committee on Baselines under the International Law of the Sea, including the dissenting view;

APPRECIATING the work done by the Committee in identifying the existing law concerning straight baselines and archipelagic baselines and assessing the need for further clarification or development of that law;

ADOPTS the Sydney Conclusions on Baselines under the International Law of the Sea annexed to this Resolution;

REQUESTS the Secretary-General of the International Law Association to forward a copy of this Resolution and its annex to the Secretary-General of the United Nations with the request that they be brought to the attention of States Parties to the United Nations Convention on the Law of the Sea and other interested States;

ALSO REQUESTS the Secretary-General of the International Law Association to forward a copy of this Resolution and its annex to the Registrar of the International Court of Justice, the Registrar of the International Tribunal for the Law of the Sea, and the Secretary-General of the Permanent Court of Arbitration;

RECOMMENDS to the Executive Council that the Committee on Baselines under the International Law of the Sea, having accomplished its mandate, be dissolved.

G *Annex: Sydney Conclusions on Baselines under the International Law of the Sea*

1. There is no agreed single interpretation of Article 7 of the 1982 UN Convention on the Law of the Sea ('LOSC') and there is no new rule of customary international law on straight baselines. Notwithstanding significant evidence of variations in state practice, many straight baselines when considered in their distinct geographic settings are in general conformity with Article 7 consistent with the indeterminate concepts that it contains.

2. The terms 'deeply indented and cut into' in Article 7(1) are criteria that are not subject to absolute precision in their interpretation. A variety of geographical factors can be taken into account in order to determine whether the particular coastline in question is one that is deeply indented and cut into, which may involve the application of a proportionality test.

3. The Article 7(1) reference to a 'fringe of islands' can be applied flexibly so as to take into account multiple different island configurations that may be located offshore a mainland. Each island must meet the criteria set by Article 121. There is no provision in the LOSC, consistency in state practice, or assessment by international courts and tribunals as to the distance between a fringe of islands and the mainland; rather the proximity of the islands to the coast is controlled by the general criteria within

Article 7. A clear distinction exists between Article 7 straight baselines being drawn to and from and between islands, and Article 47 straight archipelagic baselines, and coastal States need to be mindful of this limitation. Artificial islands or low-tide elevations without a lighthouse or similar installation cannot be utilised for the purpose of drawing Article 7 straight baselines to and from the mainland, or between the islands that comprise the 'fringe'.

4. Article 7(2) is to be read independently, and not cumulatively, with Article 7(1). The historic basis for this provision is separate and distinct from the criteria outlined in Article 7(1). Articles 7(1) and 7(2) each should be read cumulatively with Articles 7(3)–(6). The 'general direction' criterion in Article 7(3) is devoid of any mathematical precision, and is qualified by the words 'to any appreciable extent' which would permit a margin of appreciation for a coastal State seeking to draw straight baselines along a highly unstable coastline.

5. The Committee has not proposed limits on the length of Article 7 straight baselines. Nevertheless, Article 7 straight baselines cannot be of unlimited length and several controlling factors need to be taken into account including the cumulative criteria of Article 7 of which the configuration of the coastline, including the location of any fringing islands, is the most important. The Committee observes that the longer the length of a straight baseline the more difficult it will be for that baseline to comply with Article 7.

6. The legality and validity of straight and archipelagic baselines are subject to their conformity with the LOSC and customary international law. As long as the legality and validity of the baselines have not been assessed by an international court or tribunal, the opposability of those baselines largely depends upon an absence of protest from other States. State practice is variable, which also reflects the variables in coastal geography that impact upon the interpretation of Article 7.

7. With respect to Article 8(2) (Internal Waters), the recognition of the right of innocent passage within waters enclosed by Article 7 straight baselines that previously were not considered internal waters is not contentious. Article 8(2) does not require that the right of innocent passage have been previously accepted. Rather, Article 8(2) addresses waters that were previously not considered to be internal waters. Therefore, whether the coastal State had or had not previously acknowledged the right of innocent passage within those waters is not determinative of the enjoyment of the right following the establishment of Article 7 straight baselines. Other factors may need to be taken into account including the breadth of the territorial sea prior to and following establishment of a straight baseline.

8. Article 10 (juridical single-state bays) reflects general customary international law. A particular difficulty that arises with Article 10 is the multiple criteria a coastal State must apply in order to determine that the indentation along the coast is a juridical bay.

Given the ambiguity that exists with those criteria it is unsurprising that some variations exist in state practice and that the drawing of straight/closing lines has been the subject of diplomatic protest.

9. Article 14 provides certainty that a combination of methods may be utilised according to different geographical and maritime circumstances. This is appropriate and reaffirms the significance associated with the declaration of baselines for the identification of internal waters and maritime zones including the territorial sea. The Committee emphasises that the baselines methodology selected by a coastal State must be appropriate and adapted to the particular coastline under consideration.

10. With regard to Article 47 (Archipelagic Baselines), compared to Article 7 of the LOSC, there is little room for widely varying interpretation of the more technical provisions of Article 47. Variations in state practice which appear to depart from Article 47 have either been relatively minor, or subject to protest by other States, which in some instances has resulted in an adjustment of state practice and consistency with the LOSC. The term 'main islands' is not defined in Article 47(1), though the island must meet the Article 121 criteria. The main islands of an archipelagic State may be of varying geographic size.

11. In the case of offshore outlying archipelagos, a State is unable to proclaim archipelagic baselines unless it meets the criteria of being an archipelagic State. An offshore coastal archipelago may be capable of being enclosed by Article 7 straight baselines subject to the controls set by Article 7 being met. It may be possible to draw Article 7 straight baselines around an individual island located within an archipelago consistently with the LOSC where that island is not otherwise part of an archipelagic State. In nearly all cases known to the Committee, this would only be possible where the coastline of the island is 'deeply indented and cut into'.

12. Disputes arising with respect to straight and archipelagic baselines fall within the subject matter jurisdiction of the LOSC mechanisms relating to the interpretation or application of the Convention. The status of baselines has predominantly arisen in maritime boundary delimitation cases where increasingly the view of courts and tribunals has been to use their own base points. It is exceptionally rare for a case where the principal dispute relates to straight or archipelagic baselines to have arisen before an international court or tribunal. The practice of States with respect to disputes regarding straight or archipelagic baselines predominantly relies upon diplomatic means, rather than the formal means for dispute settlement found in the LOSC or general international law.

References (Sofia Report 2012 Normal Baseline)

Alexander, Lewis M., 'Baseline Delimitations and Maritime Boundaries' (1983) 23 *Virginia Journal of International Law* 503.

Anderson, David, *Modern Law of the Sea – Selected Essays* (Leiden, Martinus Nijhoff: 2008).

Antunes, Nuno Sergio Marques, 'The Importance of the Tidal Datum in the Definition of Maritime Links and Boundaries' (2000) 2(7) (IBRU) *Maritime Briefings.*

Beazley, Peter, 'Technical Considerations in Maritime Boundary Delimitations' in Jonathan I. Charney & Lewis M. Alexander (eds.), 1 *International Maritime Boundaries* 243 (1993).

Carleton, Christopher, 'Problems Relating to Man-made Basepoints under UNCLOS,' presented at *Current Problematic Issues in the Law of the Sea* (Dublin, 3–4 June 2010).

Carleton, Christopher & Clive Schofield, 'Developments in the Technical Determination of Maritime Space: Charts, Datums, Baselines, Maritime Zones and Limits' (2001) 3(3) IBRU *Maritime Briefing.*

Caron, David D., 'Climate Change, Sea Level Rise and the Coming Uncertainty in Oceanic Boundaries: A Proposal to Avoid Conflict' in Seoung-Yong Hong & Jon M. Van Dyke (eds.), *Maritime Boundary Disputes, Settlement Processes, and the Law of the Sea* 1 (2009).

Caron, David D., 'When Law Makes Climate Change Worse: Rethinking the Law of Baselines in Light of a Rising Sea Level' (1990) 17 *Ecology Law Quarterly* 621.

Churchill, R.R. & A.V. Lowe, *The Law of the Sea* 3rd (Manchester University Press, Manchester: 1999).

Commission on the Limits of the Continental Shelf, Scientific and Technical Guidelines, CLCS/11 (May 1999).

'Datums and Bench Marks,' *Resolutions of the International Hydrographic Organization* 35 2nd (2010) [updated to Mar. 2012]), IHO Res. 3/1919 (last amended by circular letter 19/2008), para. 2(a), at: http://www.iho.int/iho_pubs/misc/M3-E-MARCH12.pdf.

Egede, Edwin, 'The Nigerian Territorial Waters Legislation and the 1982 Law of the Sea Convention' (2004) 19(2) *International Journal of Marine and Coastal Law* 151.

Gihl, Torsten, *The Baseline of the Territorial Sea* (Almqvist & Wiksell, Stockholm: 1967).

Hayashi, Moritaka, 'Sea-Level Rise and the Law of the Sea: Future Options' in Davor Vidas & Peter Johan Schei (eds.), *The World Ocean in Globalisation* (Martinus Nijhoff, Leiden/Boston: 2011).

Hodgson, Robert D. & Robert W. Smith, 'The Informal Single Negotiating Text (Committee II): A Geographical Perspective' (1976) 3 *Ocean Development and International Law* 225.

Houghton, Katherine et al., 'Maritime Boundaries in a Rising Sea' (2010) 3 *Nature Geoscience*.

International Law Commission, *Summary Records of the Fourth Session*, [1952] 1 Y.B. Int'l L. Comm'n 143, UN Doc. A/CN.4/SER.A/1952, at: legal.un.org/ilc/reports/.

International Law Commission, *Régime of the Territorial Sea*, in [1952] 2 Y.B. Int'l L. Comm'n 25, UN Doc. A/CN.4/53.

International Law Commission, *Rapport du Comité d'experts sur certaines questions d'ordre technique concernant la mer territoriale*, [1953] 2 Y.B. Int'l L. Comm'n 77, UN Doc. A/CN.4/SER.A/1953/Add.1, English translation reprinted in Myron H. Nordquist (ed.), 2 *United Nations Convention on the Law of the Sea, 1982: A Commentary* 59 (2003).

International Law Commission, *Report of the International Law Commission to the General Assembly*, [1954] 2 Y.B. Int'l L. Comm'n 140, UN Doc. A/CN.4/SER.A/1954/Add.1.

International Law Commission, *Report of the International Law Commission to the General Assembly*, [1956] 2 Y.B. Int'l L. Comm'n 253, 266, UN Doc. A/CN.4/SER.A/1956/Add.1.

Jessup, Philip C., *The Law of Territorial Waters and Maritime Jurisdiction* (G.A. Jennings, New York: 1927).

Jesus, José Luís, 'Rocks, New-born Islands, Sea Level Rise and Maritime Space' in Jochen Frowein et al. (eds.), *Negotiating for Peace – Liber Amicorum Tono Eitel* 599 (Springer, Berlin: 2003).

Kapoor, D.C. & Adam J. Kerr, *A Guide to Maritime Boundary Delimitation* (Carswell, Toronto: 1986).

Klein, Natalie, *Dispute Settlement in the UN Convention on the Law of the Sea* (Cambridge University Press, Cambridge: 2005).

League of Nations, *Bases of Discussion Drawn up for the Conference by the Preparatory Committee, II. Territorial Waters*, League of Nations Doc. C.74.M.39.1929.V (1929), reprinted in Official Documents: Conference for the Codification of International Law, 24 *American Journal International Law Supplement* 29 (1930).

Lisztwan, Julia, 'Stability of Maritime Boundary Agreements' (2012) 37 *Yale Journal of International Law* 153.

McDougal, Myres and William Burke, *The Public Order of the Oceans* (Yale University Press, New Haven and London: 1962).

O'Connell, D.P., *The International Law of the Sea* (2 vols.) I.A. Shearer (ed.) (Clarendon Press, Oxford: 1982).

Park, Susin, *Climate Change and the Risk of Statelessness: The Situation of Low-lying Island States* (UNHCR, May 2011).

Pearcy, G. Etzel, 'Measurement of the Territorial Sea' 40 *Department of State Bulletin* No. 1044, at 963 (June 29, 1959).

Prescott, Victor & Clive Schofield, *The Maritime Political Boundaries of the World* 2nd (Martinus Nijhoff, Leiden/Boston: 2005).

Rayfuse, Rosemary, 'W(h)ither Tuvalu? International Law and Disappearing States' *University of New South Wales Faculty of Law Research Series*, 2009, Paper 9 at: http://law.bepress.com/unswwps/flrps09/art9/.

Rayfuse, Rosemary, 'Sea Level Rise and Maritime Zones: Preserving the Maritime Entitlements of 'Disappearing' States' in M.B. Gerrard & G.E. Wannier (eds.), *Threatened Island Nations: Legal Implications of Rising Seas and a Changing Climate* (Cambridge University Press, Cambridge: 2012).

Reed, Michael W., 3 *Shore and Sea Boundaries: the Development of International Maritime Boundary Principles through United States Practice* vol. 3 (US Government Printing Office, Washington: 2000).

Shalowitz, A.L., *Shore and Sea Boundaries* (2 vols.) (Washington, US Department of Commerce: 1962).

Schofield, Clive & I. Made Andi Arsana, 'Imaginary Islands? Options to Preserve Maritime Jurisdictional Entitlements and Provide Stable Maritime Limits in the Face of Coastal Instability' 6th IHO-IAG ABLOS Conference, 25–27 October 2010 at: http://www.iho.int/mtg_docs/com_wg/ABLOS/ABLOS_Conf6/ABLOS_Conf6.htm.

Schofield, Clive, 'Shifting Limits? Sea Level Rise and Options to Secure Maritime Jurisdictional Claims' (2009) 3 *Carbon and Climate Law Review* 405.

Sohn, Louis B. & John E. Noyes, *Cases and Materials on the Law of the Sea* (2004).

Soons, A.H.A., 'The Effects of a Rising Sea Level on Maritime Limits and Boundaries' (1990) 37(2) *Netherlands International Law Review* 207.

Stoutenburg, Jenny Grote, 'Implementing a New Regime of Stable Maritime Zones to Ensure the (Economic) Survival of Small Island States Threatened by Sea-Level Rise' (2011) 26 *International Journal of Marine and Coastal Law* 263.

United Nations Convention on the Law of the Sea, 1982: A Commentary, seven vols. Satya N. Nandan & Shabtai Rosenne (eds.) (Brill/Nijhoff, Leiden/Boston: 1993).

UN Office for Ocean Affairs and the Law of the Sea, *Baselines: National Legislation with Illustrative Maps*, UN Sales No. E.89.V.10 (1989).

UN Office for Ocean Affairs and the Law of the Sea, *Baselines: An Examination of the Relevant Provisions of the United Nations Convention on the Law of the Sea*, UN Sales No. E.88.V.5 (reissued 1989).

UN Office for Ocean Affairs and the Law of the Sea, *Handbook on the Delimitation of Maritime Boundaries*, UN Sales No. E.01.V.2 (2000).

UN Office for Ocean Affairs and the Law of the Sea, *National Legislation on the Territorial Sea, The Right of Innocent Passage and the Contiguous Zone*, UN Sales No. E.95.V.7 (1995).

UN Office for Ocean Affairs and the Law of the Sea, *National Claims to Maritime Jurisdiction: Excerpts of Legislation and Table of Claims*, UN Sales No. E.91.V.15 (1992).

UN Office for Ocean Affairs and the Law of the Sea, *Maritime Space: Legislation and Treaties* (online database), at: http://www.un.org/Depts/los/LEGISLATIONANDTREATIES/index.htm.

Walker, George K. (ed.), *Definitions for the Law of the Sea: Terms not Defined by the 1982 Convention* (Martinus Nijhoff, Leiden/Boston: 2012).

Weil, Prosper, *The Law of Maritime Delimitation – Reflections* (Grotius Publications, Cambridge: 1989).

Whiteman, M., *Digest of International Law* vol. 4 (Washington DC, Government Printing Office: 1965).

Cases

A-G of the Federation v. A-G of Abia State and 35 Others, [2002] 6 NWLR (Part 764), at 54 (Nigeria).

Award of the Arbitral Tribunal in the Matter of an Arbitration between Guyana and Suriname (Guyana v. Suriname), 47 ILM 166 (2008) (Sept. 17, 2007), at: http://www.pca-cpa.org/upload/files/Guyana-Suriname%20Award.pdf; XXX RIAA 1–144, at: http://legal.un.org/riaa/vol_30.shtml.

Award of the Arbitral Tribunal in the second stage of the proceedings between Eritrea and Yemen (Maritime Delimitation) (Eritrea/Yemen) (Dec. 17, 1999), PCA Case no. 1996-04, at: https://pca-cpa.org/en/cases/81/; XXII RIAA 335–410, at: http://legal.un.org/riaa/vol_22.shtml.

Chia Hsing v. Rankin, (1978) 141 CLR 182, 192 at: http://www.austlii.edu.au/au/cases/cth/HCA/1978/56.html.

Continental Shelf (Libyan Arab Jamahiriya/Malta), [1985] ICJ Reports 13 (June 3).

Continental Shelf (United Kingdom/France), XVIII RIAA 271 (Mar. 14, 1978).

Dispute concerning delimitation of the maritime boundary between Bangladesh and Myanmar in the Bay of Bengal (Bangladesh/Myanmar), ITLOS Case No. 16 (Mar. 14, 2012).

Fisheries (United Kingdom v. Norway), [1951] ICJ Reports 116, 132 (Dec. 18).

In the Matter of the Bay of Bengal Maritime Boundary Arbitration (Bangladesh/India), Award (7 July 2014), PCA Case no. 2010-16, at: https://pca-cpa.org/en/cases/18/.

Land and Maritime Boundary between Cameroon and Nigeria (Cameroon v. Nigeria: Equatorial Guinea intervening), [2002] ICJ Reports 303 (Oct. 10).

Maritime Delimitation in the Black Sea (Romania v. Ukraine), [2009] ICJ Reports 61 (Feb. 3).

Maritime Delimitation and Territorial Questions between Qatar and Bahrain (Qatar v. Bahrain), [2001] ICJ Reports 40 (Mar. 16).

North Sea Continental Shelf (Federal Republic of Germany/Denmark; Federal Republic of Germany/Netherlands), [1969] ICJ Reports 3 (Feb. 20).

Post Office v. Estuary Radio Ltd., [1967] 3 All English Reports 663.

Responsibilities and Obligations of States Sponsoring Persons and Entities with Respect to Activities in the Area (Request for Advisory Opinion submitted to the Seabed Disputes Chamber), ITLOS Case No. 17 (Feb. 1, 2011).

Territorial and Maritime Dispute between Nicaragua and Honduras in the Caribbean Sea (Nicaragua v. Honduras), [2007] ICJ Reports 659 (Oct. 8).

United States v. Alaska, 511 US 1 (1997).

United States v. California, 447 US 1 (1980).

United States v. Louisiana, 394 US 11 (1969), and 420 US 529 (1975).

Treaties

Convention on the Territorial Sea and the Contiguous Zone, Apr. 29, 1958, 516 UNTS 206.

United Nations Convention on the Law of the Sea, Dec. 10, 1982, 1833 UNTS 397.

Vienna Convention on the Law of Treaties, May 23, 1969, 1155 UNTS 331.

Legislation

Australia, Seas and Submerged Lands (Territorial Sea Baseline) Proclamation (2006), at: http://www.comlaw.gov.au/Details/F2006L00525.

Bahrain, Decree-Law No. 8 (1993), at: http://www.un.org/Depts/los/LEGISLATIONANDTREATIES/PDFFILES/BHR_1993_Decree.pdf.

Barbados, Territorial Waters Act, No. 1977-26 (1977), at: http://www.un.org/Depts/los/LEGISLATIONANDTREATIES/PDFFILES/BRB_1977_26.pdf.

Brazil, The Territorial Sea, the Contiguous Zone, the Exclusive Economic Zone and the Continental Shelf, Law No. 8.617 (1993), at: http://www.un.org/Depts/los/LEGISLATIONANDTREATIES/PDFFILES/BRA_1993_8617.pdf.

Brunei, Territorial Waters Act (1982), at: http://www.un.org/Depts/los/LEGISLATIONANDTREATIES/PDFFILES/BRN_1982_Act.pdf.

France, Delimitation of French Territorial Waters, Law No. 71-1060 (1971), at: http://www.un.org/Depts/los/LEGISLATIONANDTREATIES/PDFFILES/FRA_1971_Law.pdf.

Grenada, Territorial Sea and Maritime Boundaries Act, No. 25 (1989), at: http://www.un.org/Depts/los/LEGISLATIONANDTREATIES/PDFFILES/grd_act_25_1989.pdf.

Japan, Enforcement Order of the Law on the Territorial Sea and the Contiguous Zone (Cabinet Order No. 210 of 1977, as amended by Cabinet Order No. 383 of 1993, Cabinet Order No. 206 of 1996 and Cabinet Order No. 434 of 2001), 66 Law of the Sea Bulletin 71 (2008).

Namibia, Territorial Sea and Exclusive Economic Zone Act, No. 3 (1990), at: http://www.un.org/Depts/los/LEGISLATIONANDTREATIES/PDFFILES/NAM_1990_Act.pdf.

Netherlands, Territorial Sea (Demarcation) Act (9 January 1985), at: http://www.un.org/Depts/los/LEGISLATIONANDTREATIES/PDFFILES/NLD_1985_DemarcationAct.pdf.

New Zealand, Territorial Sea and Exclusive Economic Zone Act, No. 28 (1977, as amended by Act No. 146 of 1980), at: http://www.un.org/Depts/los/LEGISLATIONANDTREATIES/PDFFILES/NZL_1980_Act.pdf.

Samoa, Maritime Zones Act (1999), at: http://www.un.org/Depts/los/LEGISLATIONANDTREATIES/PDFFILES/WSM_1999_MaritimeZ.pdf;

Seychelles, Maritime Zones Act, No. 2 (1999), at: http://www.un.org/Depts/los/LEGISLATIONANDTREATIES/PDFFILES/SYC_1999_Act2.pdf.

Solomon Islands, Delimitation of Marine Waters Act, No. 32 (1978), at: http://www.un.org/Depts/los/LEGISLATIONANDTREATIES/PDFFILES/SLB_1978_Act.pdf.

Sri Lanka, Maritime Zones Law, No. 22 (1976), at: http://www.un.org/Depts/los/LEGISLATIONANDTREATIES/PDFFILES/LKA_1976_Law.pdf.

St. Kitts and Nevis, Maritime Areas Act, No. 3 (1984), at: http://www.un.org/Depts/los/LEGISLATIONANDTREATIES/PDFFILES/KNA_1984_Act.pdf.

Tuvalu, Marine Zones (Declaration) Act (1983), at: http://www.un.org/Depts/los/LEGISLATIONANDTREATIES/PDFFILES/TUV_1983_Act.pdf.

United Kingdom, Territorial Sea Act (1987), at: http://www.un.org/Depts/los/LEGISLATIONANDTREATIES/PDFFILES/GBR_1987_Act.pdf.

United States, Territorial Sea of the United States, Proclamation (1988), at: http://www.un.org/Depts/los/LEGISLATIONANDTREATIES/PDFFILES/USA_1988_Proclamation.pdf.

United States, Submerged Lands Act, 43 USC §§ 1301, 1311.

Vanuatu, Maritime Zone Act, No. 23 (1981), reprinted in UN Office for Ocean Affairs and the Law of the Sea, Baselines: National Legislation with Illustrative Maps 376, UN Sales No. E.89.V.10 (1989).

References (Sydney Conference 2018 Final Report [Straight Baselines])

Alexander, Lewis M., 'Baseline Delimitations and Maritime Boundaries' (1982–1983) 23 *Virginia Journal of International Law* 503.

Anand, R.P., *Origin and Development of the Law of the Sea* (Martinus Nijhoff, The Hague/Boston: 1983).

Baumert, Kevin and Brian Melchior, 'The Practice of Archipelagic States: A Study of Studies' (2015) 46 *Ocean Development and International Law* 60–80.

Charney, Jonathan I. and Lewis M. Alexander (eds.), *International Maritime Boundaries* vol. I (Martinus Nijhoff, Dordrecht/Boston: 1993).

Charney, Jonathan I. and Lewis M. Alexander (eds.), *International Maritime Boundaries* vol. II (Martinus Nijhoff, Dordrecht/Boston: 1993).

Charney, Jonathan I. and Lewis M. Alexander (eds.), *International Maritime Boundaries* vol. III (Martinus Nijhoff, Dordrecht/Boston: 1998).

Chinese Society of International Law 'The South China Sea Arbitration Awards: A Critical Study' (2018) 17 *Chinese Journal of International Law* 210–748.

Churchill, Robin R., 'The Impact of State Practice on the Jurisdictional Framework Contained in the LOS Convention' in Alex G. Oude Elferink (ed.), *Stability and Change in the Law of the Sea: The Role of the LOS Convention* (Martinus Nijhoff, Leiden: 2005) 91.

Colson, David A. and Robert W. Smith, *International Maritime Boundaries* vol. V (Martinus Nijhoff, Dordrecht/Boston: 2005).

Department of State (USA), Limits in the Seas series, at: https://www.state.gov/e/oes/ocns/opa/c16065.htm.

Department of State (USA), *Bahamas: Archipelagic and Other Maritime Claims and Boundaries* (Limits in the Sea No. 128) (Department of State, Washington: 2014).

Department of State (USA), *Comoros: Archipelagic and Other Maritime Claims and Boundaries* (Limits in the Seas No. 134) (Department of State, Washington: 2014).

Department of State (USA), *Dominican Republic: Archipelagic and Other Maritime Claims* (Limits in the Seas No. 130) (Department of State, Washington: 2014).

Department of State (USA), *Grenada: Archipelagic and Other Maritime Claims and Boundaries* (Limits in the Sea No. 135) (Department of State, Washington: 2014).

Department of State (USA), *Jamaica's Maritime Claims and Boundaries* (Limits in the Seas No. 125) (Department of State, Washington: 2004).

Department of State (USA), *Mauritius: Archipelagic and Other Maritime Claims and Boundaries* (Limits in the Sea No. 140) (Department of State, Washington: 2014).

Department of State (USA), *Papua New Guinea: Archipelagic and Other Maritime Claims and Boundaries* (Limits in the Sea No. 138) (Department of State, Washington: 2014).

Department of State (USA), *Seychelles: Archipelagic and Other Maritime Claims and Boundaries* (Limits in the Seas No. 132) (Department of State, Washington: 2014).

Department of State (USA), *Straight Baselines Claim: China* (Limits in the Seas No. 117) (Department of State, Washington: 1996).

Department of State (USA), *Straight Baselines: Saudi Arabia* (Limits in the Seas No. 20) (Department of State, Washington: 1970).

Department of State (USA), *Straight Baselines: Syria* (Limits in the Seas No. 53) (Department of State, Washington: 1973).

Department of State (USA), *Straight Baselines: U.S.S.R.* (Limits in the Seas No. 107) (Department of State, Washington: 1987).

Department of State (USA), *Straight Baselines: Vietnam* (Limits in the Sea No. 99) (Department of State, Washington: 1983).

Department of State (USA), *Taiwan's Maritime Claims* (Limits in the Seas No. 127) (Department of State, Washington: 2005).

Department of State (USA), *Trinidad and Tobago: Archipelagic and Other Maritime Claims and Boundaries* (Limits in the Seas No. 131) (Department of State, Washington: 2014).

Department of State (USA), *United States Responses to Excessive National Maritime Claims* (Limits in the Seas No. 112) (Department of State, Washington: 1992).

Fitzmaurice, Sir Gerald, *The Law and Procedure of the International Court of Justice*, vol. 1 (Cambridge, Grotius: 1986).

Fitzmaurice, Sir Gerald, 'Some Results of the Geneva Conference on the Law of the Sea: Part 1 – The Territorial Sea and Contiguous Zone and Related Topics' (1959) 8 *International and Comparative Law Quarterly* 73.

François, J.P.A. *United Nations Conference on the Law of the Sea, Volume III: First Committee (Territorial Sea and Contiguous Zone)*, 21st mtg, 69 [15], UN Doc. A/CONFC.13/C.1/L.10 (1958).

Goldie, L.F.E., 'Historic Bays in international law: an impressionistic overview' (1984) 11 *Syracuse Journal of International Law and Commerce* 211–273.

'Historic Bays: Memorandum by the Secretariat of the United Nations' (United Nations Conference on the Law of the Sea, 24 February–27 April 1958) UN Doc. A/CONF.13/1.

Hoque, Muhammad Nazmul, *The Legal and Scientific Assessment of Bangladesh's Baseline in the Context of Article 76 of the United Nations Convention on the Law of the Sea* (United Nations, New York: 2006).

Kwiatkowska, Barbara and Etty R. Argoes, *Archipelagic State Regime in Light of the 1982 UNCLOS and State Practice* (ICLOS/UNPAD, Bandung: 1991).

International Law Association, *Baselines under the International Law of the Sea* (Sofia Conference 2012) at: http://www.ila-hq.org/index.php/committees.

International Law Association, 'First Report' in *Report of the Seventy-Sixth Conference, Washington 2014* (International Law Association, London: 2014) at: http://www.ila-hq.org/index.php/committees.

International Law Association, 'Second Report' in *Report of the Seventy-Seventh Conference, Johannesburg 2016* (International Law Association, London: 2016) at: http://www.ila-hq.org/index.php/committees.

Kopela, Sophia, '2007 Archipelagic Legislation of the Dominican Republic: An Assessment' (2009) 24 *International Journal of Marine and Coastal Law* 501.

Kopela, Sophia, *Dependent Archipelagos in the Law of the Sea* (Martinus Nijhoff, Leiden/Boston: 2013).

Lauterpacht, Hersch, *The Development of International Law by the International Court* (Stevens, London: 1958).

Lowe, Vaughan and Antonios Tzanakopoulos, 'The Development of the Law of the Sea by the International Court of Justice' in Christian J. Tams and James Sloan (eds.), *The Development of International Law by the International Court of Justice* (Oxford University Press, Oxford: 2013).

Nandan, Satya N. and Shabtai Rosenne (eds.), *United Nations Convention on the Law of the Sea 1982: A Commentary* vol. II (Martinus Nijhoff, Dordrecht/Boston/London: 1993).

O'Connell, D.P., 'Mid-Ocean Archipelagos in International Law' (1971) 45 *British Year Book of International Law* 1.

O'Connell, D.P., *The International Law of the Sea* vol. I (Clarendon Press, Oxford: 1982).

Prescott, J.R.V., 'Straight and Archipelagic Baselines' in Gerald Blake (ed.), *Maritime Boundaries and Ocean Resources* (Croom Helm, Beckenham: 1987) 38.

Prescott, Victor and Clive H. Schofield, *The Maritime Political Boundaries of the World* 2nd (Martinus Nijhoff, Leiden/Boston: 2005).

Proelss, Alexander (ed.), *United Nations Convention on the Law of the Sea: A Commentary* (C.H. Beck/Hart/Nomos, München/Oxford/Baden-Baden: 2017).

Reed, M.W., *Shore and Sea Boundaries: the Development of International Maritime Boundary Principles through United States Practice* vol. 3 (US Government Printing Office, Washington: 2000).

Reisman, W. Michael and Gayle S. Westerman, *Straight Baselines in International Maritime Boundary Delimitation* (Macmillan, London: 1992).

Roach, J. Ashley, 'Offshore Archipelagos Enclosed by Straight Baselines: an Excessive Claim?' (2018) 49 *Ocean Development and International Law* 176–202.

Roach, J. Ashley and Robert W. Smith, *Excessive Maritime Claims* 3rd (Martinus Nijhoff, Leiden/Boston: 2012).

Rothwell, Donald R., 'Antarctic Baselines: Flexing the Law for Ice-Covered Coastlines' in Alex G. Oude Elferink and Donald R. Rothwell (eds.) *The Law of the Sea and Polar Maritime Delimitation and Jurisdiction* (Martinus Nijhoff, The Hague: 2001) 49–68.

Rothwell, Donald R. and Tim Stephens, *The International Law of the Sea* 2nd (Hart Publishing, Oxford 2016).

Schofield, Clive and I. Made Andi Arsana 'Closing the loop: Indonesia's revised archipelagic baselines system' (2009) 1(2) *Australian Journal of Maritime and Ocean Affairs* 57.

Scovazzi, Tullio, 'The Baseline of the Territorial Sea: The Practice of Arctic States' in Alex G. Oude Elferink and Donald R. Rothwell (eds.) *The Law of the Sea and Polar Maritime Delimitation and Jurisdiction* (Martinus Nijhoff, The Hague: 2001) 69–84.

Scovazzi, Tullio, 'Baselines' in *Max Planck Encyclopedia of Public International Law* (June 2007) at: opil.ouplaw.com.

Stohl, M.P., *The international law of bays* (Martinus Nijhoff, The Hague: 1963).

Symmons, Clive R., 'Article 14 Combination of methods for determining baselines' in Proelss (ed.), *United Nations Convention on the Law of the Sea: A Commentary* , 147.

Tanaka, Yoshifumi, *The International Law of the Sea* 2nd (Cambridge University Press, Cambridge: 2015).

'Text of a Joint Declaration Undertaken by the United Kingdom of Great Britain and Northern Ireland and the United States of America in relation to the Law of the Dominican Republic Number 66-07 of 22 May 2007, Done on 18 October 2007' (2008) 66 *Law of the Sea Bulletin* 98–99.

Trümpler, Kai 'Article 7 Straight Baselines' in Proelss (ed.), *United Nations Convention on the Law of the Sea: A Commentary*, 65.

United Nations Office for Ocean Affairs and the Law of the Sea, *Baselines: An Examination of the Relevant Provisions of the United Nations Convention on the Law of the Sea* (United Nations, New York: 1989).

Walker, George K. (ed.), *Definitions for the Law of the Sea: Terms Not Defined by the 1982 Convention* (Martinus Nijhoff, Leiden/Boston: 2012).

Westerman, Gayl Shaw, *The Juridical Bay* (Oxford University Press, Oxford: 1987).

Cases

Eritrea v. Yemen (Maritime Delimitation) Award of the Arbitral Tribunal in the Second Stage of the Proceedings (17 December 1999), PCA Case no. 1996-04, at: https://pca-cpa.org/en/cases/81/; XXII RIAA 335–410, at: http://legal.un.org/riaa/vol_22.shtml.

Fisheries (United Kingdom v. Norway) [1951] ICJ Reports 116 (Dec. 18).

In the Matter of an Arbitration before An Arbitral Tribunal Constituted Under Annex VII to the 1982 United Nations Convention on the Law of the Sea between The Republic of the Philippines and the People's Republic of China, PCA Case no. 2013-19, Award of 12 July 2016, at: https://pca-cpa.org/en/cases/7/.

In the Matter of an Arbitration under the Arbitration Agreement between the Government of the Republic of Croatia and the Government of the Republic of Slovenia, signed on 4 November 2009, Final Award – 29 June 2017 (Croatia/Slovenia) (PCA Case No. 2012-04), at: https://pca-cpa.org/en/cases/3/.

In the Matter of an Arbitration between Barbados and Trinidad and Tobago (11 April 2006), PCA Case No. 2004-02, at: https://pca-cpa.org/en/cases/104/; XXVII RIAA 147–251, at: http://legal.un.org/riaa/vol_27.shtml.

In the Matter of the Duzgit Interity Arbitration (Award of 5 September 2016) (Malta/São Tomé and Príncipe) PCA Case Nº 2014-07, at: https://pca-cpa.org/en/cases/53/.

Land, Maritime and Island Frontier Dispute (El Salvador v. Honduras: Nicaragua intervening) (Judgment) [1992] ICJ Reports 351 (Sept. 11).

Maritime Delimitation in the Black Sea (Romania v. Ukraine) Judgment [2009] ICJ Reports 61 (Feb. 3).

Maritime Delimitation in the Caribbean Sea and the Pacific Ocean (Costa Rica v. Nicaragua) [2018] ICJ Reports 100 (Feb. 2).

Maritime Delimitation and Territorial Questions between Qatar and Bahrain (Qatar v. Bahrain) (Judgment) [2001] ICJ Reports 40 (Mar. 16).

Sovereignty Over Pulau Ligitan and Pulau Sipadan (Indonesia/Malaysia) [2002] ICJ Reports 625 (Dec. 17).

Territorial and Maritime Dispute (Nicaragua v. Colombia) (Judgment) [2012] ICJ Reports 624 (Nov. 19).

United States v. *Alaska*, 422 US 184.

United States v. California, 381 US 139.

United States v. Louisiana, 394 US 11.

United States v. Maine, 469 US 504.

Treaties

Convention on the Territorial Sea and the Contiguous Zone, 516 UNTS 206.

Treaty on the Delimitation of the Maritime Frontier between the Republic of Cape Verde and the Republic of Senegal (1994) 26 *Law of the Sea Bulletin* 45.

United Nations Convention on the Law of the Sea (LOSC), 1833 UNTS 397.

Legislation

UN Office for Ocean Affairs and the Law of the Sea, Maritime Space: Legislation and Treaties (online database), at: http://www.un.org/Depts/los/LEGISLATIONANDTREATIES/index.htm.

Argentina, Act No. 23.968 of 14 August 1991.

'Australian Maritime Projection around Macquarie Island – Lambert Project' (Geoscience Australia) at: https://ecat.ga.gov.au/geonetwork/srv/eng/search#!a05f7892-eeed-7506-e044-00144fdd4fa6.

Bangladesh, S.R.O. No. 328-Law/2015/MOFA/UNCLOS/113/2/15 (4 November 2015), reproduced in M.Z.N. 118.2016 (LOS) Maritime Zone Notification (7 April 2016) at: http://www.un.org/Depts/los/LEGISLATIONANDTREATIES/PDFFILES/mzn_s/mzn118.pdf.

Brazil, Decree No. 8.400 of 4 February 2015.

Dominican Republic, Law No. 66-07 of 22 May 2007.

Egypt, Royal Decree No. 2510/1977 of 5 August 1977.

France, Decree of 19 October 1967 as replaced by M.Z.N.117.2015.LOS of 12 November 2015 (UN Division for Ocean Affairs and the Law of the Sea, Office of Legal Affairs) (2008) Bulletin No. 66 *Law of the Sea* 28.

Honduras, Executive Decree No. PCM 007-2000 21 March 2000.

Japan, Enforcement Order of the Law on the Territorial Sea and the Contiguous Zone (Cabinet Order No. 210 of 1977, as amended by Cabinet Order No. 383 of 1993, Cabinet Order No. 206 of 1996 and Cabinet Order No. 434 of 2001), in UN Division for Ocean Affairs and the Law of the Sea, Office of Legal Affairs (2008) Bulletin No. 66 *Law of the Sea* 71ff.

Mauritius, Maritime Zone Act 2005 (No. 2) 28 February 2005, UN Division for Ocean Affairs and the Law of the Sea, Office of Legal Affairs (2006) Bulletin No. 62 *Law of the Sea* 52ff.

Mexico, General Act of 31 December 1941 on National Property (as amended in January 1982).

Mexico, Federal Act relating to the Sea 8 January 1986.

New Zealand, Territorial Sea and Exclusive Economic Zone Act 1977.

New Zealand, Territorial Sea, Contiguous Zone, and Exclusive Economic Zone Act 1997 as amended by Act No. 146 of 1980 (New Zealand).

Papua New Guinea, National Seas Act 1977.

Philippines, Republic Act No. 9522: An Act to Amend Certain Provisions of Republic Act No. 3046, as Amended by Republic Act No. 5446, to Define the Archipelagic Baselines of the Philippines, and for Other Purposes at: http://www.un.org/Depts/los/LEGISLATIONANDTREATIES/PDFFILES/mzn_s/mzn69.pdf.

Samoa, Territorial Sea Act 1971.

Saudi Arabia, Territorial Waters of the Kingdom of Saudi Arabia (Royal Decree No. 33 of 16 February 1958).

Sudan, Territorial Waters and Continental Shelf Act of 1970 [6(1)].

Trinidad and Tobago, Territorial Sea Act 1969, No. 38 of 6 December 1969.

United Kingdom, The Territorial Sea (Baselines) Order 2014 (2014 No. 1353) 'Explanatory Note'.

Uruguay, Act 17.033 of 20 November 1998.

Vanuatu, Maritime Zones Act No. 23 of 1981.

Vanuatu, Maritime Zones Act No. 6 of 2010.

Editor Biographies

Coalter G. Lathrop
directs Sovereign Geographic, an international law and cartography consultancy serving boundary clients throughout the world. Lathrop has represented sovereign states in land and maritime boundary disputes and provided negotiating support and advice on related issues to governments and private interests in Africa, Asia, the Middle East, and North and South America. Over the last two decades he has acted as counsel and advisor in multiple cases before the International Court of Justice and the International Tribunal for the Law of the Sea. Lathrop holds a Master of Marine Affairs from the University of Washington, and a J.D. and LL.M. in International and Comparative Law from Duke University. He has published and presented extensively on the law of the sea, the Arctic, island sovereignty, and maritime boundaries, and he serves as the editor of *International Maritime Boundaries*, a project of the American Society of International Law.

J. Ashley Roach
Captain, JAGC, U.S. Navy (retired), Visiting Senior Research Fellow, Centre for International Law, National University of Singapore, was from 2012–2018 Chair of the ILA Committee on Baselines under the International Law of the Sea. He was responsible for law of the sea matters in the U.S. Department of State Office of the Legal Adviser 1988–2009. Author (with Robert W. Smith) of *Excessive Maritime Claims* 3rd, (Martinus Nijhoff, 2012) (fourth edition in preparation), co-editor of several books on various law of the sea issues, and numerous articles on law of the sea issues, the Arctic and maritime crimes. He holds a LL.M. in international and comparative law from George Washington University School of Law and a J.D. from the University of Pennsylvania Law School.

Donald R. Rothwell
is Professor of International Law at the ANU College of Law, Australian National University where he has taught since July 2006. His research has a specific focus on law of the sea, law of the polar regions, and implementation of international law within Australia as reflected in 24 books, and over 200 articles, book chapters and notes in international and Australian publications. Rothwell's recent books include *International Polar Law* (Edward Elgar, 2018) edited with Hemmings; and *The International Law of the Sea* 2nd (Bloomsbury, 2016) with Stephens. Rothwell is also Co-Editor of the *Australian Year Book of International Law* and Editor-in-Chief of the *Brill Research Perspectives in Law of the Sea*. From 2012–2018 he was Rapporteur of the International Law Association (ILA) Committee on 'Baselines under the International Law of the Sea'.

www.ingramcontent.com/pod-product-compliance
Lightning Source LLC
Chambersburg PA
CBHW031325230926
51848CB00001B/100
* 9 7 8 9 0 0 4 3 9 8 1 3 9 *

Andrew Wommack
Leben in Gottes Fülle